Noiseless Steganography

The Key to Covert Communications

D0206045

Noiseless Steganography

The Key to Covert Communications

ABDELRAHMAN DESOKY

CRC Press
Taylor & Francis Group
Boca Raton   London   New York

CRC Press is an imprint of the
Taylor & Francis Group, an **informa** business

AN AUERBACH BOOK

CRC Press
Taylor & Francis Group
6000 Broken Sound Parkway NW, Suite 300
Boca Raton, FL 33487-2742

© 2012 by Taylor & Francis Group, LLC
CRC Press is an imprint of Taylor & Francis Group, an Informa business

No claim to original U.S. Government works

Printed in the United States of America on acid-free paper
Version Date: 20111215

International Standard Book Number: 978-1-4398-4621-6 (Hardback)

Library of Congress Cataloging-in-Publication Data

Desoky, Abdelrahman.
    Noiseless steganography : the key to covert communications / Abdelrahman Desoky.
        p. cm.
    Includes bibliographical references and index.
    ISBN 978-1-4398-4621-6 (hardback)
    1. Coding theory. 2. Data transmission systems. 3. Electronics in espionage. 4.
Confidential communications. 5. Data encryption (Computer science) I. Title.

QA268.D47 2012
003'.54--dc23
                                            2011046670

Visit the Taylor & Francis Web site at
http://www.taylorandfrancis.com

and the CRC Press Web site at
http://www.crcpress.com

Dedication

This book is dedicated to those who persist in dreaming
and striving for a better tomorrow for all.

Contents

Foreword

Steganography is the science and art of covert communications and involves two procedures. First, the required message is concealed in a particular carrier, e.g., image, audio, text, etc., that is called a steganographic cover. The second procedure is concerned with transmitting the cover to the message recipient without drawing suspicion. Fundamentally, the steganographic goal is not to hinder the adversary from decoding a hidden message, but to prevent the adversary from suspecting the existence of covert communications. When using any steganographic technique, if suspicion is raised, the goal of steganography is defeated regardless of whether a plain text is revealed. Contemporary steganography approaches camouflage data as noise in a cover that is assumed to look innocent. For example, the encoded message can be embedded as the alteration of digital images, audio files, and text without noticeable degradation. However, such alteration of authenticated covers can raise suspicion and make the message detectable. Another example is when linguistics, e.g., using synonymous words, is exploited as a means to conceal a message, causing the presence of abnormal and sometimes weird sentences in a text that become discernible by human and machine examinations. The presence of such unjustifiable noise draws attention and unravels the hidden communications.

This book introduces a novel **Noi**seless **Stega**nography (**Nostega**) paradigm. Nostega neither hides data in a noise nor produces noise. Instead, it camouflages messages in a form of unquestionable data in the generated cover. In addition, steganography approaches found in the literature have focused on how to conceal a message and not on how to camouflage its transmittal. Nostega addresses this shortcoming by not only camouflaging a message, but also its transmission. Thus, Nostega is a novel paradigm in steganographic research. In Nostega, the steganographic goal is achieved by determining a suitable domain that is capable of generating an innocent appearing steganographic cover in which a message is intrinsically embedded in the form of innocent data compatible with the chosen domain. In addition, Nostega establishes a covert channel by employing a selected domain to serve as a justification for the interaction and delivering the cover among the communicating parties.

In this book, a number of Nostega-based methodologies are presented. The first to be introduced is graph-cover, a novel cover type. Unlike image-, audio-, and text-based steganographic covers, graphs enable data to be hidden in a plotted graph. Graph covers fit very well with Nostega and are suitable for many domains. The second methodology pursues popular games such as chess, checkers, crosswords, or dominoes to conceal messages. The third, Edustega, pursues the linguistics path to generate text cover. It exploits educational documents as steganographic covers mainly by manipulating questions and answers. This methodology can employ exam generators and text substitution techniques to automate the process of cover generation. The fourth is also a linguistic steganography type that manipulates automatic summarization techniques to conceal data in textual summaries. The fifth is a linguistic steganography type that conceals data by employing Natural Language Generation (NLG), template systems techniques, and Random Series (RS) values (e.g., binary, decimal, hexadecimal, octal, alphabetic, and alphanumeric) of a Domain-Specific Subject (DSS) (e.g., financial, medical, mathematical, scientific, and economic) to generate noiseless text-cover. It embeds data in a form of RS values, functions of RS, related semantics of RS, or a combination of these.

Unlike the fifth methodology, the sixth is a linguistic steganography type as well, but it is capable of handling non-random series domains. It employs NLG techniques to generate noiseless (flawless) and legitimate text cover by manipulating the inputs' parameters of a NLG system in order to camouflage data in the generated text. The seventh is a textual linguistic steganography type that conceals data in email header fields such as the recipients' email addresses, names, and subject fields, rather than the body of the email. It encodes a message, then assigns it to steganographic carriers of email header fields. The eighth is also a textual linguistic steganography type that takes advantage of the common use of textual lists to camouflage data by exploiting itemized data to conceal messages. Simply, it encodes a message then assigns it to legitimate items in order to generate a text cover in the form of a list. Finally, the ninth methodology is a textual linguistic steganography type that takes advantage of auto-notetaking to conceal data. This method pursues the variations among both human notes and the outputs of automatic-notetaking techniques to embed a message. Unlike machine translation and automatic sum-marizers, Notestega can embed non-directly related elements to its output, including linguistic elements (e.g., sentences, words, abbre-viations), and nonlinguistic elements (e.g., lines, stars, arrows, sym-bols). Thus, the generated note cover (text cover) has ample room for concealing data. Implementation and steganalysis validation of these methodologies are presented.

Abdelrahman Desoky, Ph.D.

Acknowledgments

I would like to thank my loving parents who supported and encouraged me throughout my academic pursuits. I would also like to thank everyone who taught me to dream, pursue, and achieve.

About the Author

Dr. Abdelrahman Desoky received his PhD from the University of Maryland, Baltimore County (UMBC) and his MSc from the George Washington University; both degrees are in computer engineering. His doctoral dissertation was entitled "Nostega: A Novel Noiseless Steganography Paradigm." The paradigm explored the topic of noiseless steganography, which referred to the science and art of covert communications. His MSc degree concentrated on computer architecture and networks. His research was entitled "Security Architecture for Computers and Networks." He has more than twenty years experience in the computer field and is an experienced educator at both graduate and undergraduate levels. Additionally, his industrial expertise includes developing full life cycle systems such as software, hardware, security, and telecommunications/networks. Currently, he is CEO of The Academia Planet.

1

INTRODUCTION

In this chapter, Section 1.1 briefly covers some of the fundamental concepts related to steganography, summarizes the current state of the research, and highlights the technical concerns. Section 1.2 introduces the novel **No**iseless **Stega**nography (Nostega) Paradigm. Section 1.3 summarizes the contribution. Finally, Section 1.4 details the organization of the book.

1.1 Steganography: Definition, Current State, and Concerns

Steganography is the scientific art of concealing the presence of covert communications. The origin of steganography is traced back to ancient civilizations [1,2]. The ancient Egyptians communicated covertly using the hieroglyphic language, a series of symbols representing a message. The message simply looks as if it is a drawing, although it may contain a hidden message. Hieroglyphs contained hidden information that only a legitimate person who knew what to look for could detect. After the Egyptians, the Greeks used "hidden writing," which is the derivative of steganography [1,3].

In general, steganography approaches hide a message in a cover (e.g., text, image, audio file, etc.) in such a way that is assumed to look innocent and therefore not raise suspicion. Fundamentally, the steganographic goal is not to hinder an adversary from decoding a hidden message, but to prevent an adversary from suspecting the existence of covert communications [3]. Thus, when using any steganographic technique if suspicion is raised, the goal of steganography is defeated regardless of whether or not a plain text is revealed [4,5]. Contemporary schemes are generally categorized into text, image, or audio based on the steganographic cover type.

Textual steganography can be classified as textual format manipulation (TFM) and textual fabrication (TF) [3]. In TFM, comparing the original text with the modified text will reveal the hidden message [4,25]. On the other hand, textual fabrication techniques hide a message either by generating an entire text cover, by employing methods such as null cipher [6] and mimic functions [7,8], or manipulating an existing text using such methods as NICETEXT and SCRAMBLE [9–12], translation-based techniques [13–15]. However, the text cover that is generated by these approaches often has numerous linguistic flaws that can easily raise suspicion. Such flaws in text steganography are referred to hereafter as noise. It is argued that such noise even makes it feasible to reveal the hidden message [3,13,25,107].

On the other hand, image steganography is based on manipulating digital images to conceal a message. Such manipulation often renders the message as noise. In general, image steganography suffers from several issues, such as the potential of distortion, the significant size limitation of the messages that can be embedded, and the increased vulnerability of detection through contemporary image processing techniques [5]. Audio covers have also been pursued. Examples of audio steganography techniques include LSB [16,17], spread spectrum coding [18,19], phase coding [18,20], and echo hiding [21]. In general, these techniques are too complex, and like their image-based counterparts, are still subject to distortion and detection [5].

The inability of contemporary steganography approaches to achieve the steganographic goal can be traced back to the fact that they either introduce noise to the cover or exploit noise in hiding the data. The shortcomings of these schemes motivate the presented research in this book.

1.2 Noiseless Steganography (Nostega) Paradigm

As indicated above, contemporary steganography schemes either introduce noise to the original document used as a cover, or exploit noise in the data-hiding process. The book introduces a novel paradigm for designing steganography schemes, namely, Nostega [32,35]. Nostega opts to make the presence of the hidden data natural in the cover so that neither linguistic flaws nor peculiarities are introduced as a side effect. In addition, Nostega strives to legitimize the interaction among the communicating parties so that an adversary would not suspect the association between a sender and a receiver. To illustrate the basic concept behind Nostega, consider the following scenario.

Bob and Alice are on a spy mission. Bob and Alice must appear like any other ordinary people. To emphasize, in general, "ordinary people" have professions and personal interests. Before they go on a mission that requires them to reside in two different countries, Bob and Alice plot a strategic plan and set the rules for communicating covertly using their professions and interests as steganographic umbrellas. Bob is a professor and Alice is a student. They basically agree on concealing messages in educational documents by naturally manipulating questions and answers that legitimately occur in lecture notes, exam samples, homework, and examples, to embed data in such a way that the text cover (edu-cover) looks unsuspicious. They make sure that every time a text cover is generated it has different content and meaning, while it remains legitimate to avoid suspicion of using a steganographic tool. To make this work, Professor Bob has the right to post the text cover (e.g., lecture notes, sample exams, homework, and examples) for his students. On the other hand, Alice is one of Bob's online students, which legitimizes her communications with Bob. When Bob wants to send a covert message to Alice, Bob either posts text cover online for authorized students to access, or sends it via email to the intended students. Covert messages concealed and transmitted in this manner will not look suspicious because the relationship between Bob and Alice is legitimate. Furthermore, Alice is not the sole recipient of Bob's messages; other non-spy students also receive their educational documents, further warding off suspicion.

When Alice decides to send Bob a message, she does it in the same manner as Bob does, except that she uses her role as a student to do so. She posts educational documents, such as her homework solutions, if it is legitimate to do so, as well as other related documents that Bob or any student in class can access, or else she sends them via email to the professor. These educational documents conceal data. However, only Bob and Alice are able to unravel the hidden message because they know the rules of the game. Both Bob's and Alice's communications look legitimate and nothing is suspicious because the relationship between the communicating parties is justified. Alice and Bob are using real data from their academic field to make their covert communications legitimate. Note that even after a class is over, such relationships can still play a role, for instance, a student becoming interested in a particular topic and pursuing it as a profession (e.g., Ph.D. students). On the other hand, if Bob and Alice communicate using cipher text, suspicion can easily be raised and thus the steganographic goal will be defeated.

The above scenario shows how Nostega methodology can be effective in achieving the steganographic goal. In summary, Nostega conceals data in a steganographic cover that looks legitimate and is like any other ordinary material. The cover is then transmitted through an established covert channel such as the legitimate and innocent relationship between Bob and Alice in the above scenario.

1.2.1 The Architecture of Nostega

Nostega achieves legitimacy by basing the camouflage of both a message and its transmittal on a particular field such as education, economics, graphs, or games, as stated earlier, in the above example of Bob and Alice, using a particular profession or relationship gives legitimacy for camouflaging both a message and its transmittal. The core idea of the Nostega paradigm is basically camouflaging messages by embedding them in a form of noiseless data by employing either altered authenticated data or legitimate untraceable data, as shown in Section 1.3. The following is an overview of the Nostega architecture, which consists of five modules as shown in Figure 1.1.

1. **Steganographic field determination** (Module 1) determines the fields such as education, economics, graphs, or games for achieving the steganographic goal. A major selection criterion is the way the steganographic field facilitates the process of generating a noiseless cover in which the data is naturally embedded, so that the cover looks innocent raising no suspicion and, thus, the hidden message is undetectable. Note that the process of Module 1 is only involved at the stage of constructing a Nostega-based system.
2. **Steganographic parameters determination** (Module 2) encodes a message in an appropriate form for the camouflaging process (Module 3). The form and the component of the output of Module 1 may essentially effect how a message can

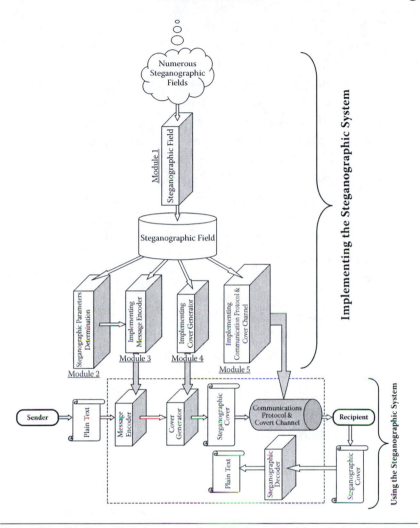

Figure 1.1   This figure Illustrates an overview of Nostega methodology. It shows the interaction of various modules required to build a Nostega system and the configurations between communication parties.

be encoded. Therefore, studying and analyzing the output of Module 1 is necessary for determining the parameters that can be used by next module (Message Encoder). In other words, this module is responsible for determining which parameters can be employed in order to implement a steganographic code that can encode messages in an effective way. For instance, if the steganographic field is a graph, then the steganographic parameters may be numerical values to plot the graph cover

[33]. On the other hand, if the steganographic field is chess games, then the steganographic parameters may be chess moves [30].

3. **Implementing message encoder** (Module 3) implements a message encoder that is capable of accommodating the requirements of the Nostega paradigm as stated earlier.

4. **Implementing cover generator** (Module 4) constructs a cover generator or uses a contemporary tool that is capable of achieving the steganographic goal. For instance, if the cover is a graph such as a chart, then employing a tool used by a wide variety of programs such as Microsoft Excel may be a good option in order to generate a steganographic cover that looks like an ordinary graph. On the other hand, if the cover is chess, then chess software such as Chessmaster [154] may legitimize the steganographic cover.

5. **Implementing communications protocol and covert channel** (Module 5) configures the basic protocol of how a sender and a recipient communicate covertly. It includes the covert channel for delivering a Nostega-based cover between the communicating parties, along with the decoder scheme to unravel a hidden message. A covert channel can be based on a justifiable reason as in the scenario of Bob and Alice discussed above.

1.2.2 Advantages of Nostega

Nostega promotes both the camouflaging of a message and its transmittal. Nostega neither hides data in a noise (errors), nor produces noise rendering the generated cover noiseless. Instead, it conceals messages in a form of noiseless dada in the generated cover using either unaltered authenticated data or untraceable data, thus avoiding wide varieties of attacks. If text is used as a steganographic carrier, the concealment process of Nostega has no effect on the linguistics of the generated cover, rendering such text cover legitimate. Unlike other approaches such as translation-based methods, Nostega can be applied to all languages. For steganographic carriers, Nostega uses materials such as graphs, text, or games, all of which have plenty of room for concealing data. The implemented metrologies based on the Nostega paradigm are keyless schemes. Yet, Nostega is a public paradigm, which implies that it is resilient even when an adversary is very familiar with this new paradigm. It is observed that a steganographic system based on Nostega is capable of fooling both machine and human examinations.

1.3 Summary of the Contributions

The key contribution of this book is the introduction of the novel **Noi**seless **Stega**nography (Nostega) Paradigm [32,35]. In addition, a number of Nostega-based steganography methodologies are developed. The following highlights the basics of the individual methodologies:

- *Graph **Stega**nography Methodology (Graphstega)* is the science and art of avoiding the arousal of suspicion in covert communications by concealing a message in a novel cover type, namely graph cover [33]. Following the Nostega paradigm, Graphstega does not embed a message as a noise in a cover. Instead, a message is camouflaged as plotted data. Graph covers can be applied to a wide variety of domains rendering it a suitable Nostega-based carrier. The popular usage of graphs in business, education, and news, and the availability of a tremendous number of graphs in electronic and non-electronic format make the investigation and detection of a hidden message extremely difficult.
- *Chess **Stega**nography Methodology (Chestega)* exploits popular games such as chess, checkers, crosswords, dominoes, etc., to embed data in steganographic game cover [30]. Chestega conceals messages in the related data of games including instructional material, game analysis, and news articles, by employing intrinsically authenticated or untraceable innocent data in the generated cover, which renders it noiseless.
- *Education-Centric **Stega**nography Methodology (Edustega)* camouflages data in educational documents primarily by manipulating questions and answers (e.g., multiple-choice, true-or-false, fill-in-the-blank, matching) of exams, examples, puzzles, and competitions in order to embed data without generating any suspicious pattern [22]. For instance,

multiple-choice questions can conceal data in the correct answers by placing the correct answers where they represent a steganographic code of a message, e.g., choices from "A" to "D" can represent binary numbers from "00" to "11". In addition, wrong answers (wrong choices) can also conceal data. While these choices must be wrong, there is no real constraint on embedding the data.

- **Sum**marization–Based **Steg**anography *Methodology (Sumstega)* takes advantage of recent advances in automatic summarization techniques to generate a text cover [23,34]. Sumstega does not exploit noise (errors) to embed a message nor produce a detectable noise. Instead, it pursues the variations among the outputs of auto-summarization techniques to conceal data. Basically, Sumstega manipulates the parameters of automatic summarization tools, e.g., frequency weights of words in the sentence selection, and employs other contemporary techniques such as paraphrasing and reordering to generate summary cover that looks legitimate. The popular use of text summaries in business, science, and education renders summary an attractive steganographic carrier and averts an adversary's suspicion.

- **Mat**ure *Linguistic Steganography Methodology (Matlist)* employs natural language generation (NLG) and template techniques along with random series (RS) values (e.g., binary, decimal, hexadecimal, octal, alphabetic, and alphanumeric) of a Domain-Specific Subject (DSS) to generate noiseless text cover [27,107]. This type of DSS (e.g., financial, medical, mathematical, scientific, and economical) has plenty of room to conceal data. It allows communicating parties to establish a covert channel, such as a relationship based on the profession of the communication parties, to transmit a text cover. Matlist embeds data in a form of RS values, functions of RS, related semantics of RS, or a combination of these.

- **Normal** *Linguistic Steganography Methodology (NORMALS)* takes advantage of recent advances in automatic Natural Language Generation (NLG) techniques to generate noiseless (flawless) and legitimate text cover by manipulating the input parameters of an NLG system in order to camouflage data in the generated text [26]. As a result, NORMALS is capable of fooling both human and machine examinations. Unlike Matlist, NORMALS is capable of handling non-random series domains.

- *Email-**Head**ers-Based **Stega**nography Methodology (Headstega)* takes advantage of the frequent exchange of emails by a wide variety of people who generate a high volume of traffic that allows communicating parties to establish a covert channel without a suspicious pattern [24]. Headstega camouflages data in email header carriers (e.g., recipient's email addresses, names, and subject fields) in order to achieve the steganographic goal, while the email contents (the body of emails) are completely legitimate and do not conceal data.

- *Automatic **Joke** Generation Based **Stega**nography (Jokestega).* Who does not joke? The obvious answer is no one. Yet, when someone is joking, anything can be said. This legitimizes the use of joke-based steganography. Jokestega methodology takes advantage of recent advances in Automatic Joke Generation (AJG) techniques to automate the generation of textual steganographic cover [28]. Jokes and puns can be retold with totally different vocabularies while still retaining their identities; therefore, Jokestega pursues the common variations among jokes to conceal messages and deliver them covertly.

- ***List**-Based **Stega**nography Methodology (Listega).* The use of textual lists of items such as products, subjects, books, etc., is widely popular and linguistically legible. Listega takes advantage of such textual lists to camouflage data by exploiting itemized data to conceal messages [28]. Simply, it encodes a message then assigns it to legitimate items in order to generate a text-cover in a form of a legitimate list. Listega establishes a covert channel among communicating parties by employing justifiable reasons based on the common practice of using textual lists of items in order to achieve unsuspicious transmission of generated covers.

- ***Note**s-Based **Stega**nography Methodology (Notestega).* The wide use of notes in business, science, education, and news renders notes attractive steganographic carriers, and allows communicating parties to establish a covert channel capable of transmitting messages in an unsuspicious way. Therefore, Notestega takes advantage of the recent advances in automatic notetaking techniques to generate a text-cover [31]. It pursues the variations among both human-notes and the outputs of automatic-notetaking techniques to conceal data. Unlike machine translation and automatic summarizers, Notestega can embed non-directly related elements to its output, including linguistic elements (e.g., sentences, words, abbreviations), and nonlinguistic elements (e.g., lines, stars, arrows, symbols). Thus, the generated note cover (text cover) has ample room for concealing data without raising a suspicious pattern while embedding a message.

The implementation, validation, and experimental results demonstrate that these methodologies are capable of achieving the steganographical goal.

1.4 Book Outline

Chapter 2 describes the related work. Chapters 3 to 11 describe the details of Graphstega, Chestega, Edustega, Sumstega, Matlist, NORMALS, Headstega, Listega, and Notestega, respectively. Chapter 12 presents the steganalysis validation of the Nostega paradigm. Chapter 13 concludes the presented work and highlights directions for future research.

2
RELATED WORK

This chapter discusses the contemporary steganography approaches found in the literature and highlights their shortcomings. The published schemes are categorized, based on the steganographic cover type, into textual and non-textual schemes; each is discussed in a distinct section.

2.1 Textual Steganography

Textual steganography approaches conceal data in a text cover. These approaches can be categorized as follows.

2.1.1 Textual Format Manipulation (TFM)

This is a nonlinguistic steganography technique that hides data by exploiting the format of text [23]. TFM modifies an original text by employing spaces, misspellings, fonts, font size, font style, colors, and non-color (as invisible ink) to embed an encoded message. However, comparing the original text to the modified text triggers suspicion and enables an adversary to detect where a message is hidden. In addition, TFM can be distorted and may be discerned by human eyes or detected by a computer [25,37].

2.1.2 Series of Characters and Words

During World War I, the Germans communicated covertly using a series of characters and words known as a null cipher [6]. A null cipher is a predetermined protocol of character and word sequence that is read according to a set of rules, such as read every seventh word or every ninth character in a message. Suspicion can be raised because the user is forced to fabricate a text-cover according to a predetermined protocol, which may introduce some peculiarity in the text that draws suspicion and defeats the steganographic goal. In addition, applying a brute force attack may reveal the entire message. The following is a famous example of null cipher:

President's embargo ruling should have immediate notice. Grave situation affecting international law. Statement foreshadows ruin of many neutrals. Yellow journals unifying national excitement immensely.

Apparently neutral's protest is thoroughly discounted and ignored. Isman hard hit. Blockade issue affects pretext for embargo on byproducts, ejecting suets and vegetable oils.

At the time of World War I, the above telegram messages were sent to Berlin by the German Embassy in Washington, D.C. A series of characters and words (null cipher) was used and the predetermined protocol was to read a character from each word based on the message number. The first message was to be read by reading the first character of each word. On the other hand, the second message was to be read by reading the second character of each word. Following the protocol reveals the message below.

"PERSHING SAILS FROM N.Y. JUNE 1[9]"

2.1.3 Statistical Based

Wayner introduced the mimic functions approach [7,8]. The word mimic means "imitate" and that is what the mimic function does; it imitates some of the statistical properties of legitimate text. The final product of mimic functions should fit the statistical profile of the chosen legitimate text. It employs the inverse of the Huffman Code by inputting a data stream of randomly distributed bits to produce text that obeys the statistical profile of a particular normal text. Therefore, the text generated by mimic functions is resilient against statistical attacks. Mimic functions can employ the concept of both context free grammars (CFG) and Van Wijnaarden grammars to enhance the output. The output of regular mimic functions is gibberish, which renders it extremely suspicious [1,3,7,8,25]. However, the combination of mimic functions and CFG slightly improves the readability of the text [7,8], even though detectability issues persist. Furthermore, if an adversary were to guess the generation of the "seed text" he might be able to reveal the original plain text [25,35].

The following example is generated by spammimic [38], which is an online tool that employs mimic functions. The text is the cover that hides the short message, "Author: Abdelrahman Desoky". Clearly the tool renders lengthy and linguistically poor text.

It's time for another game between the Whappers and the Blogs in scenic downtown Blovonia. I've just got to say that the Blog fans have come to support their team and rant and rave. Play Ball! Top of the inning. No outs. Now, Sal Sauvignon comes to the plate. Here we go. Here's the pitch It's a screamer. No good. Ball. He's winding up. What a fast one that looked like it was rising. He knocks a line-drive into the head of Robby Rawhide No trouble yet. The pitcher spits. Prince Albert von Carmicheal adjusts the cup and enters the batter's box. Okay. The next pitch is a fastball with wings. High and outside.

2.1.4 Synonym Based

Chapman and Davida introduced a steganographic scheme consisting of two functions called NICETEXT and SCRAMBLE that use a large dictionary [9–12]. NICETEXT uses a piece of text to manipulate the process of embedding a message in the form of synonym substitutions. This process preserves the meaning of text cover (the original piece of text) every time it is used. The synonym-based approach attracted the attention of numerous researchers in the last decade, including Winstein [39], Bolshakov et al. [40,41], Calvo et al. [42], Chand et al. [43], Nakagawa [44], Niimi et al. [45], Topkara et al. [46], Murphy et al. [47], and Atallah et al. [48,49]. Although the text-cover of the synonym-based approach may look legitimate from a linguistics point of view given the adequate accuracy of the chosen synonyms, reusing the same piece of text to hide a message is a steg-anographic concern. If an adversary intercepts the communications and sees a piece of text that has the same meaning over and over again with just a different group of synonyms between communicating parties, he will question such communication.

The following is an example of the text generated by NICETEXT [9–12]:

Advance around the Third Half during 1997. Either, the generally operative down ago relationships has financial. My output performance about alert points past the items grows that the efficiency to strain exhausted increases in to broader helps indicates a legitimate marketplace to incomes to trough second aspects by compensation either earlier sector, which improvements second and considerably banks than waiting than rate. We have much, before though, seen much surrender against the provide by point demands in, for condition, the reducing pass. Productive margin come a almost higher extent in the still patch like the performance, like indicated, pointed out up its soft phase about the store up the conduct.

It is observed that the text generated by NICETEXT, as shown by the above example, does not make sense and is semantically incoherent. This approach was later enhanced in [9–12] to tackle these shortcomings. The following is an example using the enhanced version [10]:

It took me a long **time** to complete the project.
It took me a long **duration** to complete the project.
It took me a long **period** to complete the project.
It took me a long **span** to complete the project.

The above examples reveal that the robustness of the synonym-based approach remains questionable, even if the enhanced version is capable of generating a better text. Linguistically, it is extremely difficult, if not impossible, to find a large number of synonyms that can be generally used in various contexts.

2.1.5 Noise Based

Grothoff et al. introduced the translation-based steganographic scheme [13–15] to hide a message in the errors (noise) that are naturally encountered in a machine translation (MT). This approach embeds a message by performing a substitution procedure on the translated text using translation variations of multiple MT systems. In addition, it inserts popular errors of MT systems, and also uses synonym substitutions in order to increase the bitrate. Unlike synonym-based steganography, linguistic flaws in the noise-based approach are not a concern unless they appear excessively. However, the authors state that one of the concerns is that the continual improvement of machine translation may narrow the margin of hiding data. In addition, the translation-based approach, as pointed out in [13–15], cannot be applied to all languages because the fundamental structures are radically different. This generates severely incoherent and unreadable text [13–15,25,35].

The following example [14] of a translation-based steganographic scheme renders a lengthy linguistically illegitimate text just to hide the two letters "hi":

That bourgeoisie has played a most revolutionary role in who history. The Bourgeoisie, Where they has to the rule come, all feudalen, patriarchalischen, idyllischen conditions destroys. The Bourgeoisie undressed every venerable and activities of their holy light regarded cum pious shyness. It has the physician, the lawyer, the pfaffen, the poet, whom man of the science transforms into her paid hired hands. The Bourgeoisie tore their agitate-sentimental veil from the family relationship off and attributed it at on pure money relationship. The bourgeoisie has revealed like the brutal Kraftaeusserung which admires the reaction on the Middle Ages so much in which traegsten Baerenhaeuterei found its suitable addition. Only she has proved what which activity of which people can manage. It has completely different wonder works achieved than Egyptian pyramids, Roman water pipelines and gotische cathedrals, it completely different courses implemented than people migrations and crusades. Which bourgeoisie cannot exist without constantly revolutionizing that instruments of production, and thereby which relations of production, and with them the whole relations of society. An unchanged retention of that old production way was which first existence condition of all former industrial classes against this. The continual circulation of production, the continuous vibration of all social conditions, the eternal uncertainty and movement distinguish the Bourgeoisepoche before all different. The need for always more extensive sales for her products chases that bourgeoisie over that whole world.

Another noise-based approach, called the confusing approach, has been proposed by Topkara et al. [50]. The approach basically employs typos and ungrammatical abbreviations in a text (e.g., emails, blogs, and forums) for hiding data. Moreover, Shirali-Shahreza et al. have introduced an abbreviation-based scheme [51] to conceal data using the short message service (SMS) of mobile phones. Due to the size constraints of SMS and the use of the phone keypad instead of the keyboard, a new language was defined for text messaging to make the approach more practical. However, these approaches are sensitive to the amount of noise (errors) that occur in human writing. Such a shortcoming not only increases the vulnerability of the approach, but also narrows the margin for hiding data. The following example of the confusing approach [50] renders the lengthy and linguistically inadequate text, along with an unacceptable level of flaws, just to hide the 16 bits:

A substantial portion of the text available online is of a kind that tends to contain mane typos and ungrammatical abbreviations, e.g., emails, blogs, forums. It is therefore not surprising chat, in suck tests, one can tarry out information-hiding by the judicious injection of tyros. The resilience is achieved through the use of computationally asymmetric transformations (CAT for short): Transformations that can be married out inexpensively, yet reversing them requires much mere extensive semantic analyses (easy for humans to carry out, but hark to automate).

2.2 Non-Textual Steganography

A number of steganography approaches employ non-text based covers such as digital images and audio files. Image steganography is based on manipulating digital images to conceal a message. Such manipulation often renders the message as noise. In general, image steganography suffers from several issues such as the potential for distortion, the significant size limitation of the messages that can be embedded, and the increased vulnerability to detection through digital image processing techniques [5]. Audio covers have also been pursued. Examples of audio steganography techniques include LSB [16,17], spread spectrum coding [18,19], phase coding [18,20], and echo hiding [20,21]. In general, these techniques are too complex, and like their image-based counterpart, are still subject to distortion and vulnerable to detection [3,5,17,23]. To a great extent, the hidden message may become a foreign body in the cover. In addition, image and audio steganography schemes rely on private or restricted access to the original unaltered cover in order to avoid the potential of comparison attacks, which is considered a major threat to covert communication. Basically, an adversary can detect the presence of a hidden message by comparing a particular image cover or audio cover to the original image or audio file, thus discovering that some alterations have been made. It is worth noting that these techniques most likely use a stega-key as a password to prevent the revelation of an embedded message.

Exploiting the use of Go games to hide messages has been another way considered by Hernandez-Castro et al. [52]. Basically, Go game scripts are suggested as covers wherein messages are hidden in moves or comments. However, this work is limited to Go games and its options for concealing messages are also very limited. This work has considered neither the coding implication on the sequence of moves, nor the use of authenticated data in terms of documented tournaments and games among known players. Only fabricated Go games are pursued as covers. In addition, the proposed approach is vulnerable to contrast attacks where the sequence of moves does not logically match the game flow, mostly caused by the message concealment process. Moreover, it is vulnerable to comparison and traffic attacks.

TCP/IP packets and storage media have also been pursued as steganographic carriers. Handel and Sandford [53] exploit the unused space in the header of TCP/IP packets to hide and deliver data across the Internet. The TCP packet header has six unused (reserved) bits and the IP packet header has two reserved bits. There are a tremendous number of packets that are transmitted over the Internet, which can convey and transmit a secret data. On the other hand, information can be hidden in unused or reserved space in computer systems [54,55]. For example, the Windows 95 operating system had around 31 kB of unused hidden space which could be used to hide data. Unused space in file headers of images, audio files, etc., can also be used to hide data. However, these techniques are detectable and vulnerable to distortion attack [3,4,23].

3

GRAPHSTEGA

Graph Steganography Methodology

This chapter presents the **Graph Stega**nography (Graphstega) Methodology [33], which is one of many methodologies developed in this book based on Nostega. Graphstega does not embed a message as a noise in a cover. Graphstega avoids the arousal of suspicion in covert communications by concealing a message as data points in a graph. This novel cover type is referred to hereafter as a graph-cover. The popular usage of graphs in business, education, and news, and the availability of a tremendous number of graphs in electronic and nonelectronic format make the investigation and detection of a hidden message extremely difficult. As will be shown later in the book, Graphstega is resilient to contemporary attacks, such as traffic analysis, and contrast and comparison attacks, even when launched by an adversary who is familiar with Graphstega.

The remainder of this chapter is organized as follows: Section 3.1 demonstrates Graphstega, Section 3.2 shows the capability of converting graph-cover to all other steganographic cover types, and Section 3.3 discusses communications protocol (CP). Finally, the chapter concludes with Section 3.4

3.1 Graphstega Methodology

According to Nostega, five modules are applied in order to implement a successful steganographic system. The first is to determine a particular field (domain) that can be employed to achieve the steganographic goal. For Graphstega, this module is concerned with the selection of a suitable subject for which a graph-cover is to be generated. The second module identifies steganographic parameters (steganographic carriers) that are capable of concealing data without creating noise. Graphstega exploits representational data such as numerical and non-numerical values that can be easily plotted. In the third module, the message is encoded in a way that neither raises suspicions nor constrains the generation of the steganographic cover. Graphstega employs either authenticated data or untraceable data (private data). Fourth, if there are contemporary non-steganographic tools that can be employed to generate the steganographic cover in such way to appear legitimate and innocent, then such tools should be used. In Graphstega, a graph cover is generated using non-steganographical tools such as MS Excel. Finally, the fifth module is the communications protocol, which is concerned with how a sender and a recipient communicate covertly. This module includes the establishment of the covert communications channel.

The focus in the balance of this section is on the third and forth modules, which address the encoding and camouflaging processes, given their relevance to the novel graph cover presented in the chapter. In other words, a graph cover is generated in two steps. First, a message is encoded in a form that can be camouflaged in a graph. Second, the steganographic code (the encoded message) is represented in a graph as data points. In Section 3.3, a few notes about the communications protocol, i.e., the fifth module, are presented.

3.1.1 Message Encoding

Graphstega creates an encoded representation of the plain text message and then camouflages it in a graph. In general, Graphstega does not impose any constraint on the message encoder scheme as long as it generates a set of data values that can be embedded in a graph cover. However, the subject of the graph has to be factored into the selection of the most appropriate encoding scheme. For example, a graph that reports weather changes will restrain the values of the data to a range within which the encoded message has to stay. In addition, the variations in the data values have to be considered, especially when the graph is not shared in a form that allows the recipient to access the table on which the graph is based. For example, showing a graph in which data varies between 1 and 2,000 would most probably make it difficult, and even infeasible, for the recipient to accurately determine the values unless they are annotated on the graph. The same applies if the message is encoded using real numbers, which sometimes lose precision when plotted. Given the availability of numerous encoding techniques in the literature that can meet these constraints [1–4,56], the discussion in the balance of this section will be focused on the graph cover rather than the message encoding.

In the examples shown in this chapter, messages are encoded as follows. First, the plain text message is converted to a binary string which is then partitioned into groups of a particular number of bits that is agreed upon among communicating parties. Finally, a decimal representation is generated for the individual groups. For example, in a 7-bit based grouping, the value of each group would range between 0 and 127 (0000000 to 1111111 in binary). The following describes the encoding of a sample message:

- The plain text of the message is *"Use my secret key"*.
- The concatenated binary string of the ASCII representation of this message is:

  "0101010101110011011001010010000001101101011110010
  01000000111001101100101011000110111001001100101011
  101000010000001101011011001010101111001"

- Slicing this string (from the previous step) into 7 bits each, as set and agreed upon by communicating parties, will result in:

  0101010 1011100 1101100 1010010 0000011 0110101
  1110010 0100000 0111001 1011001 0101100 0110111
  0010011 0010101 1101000 0100000 0110101 1011001
  0101111 001

- Converting the individual slices (from the previous step) into decimals results in:

  "42 92 108 82 3 53 114 32 57 89 44 55 19 21 104 32 53 89 47 1 ".

It is worth noting that the range of the resulting decimal values can be easily narrowed or widened by partitioning the binary string into groups of less or more than 7 bits. Again, this encoding scheme is just for illustration and many alternative schemes can be employed.

3.1.2 Graph Cover

As mentioned, Graphstega camouflages a message by embedding the encoded message as data points in a graph cover. In other words, the encoded message will be the data that is represented in a graph. The message may constitute a subset or a full set of the data in the graph. The latter case makes the message's decoding a straightforward exercise; basically, by applying the reverse process using all data items. However, the use of a partial data set requires a preagreement among the communicating parties on how to pick the data items relevant to the decoding of the message. For example, the sender may agree with the recipient on considering only every other data item on the list. The use of a subset of the plotted data can make Graphstega more resilient to attacks as observed. Basically, an adversary would have to try all possible subsets of the plotted data in order to identify the relevant items, assuming that he will suspect the presence of a hidden message in a particular set of communications traffic and attempt to guess the encoding scheme.

The subject and context of graphs are usually dependent. Obviously, the subject determines the correctness of the data. For example, a graph that shows the blood pressure over a period of time cannot have data values that are out of the known range for a live human being. The context would most probably influence the choice of the graph style. For example, pie charts would suit high level summaries, while a Pareto chart captures the relative importance of the differences among groups of data. Therefore, the communicating parties should first agree on the subject that each will use to conceal messages. Examples include finance, medicine, math, and economics reports and analysis. The selection criteria include the suitability of the chosen subject for concealing the encoded message and for averting suspicion. In general, the chosen subject has to fit the communicating parties and provide some grounds for justifying the communications. The selected subject also has to suit the desired frequency of communications. Through the use of some subjects, it may be possible to generate a new graph every hour or less. For example, it is customary for a stockbroker to receive a market update every half hour, and even more frequent updates on stocks of monitored companies. On the other hand, some subjects may not justify more than one message per month, season, or even year. For example, it is not very often that someone will receive an email message or a letter from the utility company about the rate of energy consumption or payment history. Finally, some subjects enable broadcasts or nonprivate announcements to a set of interested parties and would thus make the association between the sender and the recipient unsuspected. Unsolicited marketing is a perfect example in this category, where a sender emails a brochure to multiple recipients in order to sell some unpopular products, or promotes a stock of a new company.

One of the obvious concerns about the use of graph cover is the size constraint on the message that can be hidden. One would argue that only small messages may be embedded in a graph. While the concern is legitimate, Graphstega is capable of concealing both short and long messages. For short messages, the encoded version will be used as the data plotted in the graph. In this chapter, MS Excel is employed by Graphstega to generate the graph cover. Figure 3.1 shows an example, which hides the message "Use my secret key" encoded in Section 3.1.1, basically plotting the following set of values: *"42 92 108 82 3 53 114 32 57 89 44 55 19 21 104 32 53 89 47 1"*. Often in that case, it would suffice for the recipient to visually inspect the graph in order to note down the data values and decode the message. For long messages, however, data cannot easily be noted from the graph due to the constraints on the scale and plotting area. In other words, the scale would hinder the determination of the data values with high resolution so that the message could be accurately decoded. Therefore, Graphstega requires that long messages to be embedded in a graph are included as an object in the cover so that the data can be accurately retrieved. Examples include attaching an Excel file to an email message, or posting a graph on a website with access to a downloadable version of it.

Figure 3.2 shows a sample graph cover that conceals a long message and lists its relevant characteristics.

The message is the Consumer Prices Index of July and August 2007 [57]; the size of the long message is 47.5 KB. It is encoded by applying the scheme described in Section 3.1.1 using groups of 8 bits, i.e., each decimal number is in the range [0, 255]. The frequency of appearance of the decimal numbers in the range [1, 81] is plotted and portrayed as packet delay measures of an experiment. The graph can be inserted as an object in an MS Word document. The recipient

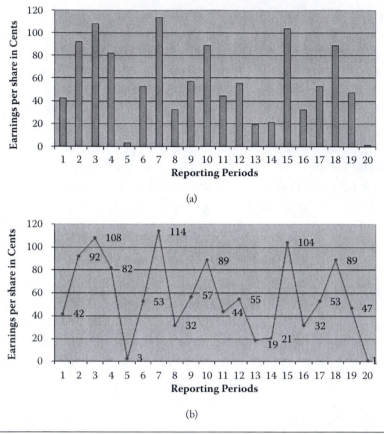

Figure 3.1   This figure illustrates the capability of Graphstega to conceal the message, *"Use my secret key."*

can double click the graph in order to open the accompanying Excel file, access the row data, and finally decode the message. It is argued that most published steganography approaches would highly recommend small messages to avoid detection since they embed them as noise. The bitrate for concealing the above examples of long and short messages is 4.37 percent and 1.0061 percent, respectively. Therefore, Graphstega is, in fact, superior to contemporary steganography when it comes to effectiveness and flexibility in hiding all sorts of messages.

3.2 Other Steganographic Cover Types

Graphstega has a very unique feature that sets it apart from all other steganographic approaches. Basically, the pursued graph cover can

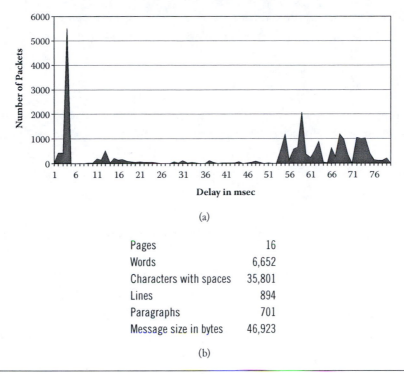

(a)

Pages	16
Words	6,652
Characters with spaces	35,801
Lines	894
Paragraphs	701
Message size in bytes	46,923

(b)

Figure 3.2 An example of a graph cover that conceals a long message.

be presented in different cover types. In other words, Graphstega is capable of converting the graph cover to an image cover, text cover, or audio cover without distortion or significant complexity. However, Graphstega's use of the other cover types is somehow constrained by the message size, as explained in this section.

3.2.1 Graph in Image Cover

Converting the graph cover that conceals the message into an image cover is straightforward. The graph can simply be converted to bitmap, GIF, JPEG, PNG, or any other digital image format. Presenting the graph in an image cover will not cause the loss or distortion of the hidden message because the message is concealed as data points rather than pixels. Unlike image steganography, an adversary will not suspect the image cover since no noise is exploited in the message-concealing process. Obviously, the data should be visually identifiable from the image (which may require scaling) in order to allow the recipient to reveal the encoded message. Thus, an image cover may be unfit for large messages, but suitable for short messages.

3.2.2 Presenting the Graph's Data in Text Cover

Graphstega can also employ a text cover. In this case, the data values used in the encoded message will be enumerated and mixed with some text. Obviously, an appropriate subject and text cover need to be generated to suit the data values so that the cover looks legitimate. An example is shown in Figure 3.3, employing a set of authenticated data that is collected through the use of Internet search engines such as Google, in which a list of authenticated books from www.amazon.com is used to justify the values.

Other examples are shown in Figure 3.4. The user must have legitimate reasons when using these techniques in order to fool an adversary. Downloading a free trial of software can be a legitimate reason for concealing a message in a software key. It is worth noting that the auto generation of appropriate textual covers involves numerous techniques from natural language processing and is beyond the scope of this chapter. Graphstega is resilient to distortion and it is capable of passing both human and machine examinations without raising suspicion. As shown by the examples in Figure 3.4, linguistically, the presented text-cover is flawless and looks legitimate.

3.2.3 Presenting the Graph's Data in Audio Cover

The use of audio covers is also possible for presenting the graph data. In order for Graphstega to do so, a textual cover has to be generated first, as explained above, and then the Graphstega scheme converts the text cover to a voice message. The latter step can be done easily by using the text-to-speech software that is widely available in the market for a nominal fee, or even downloadable for free on the Internet. The audio file can be for an oral presentation during which the graph is explained or used during news coverage. Again, an audio cover in this case is resilient to both distortion and destruction, implying that the message will not be lost, damaged, or altered during transmission because the message is concealed as data points.

BOOK TITLE	AUTHOR	PRICE
My Southern Friends	James R. (James Roberts) Gilmore	$42.00
Designing with Solar Power	Deo Prasad (Editor), Mark Snow (Editor)	$92.00
Anthology of Bulgarian Folk Musicians	Todor Bakalov	$108.00
¡Buen viaje! Level 1, Student Edition	McGraw-Hill	$82.00
Horticulture Magazine. June 1972	Horticulture Magazine Editors	$3.00
The Architect's Handbook of Professional Practice	The American Institute of Architects and Joseph A. Demkin	$53.00
Molecular Anatomy of Cellular Systems	I. Endo, I. Yamaguchi, T. Kudo, H. Osada, and T. Shibata	$114.00
The Jazz Piano Book	Mark Levine	$32.00
Tracking and Monitoring Legislation	TheCapitol.Net and Christopher Davis	$57.00
The LabVIEW Style Book	Peter A. Blume	$89.00
How the Best Get Better, Book and CD set	Dan Sullivan	$44.00
Couples and Family Client Education Handout Planner	Laurie Cope Grand	$55.00
The Well Cat Book	Terri McGinnis, DVM	$19.00
4 Blondes	Candace Bushnell	$21.00
Differential Equations and Dynamical Systems	J.K. Hale and J.P. LaSalle	$104.00
Parkett No. 70	Christian Marclay, Wilhelm Sasnal, and Gillian Wearing	$32.00
The Ceo's Guide to Health Care Information Systems	Joseph M. Deluca and Rebecca Enmark Cagan	$53.00
Preparatorio para o Exame de PMP	Rita Mulcahy	$89.00
Particles, Sources, and Fields: Volume 3	Julian Seymour Schwinger	$47.00
A Dollar = $1.00	Carey Molter and Monica Marx	$1.00

Figure 3.3   A graph cover presented in textual cover to conceal the message *"Use my secret key"* using book prices from www.amazon.com on Friday, September 07, 2007.

It is important to note that choosing the appropriate subject cover is crucial in this case and, in fact, in all other cover types pursued by Graphstega. In addition, the user must have a convincing reason for using the chosen technique for legitimizing the transmittal of a hidden message. For instance, although a bookstore receiving booklists seems innocent, receiving it as an audio file may raise suspicion. Meanwhile, one would not question the motive for sending the commentary of a CEO of a startup or an oral summary of a meeting. The ability of Graphstega to employ multiple types of cover makes it a very versatile approach and enables robust communications among the involved parties.

Tracking Number:

4292-108-82-3-53-114-32578944551921-104-32538947-1

Please keep the tracking number. In case of calling customer support have the tracking number ready.

(a)

Confirmation Number:

4292-108-82-3-53-114-32578944551921-104-32538947-1

Please keep the tracking number. In case of calling customer support have the Confirmation Number ready.

(b)

Software Key License:

4292-108-82-3-53-114-32578944551921-104-32538947-1

Please keep the tracking number. In case of calling customer support have the Software Key License ready.

(c)

Figure 3.4 Examples for possible textual covers that can be employed by Graphstega.

3.3 Communications Protocol

As a methodology based on the Nostega paradigm, Graphstega enables a powerful solution to the issue of a cover's transmittal to recipients. The use of graphs allows a legitimate association among the communicating parties and thus makes sharing the cover very ordinary. Graphs are popular in all sorts of reports, articles, educational material, and marketing brochures. Such popularity makes the transmission of the cover via email, posting the graphs on web pages, or even downloading articles that include graphs a very natural matter. For example, camouflaging a message in a stock market report, in the form of a graph cover, a text cover, or any other cover type, that is sent or posted on the Internet from a broker to a client would not be unusual. In fact, such a report can be sent to many clients with only one of them being able to reveal the hidden message. In addition, casual message exchanges that include no hidden messages can be pursued in order to avoid the formation of a communications pattern that may draw attention. Explicit message transmission is not the only means for sharing the cover. Web posting, postal mail and printed articles are samples of others that can be pursued. In summary, the way a hidden message is delivered can raise suspicion even if using a secure hiding technique. Graphstega averts the suspicion that may arise during covert communications not only by camouflaging a message, but also its transmittal. Therefore, Graphstega imposes that intended users make the appropriate arrangements, techniques, policy, rules and any other related specifications for achieving its goal. In general, a sender and recipient communicating covertly using Graphstega should agree to the following:

1. The specifications and configurations of Graphstega encoder and decoder.
2. The arrangements for the covert transmission of a hidden message. This step is to establish a legitimate channel for communications among intended users, including picking an appropriate subject and format for the cover.

The Graphstega communications protocol is illustrated in Figure 3.5.

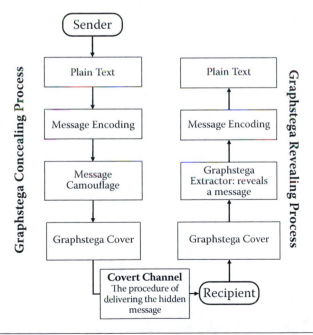

Figure 3.5 A summary of the Graphstega communications protocol followed by a sender and a receiver.

3.4 Conclusion

This chapter has introduced Graphstega, a novel steganography methodology, which employs graphs as a cover for concealing messages. Graphstega, unlike other approaches, does not embed the message as a noise in the cover; instead the message is encoded and used as the data plotted in a graph. Graphstega is a keyless approach and can be employed without difficulty using popular software tools such MS Excel. Through multiple examples, the chapter has confirmed the ability of Graphstega to camouflage both short and long messages. In addition, Graphstega can convert the graph cover to all other steganographic cover types, e.g., text cover, image cover, and audio cover. Such diverse representation of the graph cover allows flexibility in generating the steganographic cover that will fool both human and machine examinations. Graphstega camouflages both a message and its transmittal. Graphstega has been shown to be resistant to all contemporary attacks such as traffic analysis and contrast and comparison. The tremendous number of graphs in electronic and nonelectronic format, and the high volume of traffic accessing these materials, make it impossible to investigate each and every piece of content and transaction. Therefore, graphs are rendered a favorable steganographic cover.

4

CHESTEGA

Chess Steganography Methodology

This chapter presents yet another novel methodology based on the Nostega paradigm. The introduced **Che**ss **Stega**nography (Chestega) Methodology exploits popular game domains such as chess, checkers, crosswords, and dominoes to conceal messages in the form of instructional material, game analysis, news articles, or any other form of game that is capable of camouflaging data [30]. Since it is based on Nostega, Chestega does not exploit noise to embed a message nor produce a detectable noise. Instead, authenticated data can be employed in the cover, which makes it resilient to comparison attacks. This chapter demonstrates the feasibility of employing authenticated Chess Cover generated by Chessmaster 8000. Chestega is also a public approach that neither relies on the secrecy of its technique, nor needs to employ a stega-key. As will be shown later in this chapter and Chapter 13, Chestega is resilient to contemporary attacks, such as traffic analysis, and contrast and comparison attacks, even when launched by an adversary who is familiar with Chestega.

The remainder of this chapter is organized as follows. Section 4.1 describes Chestega in detail and highlights its advantages. Section 4.2 describes and discusses the implementation of Chestega. Finally, the chapter is concluded in Section 4.3.

4.1 Chestega Methodology

As indicated above, Chestega follows the Nostega paradigm and exploits popular game domains such as chess, checkers, crosswords, and dominoes to conceal messages. Referring back to the five modules of Nostega, the first step for Chestega is to determine a particular game field (domain) such as chess, checkers, crosswords, or dominoes that can be employed to achieve the steganographic goal. The second module identifies some steganographic parameters (steganographic carriers) that are capable of concealing data without creating noise. Chestega exploits representational data of games such as moves, game analysis, teaching, etc., from either authenticated data or untraceable data (private data) in order to generate noiseless steganographic cover. The third module is concerned with the message encoding and the fourth addresses cover generation. In Chestega, the message encoder will depend on the steganographic parameters and the cover is generated using non-steganographic tools such as Chessmaster 8000. The final step is implementing a communications protocol that is responsible for how the intended parties communicate covertly. The last module includes the implementation and establishment of the covert communication channel for transmitting a steganographic cover. Without loss of generality, the rest of this chapter assumes that chess is the game picked by the first module. The next section gives an overview of Chestega and is then followed by a detailed discussion of the Chestega modules.

4.1.1 Chestega Overview

Chess is a popular game that appeals to people of all ages worldwide. In addition to international competitions, numerous local, regional and national chess tournaments are held almost everywhere. Chess games are reported and rated by an international chess federation or local chapters. To standardize the storage and reporting of chess games, they are represented using specific keywords and syntax, called the Portable Game Notation (PGN) [58]. PGN is not the only chess notation that exists. However, in this chapter PGN is used since it is the official and most popular chess notation.

Chestega averts suspicion in covert communication by concealing a message using chess data. Chess data in this context includes chessboard positions, pieces and their colors, moves, tournament names, places, results, and players. This data can be exploited to conceal a message within a script of moves in a game, teaching sessions, or game analysis. The chess data can be authenticated, e.g., citing actual games or tournaments, players, etc., or fabricated as part of teaching material or a made-up scenario. The fabricated data does not always have to look normal and legitimate (e.g., reflecting only legal moves), instead it may be in a form of a natural noise such as an illegal move or a position; the use of illegal moves is often pursued by the chess community for teaching purposes.

The Chestega cover can be in the form of a graph such as game statistics, an image such as a snapshot of the chessboard during a game, text that teaches tactics, audio (e.g., game analysis), or a combination of these. The tremendous volume of chess data in electronic and non-electronic format makes an adversary's job extremely difficult and renders Chestega an effective steganographic methodology.

Chestega is composed of three core modules. Each core module's ultimate goal is to define a configuration for the communicating parties to use. The first module mainly determines Chestega encoding parameters, meaning what aspect of the game would be used to hold steganographic code. These parameters are then used by the second and third modules to define a message encoder and a camouflage scheme, respectively. Figure 4.1 shows the interaction among the Chestega modules and how the generated configuration is used by the sender and recipient. The following sections explain the core Chestega modules in detail. Section 4.2 elaborates on how the communicating parties employ the Chestega configuration for covert message exchange.

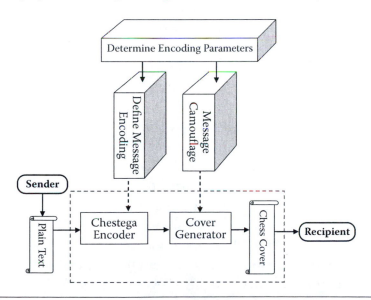

Figure 4.1   This figure demonstrates the interaction between Chestega modules and shows the way a generated configuration is used by the sender and recipient.

4.1.2 Determining Encoding Parameters

Numerous parameters in chess can be exploited as a vehicle for concealing a message. A parameter in this context means some aspect of the game that is referred to with multiple values throughout the game. Examples of these parameters include the squares on the chessboard, pieces, moves, players, or thinking time. The encoding module of Chestega exploits these choices and determines the parameter(s) that will be employed to conceal a message. The selection criteria will be mostly driven by the message size, the style of the cover, and the availability of authenticated data that would match the encoded message.

While the use of the chessboard is the most intuitive choice for message encoding, it puts a cap on the size of the message. For example, assume that the squares in the chessboard are serially numbered and the presence of a pawn indicates that that square conceals part of the message. Obviously, the maximum size of a message would be constrained by the number of pawns (16) and the number of squares in the board (64), and thus the message would not exceed 96 bits (16 pawns × 6 bits of 64 squares). On the other hand, the use of moves as an encoding vehicle would allow the concealment of long messages. The message can simply be represented as a sequence of moves in a game. Given that most chess games, especially at the master level, last for an extended duration and involve many moves, it is feasible to conceal long messages subject to availability of authenticated data as we explain below. While concealing long messages is a challenge for all known steganography approaches, Chestega can hide relatively long messages.

Although one could argue that the selection of a suitable cover is affected by the selected coding parameter and not the other way around, an imposed style for the cover would constrain the encoding of the message. For example, if chess-teaching sessions are not an acceptable form of cover, e.g., the communicating parties are known to play well, allowing illegal moves will raise suspicion and would not be acceptable. Thus, using moves as an encoding parameter will be restricted to only legal moves. The same applies to chessboard and pieces encoding, such as having the two bishops tied to the same square color early in the game. In addition, the availability of authenticated data plays a major role in determining the encoding parameters. In general, being able to map each steganographic code to realistic data that is publicly accessible would be a major advantage to any steganography approach. For example, concealing a message within a game analysis would mean that every reference to a move in the game must match what happened in reality, since the game is documented and anyone can examine the authenticity of the used data. While the use of fabricated chess data such as reporting on a fictitious game is always possible, it requires more care in justifying the association between the communicating parties as discussed in Section 4.1.5.

4.1.3 Defining Message Encoder

Chestega creates an encoded representation of the plain text message and then camouflages it in a chess cover. The obvious constraint that Chestega imposes on the message encoder is generating steganographic code that can be embedded in the cover. For example, when a chessboard is employed as an encoding parameter, the message encoder should not refer to a nonexistent square. In addition, the variations in the data values may have to be considered. For example, when moves are pursued as an encoding vehicle, the target square has to abide with the chess rules for movement of a piece. Encoding the message as numerical values is not the only option. As discussed in the previous section, the use of characters can be a feasible choice. Messages can be concealed using the names of players, tournament locations, or opening techniques. Character-based encoding will be mostly challenged by finding the appropriate authenticated data that can be referenced in the same chess cover.

Given the availability of numerous encoding techniques in the literature that fit [3,4,56], the balance of this section will focus on an example that illustrates how to meet the message encoding constraint. This example will be used in Section 4.2 to demonstrate the applicability of Chestega. A message is encoded as follows. First, the message is converted to a binary string which is then partitioned into groups of a particular number of bits that is agreed upon among communicating parties and such that all constraints on the range of steganographic code values are met. Finally, a decimal representation is generated for the individual groups. For example, in a 7-bit based grouping, the value of each group would range between 0 and 127 (0000000 to 1111111 in binary). The following describes the encoding of a sample message:

- The plain text of the message is "*he doesn't love you*".
- The concatenated binary string of the ASCII representation of this message is:

  "0110100001100101001000000110010001101111011001010111001101101110100100100111010000100000011011000110111101110110011001010010000001111001011011110111010100100000"

- Slicing this string (from the previous step) into 7 bits each, as set and agreed upon by communicating parties, will result in:

  0001111 0010110 1111011 1010100 100000

- Converting the individual slices (from the previous step) into decimals results in:

  "52 25 36 6 35 61 74 115 55 36 78 66 3 49 94 118 50 72 15 22 123 84 32".

It is worth noting that the range of the resulting decimal values can be easily narrowed or widened by partitioning the binary string into groups of less or more than 7 bits. Again, this encoding scheme is only for illustration; many alternative schemes can be employed.

4.1.4 *Message Camouflaging Scheme*

As mentioned before, Chestega camouflages a message by concealing the encoded message as data in a chess cover. In other words, the encoded message will be the data that is referenced in the cover. The message may constitute a subset or a full set of the data in the cover. The latter case makes the message's decoding a straightforward exercise by applying the reverse process using all data items. However, the use of a partial data set would require a preagreement among the communicating parties on how to select the data items that are relevant to the decoding of the message. For example, the sender may agree with the recipient on considering only every other data item according to the order of appearance in the cover. The use of a subset of the chess data can make Chestega more resilient to attacks. Basically, an adversary would have to try all possible subsets of the data in order to identify the relevant items, assuming that he suspected the presence of a hidden message in a particular set of chess-related documents, and he would have to attempt to guess the encoding scheme. The same applies when multiple encoding parameters are pursued. It would be very difficult for an adversary to identify which parameter to investigate, especially when an explicit interaction between the sender and the receiver does not take place, e.g., by posting the cover on a publicly accessible web site. Note that in this chapter a plain text is concealed for simplicity. In reality, the cipher text is concealed rather than plain text, which is common practice in steganography.

Chestega supports multiple cover styles and types. A style in this context means how and why chess data is presented. Examples of cover styles include teaching documents, puzzles, game reports, and news articles. A cover can be focused on a single game or discuss multiple games. While it is a common practice for a chess player to read and analyze unrelated games, e.g., checking various postings on the Internet, it is feasible nonetheless to relate various chess games appearing in a cover. Themes for relating a collection of games in a cover could include:

1. The opening strategies of a chess game
2. Similar positions of some pieces or the application of similar concepts such as scarifying piece(s), controlling open files, short castle, or opposite castle
3. The names of chess players, tournaments, and events
4. The date and place of games, e.g., country and city
5. Political or rivalry aspects of the played games, e.g., U.S. versus the former Soviet Union

It is worth noting that identifying the theme and generating text to legitimize the appearance of unrelated games in a chess cover can be automated through the use of a natural language generation (NLG) system [59]. Many of the computer-based chess tools such as Chessmaster employ NLG systems to generate analysis and comments.

Meanwhile, the type of cover indicates its format. The most intuitive cover type is the use of images when using the chessboard for encoding. Basically, the relevant pieces are placed in the right squares and a capture of the chessboard then constitutes the cover. Alternatively, text covers can be employed in the form of detailed descriptions, game analyses, and teaching sessions. The use of the PNG notation would be appropriate in that case. In addition, a graph cover [30,33] can be employed when game or tournament statistics are used to conceal a message. Moreover, an audio cover may be pursued in the form of expert commentary, or a live update of a game. The encoding parameters, chosen by the first module, guide the process of selecting the most suitable type and style of cover. As mentioned earlier, long messages make some encoding parameters such as moves an appropriate choice for concealing a message, and also make detailed description and analysis of games a favorable cover. Also, an encoding that causes illegal moves mandates the use of educational chess documents as cover. It is worth noting that multiple cover types may be involved. For example, the game analysis can include a number of images of the chessboard that summarize the status of the game at different instants.

The selected cover style also has to suit the desired frequency of communications. Through the use of some styles it may be legitimate to generate a new cover every day or so. For example, it is customary for a chess website to report on recent games on a daily basis, or even more frequently. On the other hand, some covers may not justify more than one message per month, season, or year. For example, the statistics of chess activities in a local region are not reported very often. Finally, some covers enable broadcasts or nonprivate announcements to a set of interested parties, and thus make the association between the sender and the recipient unsuspected. Posting an opinion about a chess game on a website of chess fans is a perfect example in this category. Finally, the cover style may depend on whether the use of authenticated data is required. Chess covers that involve verbose documents make the use of authenticated data less favored because many constraints may be imposed to ensure consistency. For example, using moves of a publicly watched game to conceal a message requires the moves, and possibly their order, to match what happened in the game. That is obviously harder than reporting the moves of a private or fictitious game.

4.1.5 Chestega Configuration

A sender and a recipient who communicate covertly using Chestega must agree on the following, which constitutes the Chestega configuration:

1. The particular specifications of the message encoding/decoding scheme including the parameters employed for concealing the message
2. The style and type of the chess cover so that the recipient knows what to decode
3. How to establish a covert channel enabling them to communicate, i.e., delivering a Chestega cover to the recipient

The first and second items are addressed by the three modules, which are discussed in the previous sections. The third item, which is referred to as the Chestega communication protocol, mainly defines how the cover will be delivered to the recipient without raising suspicion. Contemporary steganography approaches in the literature have focused on how to conceal a message and not on how to camouflage its transmittal. It is however argued that covert transmittal of the steganographic cover is very crucial to the success of steganography. At the core of the cover transmittal issue is how to prevent the association between the sender and recipient from drawing suspicion. For example, exchanging email messages would automatically imply a relationship between the communicating parties. Similarly, downloading files from a web site indicates an interest in the accessed material. With advances in monitoring tools for network and Internet traffic, profiles of user's access pattern can be easily established. An adversary most probably will suspect the presence of a hidden message, even if the content does not look suspicious, because of the observed traffic pattern and the lack of a justification for the interest in the contents of such message traffic. Therefore, it is very important to rationalize the receiving of the steganographic cover in order to avoid attracting any attention that may trigger an attack.

Chestega enables an effective solution to the issue of a cover's transmittal to recipients. The use of chess allows a legitimate association among the communicating parties and would thus make sharing a chess cover an ordinary practice. Chess is a very popular game and has many fans and players all over the world. Such popularity makes the transmission of the chess covers via email, posting them on web pages, or even downloading chess-related articles a natural matter. In addition, casual message exchanges that include no hidden messages can be sent to avoid the formation of a communications pattern that may draw attention.

Explicit message transmission is not the only means of sharing the cover. Web posting in public discussion forums and mailing magazines via postal services are samples of other means that can be pursued. In summary, the way of delivering the hidden message can raise suspicion even when using a resilient steganographic technique. Chestega averts the suspicion that may arise during covert communications not only by camouflaging the message but also its transmittal.

4.2 Chestega Implementation

The following scenario illustrates how Chestega can be used. Bob and Alice are undercover agents and they communicate covertly using chess. They agree on a date and time using a specific online chess provider to play a game, examine games, or teach chess for the purpose of communicating covertly.

This section demonstrates the applicability of Chestega and validates the feasibility of the concealment process through two examples. In the first example, only the chessboard is used to encode a message. The second example employs the first letter of a real chess player as an encoding scheme. These examples are also indented to show how one can define his Chestega configuration. It should be noted that this section shows just a few examples of possible implementations. In addition, the goal of this section is to show Chestega capabilities in concealing data, rather than making the adversary's task difficult to decode a message. Using a cryptosystem to protect a message is straightforward and is not the focus of this chapter.

4.2.1 Chessboard-based Example

Intuitively, the chessboard is the most basic encoding venue. The encoding scheme of this example is similar to the one discussed in Section 3.3 of Chapter 3. A chessboard is an 8x8 square, which renders 64 squares, as shown in Figure 4.2. Since the chess pieces are two colors, white and black, the encoding of the chessboard will be the double

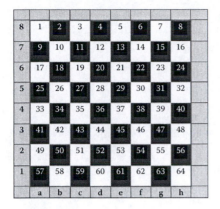 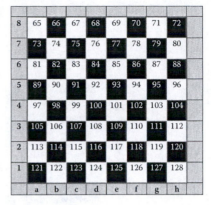

Figure 4.2 The steganographic code when encoding the white side (left) and the black side (right) of a chessboard.

of 64 squares which is 128 squares. The squares are encoded from 0 (in binary 0000000) to 127 (in binary 1111111). Employing an index that starts at 1 referring to 0 in decimal (in binary 0000000) up to 128 referring to 127 in decimal (in binary 1111111), as shown in Figure 4.2, each move will be thus represented by 7 binary digits (7 bits), referring to the index of the target square by a piece of a particular color. Note that these 7 bits per move represent the bitrate of the presented implementation example of Chestega, which can be different from one implementation to another. The message to be concealed is "*he doesn't love you*", which will be encoded as detailed in this section and also explained in Section 3.2 to "*52 25 36 6 35 61 74 115 55 36 78 66 3 49 94 118 50 72 15 22 123 84 32*". Table 4.1 shows each steganographic code and its corresponding move in the PNG notation. The PNG moves are then used to conceal the message in a chess-cover (Figure 4.3). In this cover, particular chess moves from unaltered authenticated games are used to camouflage the message in a chess training lesson. A collection of games are included, each starts with a move that corresponds to a steganographic code in the encoded message. The theme of the cover is that sacrificing a piece in chess may be the gate to winning the game. The order of the games corresponds to the moves in Table 4.1. The selection of games was done by querying the Chessmaster database. There are multiple databases for chess games and distinct moves, which enable the automation of identifying the contents of a chess-cover. The text in the cover, other than the first paragraph, is auto-generated using Chessmaster. Given the size of the full cover, only the

This lesson is about trading off pieces in order to gain a superior position. The following games demonstrate that having less material and good position can lead to winning.

Anderssen defeated Dufresne by sacrificing a piece to open the central files against the uncastled Black King, and despite his seemingly adequate development and counterattacking chances, Black comes out a tempo short in one of the finest combinations on record, justly known as the "Evergreen Game."

1. e4	e5	
2. Nf3	Nc6	
3. Bc4	Bc5	
4. b4	Bxb4	
5. c3	Ba5	
6. d4	exd4	
7. O-O	d3	
8. Qb3	Qf6	
9. e5	Qg6	
10. Re1	Nge7	
11. Ba3	b5	
12. Qxb5	Rb8	
13. Qa4	Bb6	

The Chessmaster recommends: Knight at b1 to d2.

Analysis: You move your knight at b1 to d2, which blocks Black's pawn at d3. Black answers with a castle. You move your knight to e4, which threatens Black's pawn at d3. Black responds with the pawn to d5, which disengages the pin on Black's pawn at f7 and forks your bishop at c4 and your knight at e4. Your pawn captures pawn en passant, which pins Black's pawn at f7, protects your bishop at c4 and your knight at e4, and attacks Black's knight at e7.

Black counters with pawn takes pawn, which removes the threat on Black's knight at e7 and isolates your pawn at c3. Your bishop at a3 takes pawn, which pins Black's knight at e7, attacks Black's rook at b8, and creates a passed pawn on c3. Black responds with the bishop to h3, which threatens checkmate (queen mates), pins your pawn at g2 with a partial pin, and blocks your pawn at h2. You move your knight at f3 to g5, which frees your pawn at g2 from the pin. As a result of this line of play, you win two pawns for a pawn. Additionally, your mobility is greatly increased. Also, Black's pawn structure is somewhat weakened. Finally, the pressure on Black's King is slightly increased.

14. Nbd2	Bb7	
15. Ne4	Qf5	
16. Bxd3	Qh5	
17. Nf6+	gxf6	
18. exf6	Rg8	
19. Rad1	Qxf3	
20. Rxe7+	Nxe7	
21. Qxd7+	Kxd7	
22. Bf5+	Ke8	

23. Bd7+	Kd8	
24. Bxe7#	1-0	

This brilliancy-prize game by Henry Edward Bird, one of England's premier players for half a century, features a speculative queen sacrifice with the unusual combination of two rooks and knights against queen, rook and ;knight. A delight!

1. e4	e6	
2. d4	d5	
3. Nc3	Nf6	
4. exd5	exd5	
5. Nf3	Bd6	
6. Bd3	O-O	
7. O-O	h6	
8. Re1	Nc6	
9. Nb5	Bb4	
10. c3	Ba5	
11. Na3	Bg4	
12. Nc2	Qd7	
13. b4	Bb6	
14. h3	Bh5	
15. Ne3	Rfe8	
16. b5	Ne7	
17. g4	Bg6	
18. Ne5	Qc8	
19. a4	c6	
20. bxc6	bxc6	
21. Ba3	Ne4	
22. Qc2	Ng5	
23. Bxe7	Rxe7	
24. Bxg6	fxg6	
25. Qxg6	Nxh3+	
26. Kh2	Nf4	
27. Qf5	Ne6	
28. Ng2	Qc7	

The Chessmaster recommends: Queen to d3.

Analysis: You move your queen to d3. Black counters by moving the rook to f8, which attacks your pawn at f2. You move your king to g1, which frees your knight at e5 from the pin and protects your pawn at f2. Black responds by moving knight to c5, which attacks your queen. You move your queen to e2, which moves it to safety. Black replies by moving the rook at f8 to e8. You move your queen to a2, which frees your knight at e5 from the pin. Black responds with rook captures knight. Your pawn captures rook, which pins Black's pawn at d5 and creates a passed pawn on e5. Black answers with rook captures pawn. As a result of this sequence of moves, you win a rook for a knight and a pawn.

29. a5	Bxa5	
30. Rxa5	Rf8	
31. Ra6	Rxf5	
...		
.....		

Figure 4.3 The chess cover that conceals *"he doesn't love you,"* using a chessboard-based encoding.

first two games are included. It is worth noting that in practice, links to the individual games can be used in order to avoid lengthy text and make it easy to browse the contents.

4.2.2 Non-game Example

This example (shown in Figure 4.4) demonstrates how a message can be concealed without using contemporary chess parameters such as pieces, a chessboard, or moves. The idea is to use data that is not

Table 4.1 Encoded Message Using
Steganographic Code in Figure 4.2

BINARY	DECIMAL	COLOR	PGN SQUARE
0110100	52	W	d2
0011001	25	W	a5
0100100	36	W	d4
0000110	6	W	f6
0100011	35	W	c4
0111101	61	W	e1
1001010	74	B	b7
1110011	115	B	c2
0110111	55	W	g2
0100100	36	W	d4
1001110	78	B	f7
1000010	66	B	b8
0000011	3	W	c8
0110001	49	W	a2
1011110	94	B	f5
1110110	118	B	f2
0110010	50	W	b2

related to how the game is played, e.g., components and rules, but rather related to the players, tournaments, place, and date. That is why the example is called "non-game." Again the message "*he doesn't love you*" is to be concealed. The bit string for this message shown in Section 3.2 is again used here. However, the bit string is sliced into 4-bit sets. The encoding scheme for this example is to pick any 16 letters in the English alphabet and map each to a distinct combination of 4 bits. Table 4.2 shows the mapping used in this section. It is worth noting that other mappings will work as well. In fact, unordered mapping may be even better from a security point of view. In addition, it is important to mention that slicing the message into 5 bits or more is still feasible. However, some combinations would then need to be mapped to a sequence of two letters and would slightly restrict the cover generation as explained.

Now the corresponding letter for every 4-bit slice of the message's bit string is determined and a name of a chess player that starts with the same letter is identified. Table 4.3 shows the results of this step. Again multiple databases of chess players do exist with a large number of names on record. The names listed in Table 4.3 are found by

This lesson is about trading off pieces in order to gain a superior position. The following games demonstrate that having less material and good position can lead to winning.

Anderssen defeated Dufresne by sacrificing a piece to open the central files against the uncastled Black King, and despite his seemingly adequate development and counter-attacking chances, Black comes out a tempo short in one of the finest combinations on record, justly known as the "Evergreen Game."

1.	e4	e5
2.	Nf3	Nc6
3.	Bc4	Bc5
4.	b4	Bxb4
5.	c3	Ba5
6.	d4	exd4
7.	0-0	d3
8.	Qb3	Qf6
9.	e5	Qg6
10.	Re1	Nge7
11.	Ba3	b5
12.	Qxb5	Rb8
13.	Qa4	Bb6

The Chessmaster recommends: Knight at b1 to d2.

Analysis: You move your knight at b1 to d2, which blocks Black's pawn at d3. Black answers with a castle. You move your knight to e4, which threatens Black's pawn at d3. Black responds with the pawn to d5, which disengages the pin on Black's pawn at f7 and forks your bishop at c4 and your knight at e4. Your pawn captures pawn en passant, which pins Black's pawn at f7, protects your bishop at c4 and your knight at e4, and attacks Black's knight at e7.

Black counters with pawn takes pawn, which removes the threat on Black's knight at e7 and isolates your pawn at c3. Your bishop at a3 takes pawn, which pins Black's knight at e7, attacks Black's rook at b8, and creates a passed pawn on c3. Black responds with the bishop to h3, which threatens checkmate (queen takes pawn), pins your pawn at g2 with a partial pin, and blocks your pawn at h2. You move your knight at f3 to g5, which frees your pawn at g2 from the pin. As a result of this line of play, you win two pawns for a pawn. Additionally, your mobility is greatly increased. Also, Black's pawn structure is somewhat weakened. Finally, the pressure on Black's King is slightly increased.

14.	Nbd2	Bb7
15.	Ne4	Qf5
16.	Bxd3	Qh5
17.	Nf6+	gxf6
18.	exf6	Rg8
19.	Rad1	Qxf3
20.	Rxe7+	Nxe7
21.	Qxd7+	Kxd7
22.	Bf5+	Ke8
23.	Bd7+	Kd8
24.	Bxe7#	1-0

Figure 4.4 The chess cover that conceals "he doesn't love you" using a chessboard-based encoding.

This brilliancy-prize game by Henry Edward Bird, one of England's premier players for half a century, features a speculative queen sacrifice with the unusual combination of two rooks and knights against queen, rook, and knight. A delight!

1.	e4	e6	15.	Ne3	Rfe8
2.	d4	d5	16.	b5	Ne7
3.	Nc3	Nf6	17.	g4	Bg6
4.	exd5	exd5	18.	Ne5	Qc8
5.	Nf3	Bd6	19.	a4	c6
6.	Bd3	O-O	20.	bxc6	bxc6
7.	O-O	h6	21.	Ba3	Ne4
8.	Re1	Nc6	22.	Qc2	Ng5
9.	Nb5	Bb4	23.	Bxe7	Rxe7
10.	c3	Ba5	24.	Bxg6	fxg6
11.	Na3	Bg4	25.	Qxg6	Nxh3+
12.	Nc2	Qd7	26.	Kh2	Nf4
13.	b4	Bb6	27.	Qf5	Ne6
14.	h3	Bh5	28.	Ng2	Qc7

The Chessmaster recommends: Queen to d3.

Analysis: You move your queen to d3. Black counters by moving the rook to f8, which attacks your pawn at f2. You move your king to g1, which frees your knight at e5 from the pin and protects your pawn at f2. Black responds by moving knight to c5, which attacks your queen. You move your queen to e2, which moves it to safety. Black replies by moving the rook at f8 to e8. You move your queen to a2, which frees your knight at e5 from the pin. Black responds with rook captures knight. Your pawn captures rook, which pins Black's pawn at d5 and creates a passed pawn on e5. Black answers with rook captures pawn. As a result of this sequence of moves, you win a rook for a knight and a pawn.

29.	a5	Bxa5
30.	Rxa5	Rf8
31.	Ra6	Rxf5

. . .

Figure 4.4 (continued).

searching the Chessmaster database. If 5-bit slices of the bit string are used, names that match 2 consecutive letters will be needed for some combinations and the search becomes somewhat constrained.

The chess cover, Figure 4.5, is simply generated by looking for games for the identified players. Again, Chessmaster is used to collect the description of the individual games. In other words, unaltered authenticated game information is used for camouflaging the message. It should be noted that some details are omitted from the games in Figure 4.5 in order to simplify the presentation and to highlight the key features. The cover basically lists the games such that the name

Table 4.2   The Letter to Binary
Mapping for the Encoding Scheme

INDEX	BINARY	LETTERS
1	0000	A
2	0001	B
3	0010	C
4	0011	D
5	0100	E
6	0101	F
7	0110	G
8	0111	H
9	1000	I
10	1001	J
11	1010	K
12	1011	L
13	1100	M

of the player with white pieces matches that in Table 4.3. The cover includes many other names that are not related to the message. The appearance of other player names in the cover creates a huge fugue that confuses the adversary and convinces him that nothing is hidden.

4.3 Conclusion

In this chapter, Chestega, a novel methodology for steganography, has been presented. Chestega promotes the use of popular games like Chess as effective venues for covert communication. Chestega averts suspicion in covert communication by concealing a message using chess data. Chess data in this context includes chessboard positions, pieces and their color, moves, tournament name, place, results, and players. This data is exploited to conceal a message within a script of moves in a game, teaching sessions, or game analysis. Unlike most contemporary approaches, Chestega does not exploit noise to embed a message, nor introduce a detectable noise. Instead, authenticated data can be employed in the cover, which makes Chestega resilient to comparison attacks. Chestega also legitimizes the interactions between a sender and a recipient based on their interest in chess and thus makes

Table 4.3 Encoded Message Using Player Names

BINARY	DECIMAL	LETTER	PLAYER NAME
0110	6	G	Grunfeld, E.
1000	8	I	Ivanchuk, V.
0110	6	G	Grunfeld, E
0101	5	F	F. A. Hoffmann
0010	2	C	Chigorin, M.
0000	0	A	Anderssen, A.
0110	6	G	Geller, E.
0100	4	E	Edinburgh
0110	6	G	Gheorghiu, F.
1111	15	P	Pierre de Saint-Amant
0110	6	G	Gligoric, S.
0101	5	F	Frederic Lazard
0111	7	H	Henry Bird
0011	3	D	David Bronstein
0110	6	G	Glucksberg
1110	14	O	Ossip Bernstein
1001	9	J	Johannes Zukertort
0010	2	C	Chigorin, M.
0111	7	H	Hebden, M.
0100	4	E	Emanuel Lasker
0010	2	C	Captain Smith
0000	0	A	Anderssen, A
0110	6	G	Gaspariantz
1100	12	M	MacDonnell, A.
0110	6	G	Gligoric, S.
1111	15	P	Paulsen, L.
0111	7	H	Hennings, A.
0110	6	G	Geller, Y.
0110	6	G	Garcia, G.

traffic analysis ineffective. Numerous types of Chestega cover such as textual, image, graph, or audio can be pursued. In addition, the cover can be auto-generated by contemporary tools like Chessmaster, which employs natural language generation systems, and is thus resilient to linguistic and statistical profile attacks. Chestega is also applicable to other games such as checkers, crosswords, or dominoes.

The following is a list of good games for beginners to check and enrich their tactics.

[White "Grunfeld, E."]
[Black "Bogoljubow, E."]
[Result "1-0"]

Austria's Ernst Grunfeld was a great theoretician who possessed an encylopedic knowledge of the openings. A prominent star in the 1920s, he later became too content with colorless draws. Here is one of his finest early efforts.

1.	d4	Nf6
	....	
19.	Rd8#	1-0

=====================================

[White "Ivanchuk, V."]
[Black "Angelov, K."]
[Result "1-0"]

After a weirdly violent opening exchange, Black finds his Knight difficult to extract.

1.	e4	d5
	....	
29.	Rc1	1-0

=====================================

[White "Grunfeld, E."]
[Black "Alekhine, A."]
[Result "0-1"]

Another superb Alekhine combination, as he outplays opening expert Grunfeld in the middle game.

1.	d4	Nf6
	....	
34.	Qf1	Bd4+

=====================================

[White "Hoffmann, F. A."]
[Black "Petrov, A. D."]
[Result "0-1"]

The main feature of this ancient game is the simultaneous assault by White on f7 and Black on f2, the weakest square on each side. Black's maneuvers culminate in a magnificent queen sacrifice and a relentless king hunt.

1.	e4	e5
	....	
22.	gxh4	Be3#

=====================================

[White "Alekhine, A."]
[Black "Yates, F."]
[Result "0-1"]

Frederick Yates was England's outstanding representative after Blackburne was no longer on the scene. Here is his most celebrated victory which earned him a brilliancy prize.

1.	d4	Nf6
	....	
50.	Kf3	Bg1+

Figure 4.5   A chess cover that conceals a message using the first letter in the name of the player with the white pieces.

5

EDUSTEGA

Education-Centric Steganography Methodology

Unlike previous methodologies, this chapter presents a novel linguistic steganography methodology based on the Nostega paradigm, namely an **Edu**cation-Centric **Stega**nography (Edustega) Methodology [22]. Since the use of educational documents is widely popular within both academic and nonacademic communities, Edustega exploits such documents to conceal data. Because Edustega is based on the Nostega paradigm, it neither hides data in a noise (errors) nor produces noise. Instead, it camouflages the data primarily by manipulating questions and answers of exams (e.g., multiple-choice, true-or-false, fill-in-the-blank, or matching), examples, and puzzles.

The frequent exchange of educational documents, both in electronic and printed formats, creates a high volume of traffic without a suspicious pattern that can draw an adversary's attention, rendering Edustega an attractive approach. The implementation validation of Edustega shows that there is adequate room for concealing data with a bitrate superior to other contemporary steganography techniques found in the literature. The steganalysis validation demonstrates the robustness of Edustega for achieving the steganographic goal, as shown later in the book.

The remainder of this chapter is organized as follows. Section 5.1 explains the Edustega methodology in detail. Section 5.2 demonstrates the Edustega implementation. Finally, Section 5.3 concludes the chapter.

5.1 Edustega Methodology

According to Nostega, there are five modules applied in order to implement a successful steganographic system. The first is to determine a particular field (domain) that can be employed to achieve the stegano-graphic goal. For Edustega, this module is concerned with the selection of a suitable subject for which an edu-cover is to be generated. The second module identifies steganographic parameters (stegano-graphic carriers) that are capable of concealing data without creating noise. Edustega primarily exploits questions and answers of exams (e.g., multiple-choice, true-or-false, fill-in-the-blank, and matching), examples, and puzzles. In the third module, the message is encoded in a way that does not arouse suspicions or constrain the generation of the steganographic cover. Edustega may employ either authenticated data that is publicly available, e.g., questions, or untraceable data (private data) such as made-up questions. Fourth, if contemporary non-steganographic tools are available, these can and should be employed to generate the steganographic cover in such way to appear legitimate and innocent. In Edustega, an edu-cover (text cover) can be generated using non-steganographic tools such as exam generators. Finally, the fifth module is concerned with the communications protocol, which is responsible for how a sender and recipient will communicate covertly. Obviously, it includes the covert channel for transmitting a stegano-graphic cover. The next section gives an overview of Edustega.

5.1.1 Edustega Overview

To illustrate Edustega, consider the following scenario, introduced in Chapter 1. Bob and Alice are on a spy mission, which requires them to reside in two different countries. Before traveling, they plot a strategic plan and set the rules for communicating covertly while portraying themselves as a professor and a student. They basically agree on concealing messages in educational documents by manipulating questions and answers that naturally appear in lecture slides, exam samples, homework, and examples in order to embed the secret data. The manipulated text document serves as a cover (edu-cover). Bob and Alice make sure that every time an edu-cover is generated it has different content and meaning in order to avert suspicion. To make this work, Professor Bob posts or email an edu-cover, e.g., class notes, exam samples, or homework to his students. Alice is one of Bob's students, which legitimizes her interest in Bob's class's web page and getting his email announcements. These covert transmissions will not look suspicious because the relationship between Bob and Alice is legitimate. Furthermore, Alice is not the sole recipient of Bob's messages; other non-spy students also receive their educational documents, further warding off suspicion.

When Alice decides to send Bob a message, she does it in the same manner as Bob does, except that she uses her role as a student to do so. She sends educational documents such as her homework solutions via email to the professor. These educational documents conceal data. However, only Bob and Alice will be able to unravel the hidden message because they know the rules of the game. In other words, nothing is suspicious about the communications traffic between Bob and Alice because they are using real data from their academic field to make their covert communications legitimate. Note that even after a class is over, the relationship can still be exploited. For example, Alice may become interested in a particular topic and pursue an independent study or a Ph.D.

The above scenario demonstrates how Edustega methodology can be used. Edustega achieves legitimacy by basing the camouflage of both a message and its transmittal on a particular educational topic. In the above example, Bob and Alice use a particular educational topic which justifies the interaction as well as the content of the exchanged text. The core idea of the Edustega methodology is to hide data using questions and answers in educational documents such as questionnaires, exams, quizzes, and homework. Obviously, such steganographic cover is linguistically valid and scientifically meaningful. The architecture of Edustega is composed of the following three modules whose ultimate goal is to define a configuration for the communicating parties to use:

1. **Establishing Covert Channel (Module 1):** Determines an appropriate educational topic for achieving the steganographic goal and the means for covert delivery of covers that hide data. Module 1 is only involved in the stage of generating an Edustega configuration.

2. **Message Encoding (Module 2):** Encodes a message in an appropriate form for the camouflaging process (Module 3). The process of generating an edu-cover (Module 3) may influence how a message should be encoded. Therefore, studying

and analyzing the output of Module 3 may be necessary for implementing an effective encoder.

3. **Message Camouflager (Module 3):** Generates an edu-cover (text-cover), in which data is embedded by employing the output of Module 2. The edu-cover may be in the form of a list of questions and answers such as tests, homework, examples, exercises, puzzles, and competitions.

Once the Edustega system is implemented, the covert communications will be accomplished in three steps. First, Module 2 encodes a message. Second, Module 3 camouflages the steganographic code (encoded message) generated by Module 2. Third, the sender transmits the edu-cover over the established covert channel (Module 1). Figure 5.1 shows the interaction among the Edustega modules and how the configured system is used between a sender and recipient. The following sections explain the Edustega modules in detail.

5.1.2 Establishing Covert Channel (Module 1)

The scenario discussed above demonstrates that the communication between Bob and Alice would not be unusual because their interests play a role in camouflaging the delivery of an edu-cover. To employ Edustega, the communicating parties first need to define and agree on the basic configuration of the covert channel. This step includes determining (1) the topic of the educational documents that will be used as a cover, (2) how the cover will be delivered from the sender to the recipient, and (3) how their interaction will be justified. Selecting a suitable topic can play an essential role for securing the steganographic communications by establishing an appropriate covert channel for delivering a hidden message. The chosen topic must facilitate the process of embedding data without generating noise in order to achieve the steganographic goal. Since Edustega mainly manipulates questions and answers to camouflage messages, any topic that allows the use of a list of questions and answers, such as examples, exercises, puzzles, tests, or homework can be used. Although academic subjects such as mathematics and science are obvious choices, numerous nonacademic options can be pursued as well. Examples of nonacademic topics include training courses in industry, puzzle-based

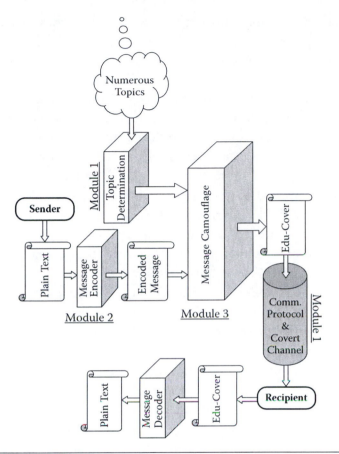

Figure 5.1 An illustration of the Edustega modules and their interface. Module 1 is functionally split to clarify how the selected parameters affect system configuration.

entertainment programs, and competitions. In addition, the chosen topic has to fit the communicating parties and provide some ground for justifying the communications, as elaborated below.

The second important configuration parameter is how the cover will be delivered to the recipient without raising suspicion. Covert transmittal of the steganographic cover is very crucial to the success of steganography. The fact that Edustega employs noiseless-based means for hiding data enables great flexibility in delivering the stegano-graphic cover to its recipient. Basically, the cover does not have to be in a digital format. Even when the cover is delivered digitally, it does not have to be sent as plain text. For example, an edu-cover can be a PDF file, MS-Word document, or even an image, yet the legitimate recipient can extract the hidden data. Therefore, Edustega enables numerous choices for delivering an edu-cover. Options may include web posts and downloads, email transmissions, mailing hardcopies, specialized publications, TV broadcasting [60], manually transferred CD-ROMs, videocassettes, or DVDs. Since the sender may mix an edu-cover in with other legitimate documents, obviously, the basic configuration of the covert channel should include how a recipient can decode only the right covers. For instance, the communicating parties may agree on putting edu-covers among other similar documents by designating a particular sequence (such as odd number, even number, every other 3, etc.), by placing edu-covers in a specific folder, or by specifying certain document contents such as homework.

At the core of the establishment of covert channels is how to prevent the association between a sender and recipient from drawing suspicion. For example, exchanging emails automatically implies a relationship between the communicating parties. Similarly, downloading files from a web site indicates an interest in the accessed material. Due to the advances in monitoring tools for network and Internet traffic, profiles of a user's access pattern can be easily established. An adversary most probably will suspect the presence of a hidden message, even if the content does not look suspicious, because of the observed traffic pattern and the lack of a justification for the interest in the contents of the transmitted materials. For example, if the pretended profession for one of the communicating parties is an elementary English teacher, and yet he sends or receives college level chemistry exams, then suspicion will likely be raised. Therefore, it is very important to rationalize the exchange of steganographic cover in order to avoid attracting any attention that may trigger an attack. The communicating parties need to agree on how to justify their interest in the education documents of the selected topic. This may include defining a role that a sender plays such as mentoring or tutoring, a profession, or simply an interest that justifies a peer relationship.

5.1.3 Message Encoding (Module 2)

Implementing the message encoder entails a two-steps process: (1) determining the encoding parameters in the topic picked by Module 1, and (2) defining a steganographic coding based on these parameters. A parameter in this context means some aspect of educational document(s) that can refer to steganographic values throughout an edu-cover. For educational documents, the order and style of questions as well as their answers can be exploited for concealing data. The definition of the steganographic code would depend on the selected parameters. For example, encoding a message using multiple-choice questions is different from encoding it using the order in which the various question styles appear and so on. The coding module of Edustega exploits these options and determines the parameter(s) that will be employed for concealing messages. The selection criteria may be driven by the size of the message to concealed, the popular question styles for the selected topic, and the availability of authenticated data (answers) that would match the encoded message. Concealing long messages is generally a challenge for most known steganography approaches. Edustega can hide long messages by simply employing more questions in an edu-cover or splitting the message over multiple documents, e.g., multiple homework assignments. Nonetheless, the popularity of certain question styles is an important factor in the selection of parameters, since excessive appearance of a certain style may draw suspicion. For example, having an exam that is mostly composed of true-or-false questions is not a usual practice in some disciplines. Finally, when certain words are exploited for message encoding, e.g., the use of the word "planner" to mean "0," there must be sufficient questions that have such a word in their answers. Finally, one would argue that the encoding parameters may actually influence the selection of a topic for the covert communication and should be defined first. While this is a valid concern, the topic selection is crucial for justifying the interaction among the communicating parties and is thus more affected by the criteria for establishing a covert channel.

Edustega does not impose any constraint on the message encoding scheme as long as it generates a set of data values that can be embedded in an edu-cover. Given the availability of numerous encoding techniques in the literature that fit [3,23,56], the balance of this section will focus on an example that will be used in Sections 5.1.4 and 5.2 to demonstrate the applicability of Edustega.

In the example, the encoding is done as follows. A message is first converted to a binary string. The string can be a binary of cipher text or a compressed representation. The binary string is then partitioned into groups of m bits. The value of m is determined based on the encoding parameters that Edustega exploits. For example, if a message will be concealed in the answer of true-or-false questions, the value of m is 1 since each answer can conceal only 1 bit. On the other hand, if the edu-cover will be in a form of a list of multiple-choice questions with four possible answers, A, B, C, and D, the binary message is partitioned it into groups of two bits, e.g., 00, 01, 10, and 11, corresponding to the possible choices. Again, this encoding scheme is just for illustration and many alternate and more sophisticated schemes can be employed, as demonstrated in Sections 5.1.4 and 5.2.

Countering Coding Patterns: One of the means for steganalysis is to investigate the steganographic cover by looking for unusual patterns. In regard to edu-covers, an adversary may use the answers of questions and look for a pattern that may imply the presence of code words. The use of a fixed steganographic coding in multiple covers may create such a pattern. For example, an adversary may correlate the answers of multiple-choice questions over time given the typical use of few choices to pick from, e.g., four.

In order to prevent such potential vulnerability, Edustega opts to introduce some randomness to how the data are embedded in the cover. One possibility is to exploit multiple parameters in encoding messages. An alternate strategy is to use multiple methods for steganographic coding and establish a protocol for when a particular coding is to be used. In all cases, the communicating parties should pre-agree on when a particular coding parameter or technique is to be used so that a receiver can successfully extract and decode the hidden message. Edustega advocates the use of combinatorics in order to support the desired randomness in edu-covers. Unlike noncombinatorics-based approaches, the coding is both predictable to the receiver and quite random to an observer who tries to analyze the steganographic cover. To illustrate the idea, the following describes how a Latin square [61,62] can be employed by Edustega in defining steganographic coding in the form of a table. It should be noted that in this chapter, a plain text message is concealed for simplicity. In reality a cipher text is concealed rather than plain text, which is common practice in steganography.

A Latin square is an $n \times n$ matrix that is filled with n distinct symbols, each occurring only once in each given row or column.

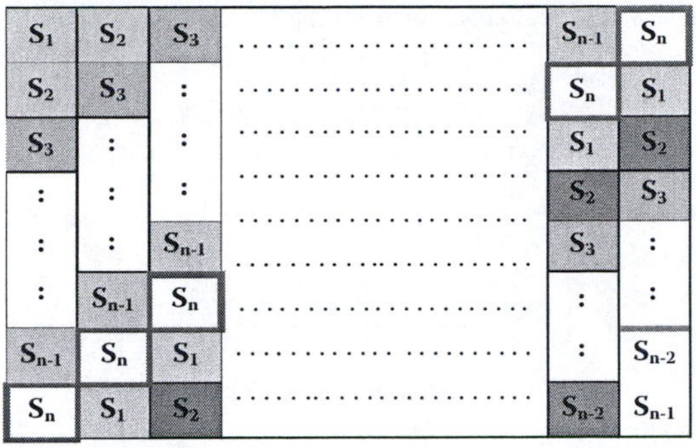

Figure 5.2   In an $n \times n$ Latin square, each row or column is a distinct permutation of n symbols.

Table 5.1   The Use of Latin Squares Introduces Randomness in the Definition of the Steganographic Code, Yet Keeps the Code Predictable for a Receiver to Successfully Decode the Hidden Message

CHOICE	A	B	C	D
1st time used	00	01	10	11
2nd time used	01	10	11	00
3rd time used	10	11	00	01
4th time used	11	00	01	10
5th time $\rightarrow$ restart at first row or use another Latin square				

An example is shown in Figure 5.2. It should be noted that the first row does not have to start from S_1. In other words, the rows can be swapped. A Latin square can be employed in Edustega by uniquely mapping a symbol to each value of the steganographic code. The mapping varies each time a message is encoded. Table 5.1 illustrates the idea through an example. Assume that multiple-choice questions are pursued for concealing messages, with each question providing four choices: A, B, C, and D. The correct answer of a particular question is to match the corresponding bit string in the encoded message. The first time the encoder is used, the first row or column of the Latin square will be used to map A, B, C, and D to "00", "01", "10", and "11" respectively. While concealing a message the second time, the sender will use the second row (or column) which re-maps (rotates) the code among the choices. The third time the sender will use the third row. After the fourth time, the first row may be used again or a different Latin square can be employed for increasing randomness. There is no known close-form formula for the number of $n \times n$ Latin squares with

Table 5.2   Demonstrating the Effect of Randomizing the Steganographic Code by Latin Squares

SENDING "X" THE 1ST TIME (USING 1ST ROW IN LATIN MATRIX)	SECOND TIME "X" IS SENT (ENCODED USING 2ND ROW)	SENDING "X" THE 3RD TIME (ENCODED USING 3RD ROW)
01 = B	01 = A	01 = B
01 = B	01 = A	01 = A
10 = C	10 = B	10 = A
00 = A	00 = D	00 = B

symbols 1, 2, ..., n. The upper and lower bounds that are deemed the most accurate by the technical community are far apart for large n, which makes Latin squares a powerful steganographic coding technique [63]. The receiver is aware of the Latin matrix and can successfully extract the message and decode it. Note that the order of the symbols can be formed differently as long as each element appears only once in each given row and column, e.g., by using another Latin square. Table 5.2 shows an example of concealing the 8-bit ASCII representation of the letter "X", which is "01011000", using the matrix in Table 5.1. It is worth mentioning that the use of empty values, i.e., a null symbol, may also be used. It will then refer to a null-coded element and can be manipulated in order to further avert suspicion.

5.1.4 *Message Camouflaging (Module 3)*

As mentioned earlier, the popularity of educational documents allows communicating parties to establish a covert channel to transmit hidden messages, rendering educational documents an attractive steganographic carrier. Edustega takes advantage of such popularity and camouflages data in educational documents by manipulating, mainly but not limited to, questions and answers (e.g., multiple-choice, true-or-false, fill-in-the-space, matching) of exams, tests, examples, or exercises in order to embed data without generating any suspicious pattern. The high demand for educational documents by a wide variety of people in both the academic and nonacademic spheres has motivated the development of numerous tools for automating the generation of exam questions. Examples of exam generator systems include:

- Bank of Chemistry Questions [64]
- Exams and practice tests such as GRE, SAT, etc. [65]
- Graduate Management Admission Test (GMAT) [66]

- Exam Pro Software [67]
- Test-generator [68]
- Chemistry Exam Generator at the Department of Chemistry, Indiana University Northwest [69]
- Chemistry Exam Generator at the Department of Chemistry, Ohio State University [70]
- Exam Generator (GRE Antonyms) [71]

From a steganography point of view, reusing or altering an existing text to hide data is not a recommended practice, since an adversary can reference the original text and detect the differences. In addition, the reuse of the same piece of text more than once may increase the vulnerability of the covert communications. If an adversary intercepts the communications and notices a similar piece of text being exchanged between communicating parties over and over again, suspicion may be raised. However, this is not a concern for Edustega because the reuse and modification of educational documents is a common practice. For example, an instructor may use and modify old documents such as lectures, examples, tests, or exams for generating new versions. Edustega eases the automation of an edu-cover using tools similar to the systems mentioned above. The automation process of edu-cover, as illustrated in Figure 5.3, is composed of three submodules:

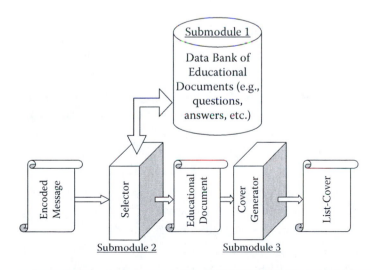

Figure 5.3   An illustration of the submodules of Module 3.

1. **Data Bank of Educational Documents** (Submodule 1): This is simply a large database of documents or pieces of text related to education, such as a bank of questions and answers. Implementing such a bank is accomplished by collecting the required pieces of text, e.g., questions, documents, or lecture notes that are initially developed by teachers, trainers, and experts. This kind of text is often linguistically legitimate given the rigor that the development of educational documents is subject to. For example, the wording of questions put on a test is often checked multiple times to ensure clarity and accuracy. In addition, the reuse of educational documents, a common practice as mentioned above, further strengthens them linguistically given the multiple review cycles that they go through. An example of such a document bank is the database of examination questions for popular standardized tests such as the GRE and SAT [65]. The document database does not have to be centralized. A distributed implementation using a peer-to-peer system or web links can also be pursued. As noted earlier, the updating of such databases is a continual process, and altering a question or document is not unusual and would not draw suspicion. It is also worth noting that a document bank is not generic and is usually limited to a certain topic. Therefore, Edustega will have to reference the appropriate bank based on the topic selected when establishing the covert channel.

2. **Selector** (Submodule 2): This picks the elements from the Data Bank of Educational Documents (Submodule 1) that will form the edu-cover. The criteria of selection are based on the topic and the message-encoding scheme. For example, if the topic is college-level calculus, the scope of the selection will be narrowed to that specific subject. On the other hand, if an edu-cover uses questions and answers, the Edustega system will select a list of questions that forms the edu-cover. The chosen questions have to enable the concealment of the encoded messages. For example, if a message will be concealed by using correct answers of multiple-choice questions, a set of questions that matches the symbols (bit string) used in the message have to be picked. The order of these picked questions in the edu-cover is handled by Submodule 3, as explained next.

3. **Cover Generator** (Submodule 3): This submodule is responsible for forming an edu-cover based on the text picked by the Selector (Submodule 2), while embedding the encoded message. For some styles of edu-covers, the generator may be as simple as listing the picked text in an order that matches the encoded message. For example, if the message is concealed in the answers of multiple-choice or true-or-false questions, the questions are then sequenced according to the symbols or the bits in the encoded message, respectively. Some other styles may require a higher level of sophistication in order to generate a wrapper. For example, the use of a sample GRE text as an edu-cover requires special formatting and the inclusion of preamble, header, or footer. Numerous tools can be employed to ease this step [65–70]. Since the sender may mix edu-cover among other legitimate documents, obviously, the basic configuration of the covert channel should include how a recipient can decode only the right covers. For instance, the Cover Generator (Submodule 3) may put edu-covers among other similar, but null-coded, documents by following a particular sequence (e.g., odd number, even number, every other 3, etc.), by placing edu-covers in a specific folder, or by specifying certain document contents such as homework.

5.2 Edustega Implementation

This section demonstrates the feasibility of Edustega and its distinct capability for achieving the steganographic goal with a higher bitrate than the linguistic steganography approaches found in the literature. It is worth noting that the focus in the balance of this section is on showing how Edustega achieves the steganographic goal, rather than making it difficult for an adversary to decode an encoded message. Employing a hard encoding system or cryptosystem to increase the protection of a message is obviously recommended and straightforward using any contemporary encoder or cryptosystem. Similarly, employing compression to boost the bitrate can easily be accomplished by using the contemporary techniques in the literature. This section shows a few examples of possible implementations following the steps outlined in the previous section.

5.2.1 Edustega System

This section first explains how Edustega modules are employed and configured to construct the overall Edustega system used by the communicating parties.

The Covert Channel Parameters: As indicated earlier, the configuration of the covert channel includes the topic of the educational documents, the relationship between the sender and receiver, and how an edu-cover can be delivered. In this section two topics are employed; namely, the Graduate Record Examination (GRE) and chemistry. Obviously, these topics are just examples and any other topics may apply as stated in Section 5.1. The GRE is very popular worldwide among postgraduate students, both native and nonnative English speakers. Both topics, the GRE and chemistry, offer numerous styles of questions that facilitate the process of camouflaging data. Tools are already available to enable the automation of the concealment process. Examples include the Exam Generator at the Department of Chemistry, Indiana University Northwest [69] or the Exam Generator at the Department of Chemistry, Ohio State University [70]. Both topics make it easy to legitimize the communications between sender and recipient, like the scenario of Bob and Alice in Section 5.1. For instance, an instructor of a chemistry class may post a homework assignment that conceals a message on the class web page. The student can conceal his message in the submitted assignment, possibly through wrong answers. For example, the student may respond to a multiple-choice question with the correct answer if it matches the corresponding symbol in the message, or intentionally mark the wrong answer that suits the symbol. The student-teacher relationship can justify the association between the communicating parties to legitimize the transmittal of an edu-cover.

Edustega Encoder: Edustega encodes a message in a form that suits the camouflaging process. The examples in this section conceal messages using multiple-choice questions. To increase the resilience to attacks, Edustega introduces randomness to the steganographic

Table 5.3 The Steganographic Code Table of the Symbols A, B, C D and E Based on the Properties of Latin Squares

CHOICE	A	B	C	D	E
1st time used	00	01	10	11	000
2nd time used	01	10	11	000	00
3rd time used	10	11	000	00	01

coding through the use of a Latin square to define the mapping of symbols to bit strings. The steganographic code in this Edustega configuration works as follows:

1. Each correct answer (choice) conceals two or three bits according to the steganographic code in Table 5.3. For example, if a correct answer is the choice "A" while using the first row of Table 5.3, the steganographic value "00" is assumed. On the other hand, if using the second row in Table 5.3, the choice "A" will then carry the steganographic value "01" instead.

2. A wrong answer (choice) is also used to conceal data. The code is not dependent on the choice though. Instead, the first letter in a wrong answer is encoded according to Table 5.4. For example, when the incorrect answer starts with the letter "B" while using the first row, it is concluded that the question conceals "01". However, if using the second row, "B" implies "10", and so on. In other words, a wrong choice is not encoded. Instead, if the answer of a question is incorrect, regardless of which wrong choice is marked, the first letter of the picked answer is checked against the table to find out its code value. The use of this table is illustrated later in this section.

3. Based on an agreed-upon protocol, for the entire edu-cover, either one particular row or all rows are used in order, one per question.

Camouflage Module: In this Edustega configuration, the edu-cover is mainly a list of multiple-choice questions. These questions are grouped in the form of exams, examples, or homework. The camouflage module employs online exam generator systems [69–71], online examples [72,73], online dictionaries [74–76], and Microsoft Thesaurus (built into Microsoft Word 97) [77] to embed the data and

Table 5.4 The Steganographic Code for Camouflaging Four Bits in the Wrong Answers of Questions

CODE VALUES

↓ ROW INDEX/ DECIMAL →	0	1	2	3	4	5	6	7	8	9	10	11	12	13	14	15	0	1	2	3	4	5	6	7	8	9
BINARY (4 BITS) →	0000	0001	0010	0011	0100	0101	0110	0111	1000	1001	1010	1011	1100	1101	1110	1111	0000	0001	0010	0011	0100	0101	0110	0111	1000	1001
1.	A	B	C	D	E	F	G	H	I	J	K	L	M	N	O	P	Q	R	S	T	U	V	W	X	Y	Z
2.	B	C	D	E	F	G	H	I	J	K	L	M	N	O	P	Q	R	S	T	U	V	W	X	Y	Z	A
3.	C	D	E	F	G	H	I	J	K	L	M	N	O	P	Q	R	S	T	U	V	W	X	Y	Z	A	B
4.	D	E	F	G	H	I	J	K	L	M	N	O	P	Q	R	S	T	U	V	W	X	Y	Z	A	B	C
5.	E	F	G	H	I	J	K	L	M	N	O	P	Q	R	S	T	U	V	W	X	Y	Z	A	B	C	D
6.	F	G	H	I	J	K	L	M	N	O	P	Q	R	S	T	U	V	W	X	Y	Z	A	B	C	D	E
7.	G	H	I	J	K	L	M	N	O	P	Q	R	S	T	U	V	W	X	Y	Z	A	B	C	D	E	F
8.	H	I	J	K	L	M	N	O	P	Q	R	S	T	U	V	W	X	Y	Z	A	B	C	D	E	F	G
9.	I	J	K	L	M	N	O	P	Q	R	S	T	U	V	W	X	Y	Z	A	B	C	D	E	F	G	H
10.	J	K	L	M	N	O	P	Q	R	S	T	U	V	W	X	Y	Z	A	B	C	D	E	F	G	H	I
11.	K	L	M	N	O	P	Q	R	S	T	U	V	W	X	Y	Z	A	B	C	D	E	F	G	H	I	J

12.	L	M	N	O	P	Q	R	S	T	U	V	W	X	Y	Z	A	B	C	D	E	F	G	H	I	J	K
13.	M	N	O	P	Q	R	S	T	U	V	W	X	Y	Z	A	B	C	D	E	F	G	H	I	J	K	L
14.	N	O	P	Q	R	S	T	U	V	W	X	Y	Z	A	B	C	D	E	F	G	H	I	J	K	L	M
15.	O	P	Q	R	S	T	U	V	W	X	Y	Z	A	B	C	D	E	F	G	H	I	J	K	L	M	N
16.	P	Q	R	S	T	U	V	W	X	Y	Z	A	B	C	D	E	F	G	H	I	J	K	L	M	N	O
17.	Q	R	S	T	U	V	W	X	Y	Z	A	B	C	D	E	F	G	H	I	J	K	L	M	N	O	P
18.	R	S	T	U	V	W	X	Y	Z	A	B	C	D	E	F	G	H	I	J	K	L	M	N	O	P	Q
19.	S	T	U	V	W	X	Y	Z	A	B	C	D	E	F	G	H	I	J	K	L	M	N	O	P	Q	R
20.	T	U	V	W	X	Y	Z	A	B	C	D	E	F	G	H	I	J	K	L	M	N	O	P	Q	R	S
21.	U	V	W	X	Y	Z	A	B	C	D	E	F	G	H	I	J	K	L	M	N	O	P	Q	R	S	T
22.	V	W	X	Y	Z	A	B	C	D	E	F	G	H	I	J	K	L	M	N	O	P	Q	R	S	T	U
23.	W	X	Y	Z	A	B	C	D	E	F	G	H	I	J	K	L	M	N	O	P	Q	R	S	T	U	V
24.	X	Y	Z	A	B	C	D	E	F	G	H	I	J	K	L	M	N	O	P	Q	R	S	T	U	V	W
25.	Y	Z	A	B	C	D	E	F	G	H	I	J	K	L	M	N	O	P	Q	R	S	T	U	V	W	X
26.	Z	A	B	C	D	E	F	G	H	I	J	K	L	M	N	O	P	Q	R	S	T	U	V	W	X	Y

Note: The table is based on the properties of Latin squares.

generate the edu-cover. The dictionaries and thesaurus are mainly used with a GRE-based edu-cover in order to pick appropriate vocabulary for the choices for a question. Since both the GRE and chemistry exams use five options in the multiple-choice, "A" to "E," the correct answers (choices) will be placed in an order that matches the bit string of an encoded message. According to Table 5.3 a correct answer may conceal either two or three bits. For instance, when using the first row in the table, if the steganographic value that needs to be embedded is "00," then the correct answer (choice) will be "A," but if it is equal to "11" then the correct answer (choice) is "D," and so on. On the other hand, this Edustega system embeds data in wrong answers as well, either by selecting particular wrong choices or substituting them according to Table 5.4. As will be shown in the examples below, the use of first letters does not impose constraints on the employed vocabulary. Based on this Edustega configuration each wrong choice (incorrect answers) may conceal four to eight bits.

5.2.2 Edustega Examples

This section shows a few examples for how the Edustega configuration discussed above can be used by the communicating parties to conceal messages. The following describes how a message is encoded and processed by the camouflage module prior to generating the cover. A number of examples of edu-covers that conceal data are demonstrated afterward.

- The plain text is: "Use my same security key".
- The Edustega Encoder converts the message to a concatenated binary string using the ASCII representation of the individual characters, as follows:

  01010101011100110110010100100000011011011110010
  01000000011100110110000101011011010110010100100 0000
  11100110110010101100011011101010111001001101001011
  10100011110010010000001101011011001010111001

- The encoder will then divide the above binary message into slices of sizes that matches those supported by the steganographic coding. The result is shown below. It should be noted

Table 5.5 The Sequence of Answers That the Edustega Camouflage Module Will Use to Embed the Encoded Version of the Message "Use my same security key" in an Edu-Cover

INDEX	CORRECT ANSWERS	WRONG ANSWERS							
1	01	0101	0101	1100	1101	1001	0100	1000	0001
2	10	1101	0111	1001	0010	0000	0111	0011	0110
3	00	0101	1011	0101	1001	0100	1000	0001	1100
4	11	0110	0101	0110	0011	0111	0101	0111	0010
5	011	0100	1011	1010	0011	1100	1001	0000	0011
6	01	0110	1100	1010	1111	0001			

that the binary string could have been encrypted or compressed prior to this step.

```
01  0101  0101  1100  1101  1001  0100  1000  0001
10  1101  0111  1001  0010  0000  0111  0011  0110
00  0101  1011  0101  1001  0100  1000  0001  1100
11  0110  0101  0110  0011  0111  0101  0111  0010
011 0100  1011  1010  0011  1100  1001  0000  0011
01  0110  1100  1010  1111  0001
```

- The camouflage module considers the sliced bit string of the encoded message, generated by the encoder, and maps every slice to a question. The answer (choice) of each question will conceal a part of the message according to Tables 5.3 and 5.4. A slice of 2-3 bits will be assigned to a correct answer, while 4 bits will be embedded in a wrong answer. The results, shown in Table 5.5, are used to finally generate an edu-cover.

Sample Edu-Covers: The following are sample edu-covers for the above message. Only part of the message is shown because of space limitation. The samples demonstrate the effectiveness and efficiency of Edustega and are grouped based on the topic into GRE and chemistry examples.

GRE Antonyms: The following GRE question conceals the 18 bits "010101010111001101" and is generated by [71]. Table 5.6 shows how the mapping of the individual slices of the bit string to the offered choices for the answer. The correct choice B, according to the first row of Table 5.3, matches the first slice. The following 4 slices are embedded into the wrong choices according to the first row of Table 5.4. The

Table 5.6   Details Encoding of a Message

	CORRECT ANSWER	WRONG ANSWERS CAMOUFLAGE DATA BY 1ST LETTER OF KEYWORDS			
INDEX →	1	2	3	4	5
Encoded message →	01	0101	0101	1100	1101
Camouflager uses this row →	B	F or V	F or V	M	N
	From 1st row of Table 5.3	From 1st row of Table 5.4			

Note: Part of the message ("Use my same security key") using a GRE Question. Part of the message is embedded using correct and wrong answers based on Tables 5.3 and 5.4, respectively.

letters of wrong choices are then matched to possible words, employing the dictionary as needed, and the picked words are sorted according to the order of the slices in the bit string. The question in the edu-cover is shown below.

```
Putative
    A. fruitful
    B. undisputed
    C. forceful
    D. modified
    E. noncommittal
```

GRE Sentence Completion: The edu-cover in this sample conceals the 34 bits "0101010101110011011001010010000001" using a GRE Sentence Completion question generated using [72]. Table 5.7 shows how the bit string is mapped, again based on Tables 5.3 and 5.4,

Table 5.7   Details Encoding of a Message (Only the First 34 Bits) Using a GRE Sentence Completion Question Style

	CORRECT ANSWER	WRONG ANSWERS CAMOUFLAGE DATA BY 1ST LETTER OF KEYWORDS							
INDEX →	1	2	3	4	5	6	7	8	9
Encoded message →	01	0101	0101	1100	1101	1001	0100	1000	0001
Camouflager uses this row →	A	G or W	G or W	N	O	K or A	F or V	J or Z	C or S
	From 2nd row of Table 5.3	From 2nd row of Table 5.4							

similar to the previous sample. Note that the second row of both Table 5.3 and Table 5.4 are used this time to embed the required data into the correct and wrong answers.

```
The pressure of population on available resources is
the key to understanding history, consequently any
historical writing that does not take cognizance
of_____ facts is _____ flawed.

    A. demographic…intrinsically
    B. guard…weak
    C. national…object
    D. keen…feeling
    E. joint…congenial
```

GRE Analogy Question: The following edu-cover, again, conceals the first 34 bits of the same bit strings using a GRE Analogy question formed using [73], which is detailed in Table 5.8.

```
Dose:medicine
    A. hubris:hold
    B. oscillation:pulsation
    C. beat:groove
    D. alternating:disturbance
    E. sentence:punishment
```

Chemistry Edu-Cover Samples: The following two chemistry-based edu-covers conceal the 18 bits "010101010111001101", generated similar to the GRE questions above. They are generated using [70]. The encoding procedure is explained in Tables 5.9 and 5.10.

Table 5.8 Details Encoding of the 34 Bits "0101010101110011011001010010000001"

	CORRECT ANSWER	WRONG ANSWERS CAMOUFLAGE DATA BY 1ST LETTER OF KEYWORDS							
INDEX →	1	2	3	4	5	6	7	8	9
Encoded message →	01	0101	0101	1100	1101	1001	0100	1000	0001
Camouflager uses this row →	E From 3rd row of Table 5.3	H or X	H or X	0 From 3rd row of Table 5.4	P	L or B	G or W	K or A	D or T

Table 5.9   Details of Encoding the First 18 Bits of the "Use my same security key" Message to Generate Chemistry Edu-Cover

	CORRECT ANSWER	WRONG ANSWERS CAMOUFLAGE DATA BY 1ST LETTER OF KEYWORDS			
INDEX →	1	2	3	4	5
Encoded Message →	01	0101	0101	1100	1101
Camouflager uses this row →	B	F or V	F or V	M	N
	From 1st row of Table 5.3	From 1st row of Table 5.4			

Table 5.10   Encoding the 18 bits "010101010111001101" in the Second Chemistry Edu-Cover

	CORRECT ANSWER	WRONG ANSWERS CAMOUFLAGE DATA BY 1ST LETTER OF KEYWORDS			
INDEX →	1	2	3	4	5
Encoded Message →	01	0101	0101	1100	1101
Camouflager uses this row →	A	G or W	G or W	N	O
	From 2nd row of Table 5.3	From 2nd row of Table 5.4			

In the 19th century, Dalton revitalized the concept of the atom, which had been dormant for close to 2000 years. Which ancient philosopher coined the term "atomos," or atom?

A. Farnsworth
B. Aristotle
C. Vonnegut
D. Mazdak
E. None of the above

An atom with a positive charge is known as

A. proton
B. WC12
C. Ga
D. neutrons
E. O

5.2.3 Bitrate

The aim of this section is to show the achieved bitrate by the presented implementation examples of the Edustega system. The bitrate

Table 5.11 The Bitrate of the Presented Edustega Examples

INDEX SAMPLE	TOPIC	EDUSTEGA BITRATE
1	GRE Antonyms	3.26%
2	GRE Sentence Completions	1.47%
3	GRE Analogies	3.86%
4	Chemistry (1st sample)	0.94%
5	Chemistry (2nd sample)	2.81%

is defined as the size of the hidden message relative to the size of the cover. Table 5.11 shows the bitrate achieved in the sample edu-covers above. It is worth noting that the bitrate differs from one question to another, from one topic to another, and from one implementation to another.

It is obvious that Edustega achieves a much more superior bitrate than all comparable approaches, making it a very effective stegano- graphic approach. The high bitrate also enables the use of reason- able cover sizes, which is a major concern for all steganographic approaches, linguistic and nonlinguistic. In Chapter 13, all bitrates of linguistic Nostega-based methodologies will be compared to all other comparable approaches (textual steganography).

5.3 Conclusion

This chapter has presented a novel Educational-Centric Steganography (Edustega) Methodology that conceals data in educational docu- ments. The high demand for educational documents by a wide variety of people in both the academic and nonacademic spheres allows the communicating parties to establish a covert channel to transmit hid- den messages, rendering educational documents an attractive steg- anographic carrier. Edustega neither hides data in a noise (errors) nor produces noise. Instead, it camouflages data in educational documents primarily by manipulating questions and answers of exams (e.g., mul- tiple-choice, true-or-false, fill-in-the-blank, matching), examples, puzzles, and competitions in order to embed data without generating any suspicious pattern. It has been shown that Edustega can conceal data in both correct and incorrect answers. An example implemen- tation has demonstrated that a bitrate ranging from 0.94% up to

3.86% can be achieved. Such bitrates are superior to contemporary linguistic steganography approaches found in the literature, confirming the effectiveness of Edustega and the high capacity educational documents provide for concealing data. Furthermore, Edustega can be applied to all languages.

6

SUMSTEGA

Summarization-Based
Steganography Methodology

This chapter presents the second novel linguistic steganography methodology that is based on the Nostega paradigm; namely, **Sum**marization-Based **Stega**nography (Sumstega) Methodology [23,34]. Sumstega neither exploits noise (errors) to embed a message, nor produces a detectable noise. Instead, it takes advantage of recent advances in automatic summarization techniques to generate noiseless text cover. This is accomplished by pursuing the variations among the outputs of auto-summarization techniques to conceal data. Basically, Sumstega manipulates the parameters of automatic summarization tools (e.g., the word frequency weights in the sentence selection), and employs other contemporary techniques such as paraphrasing and reordering to generate summary cover that looks legitimate. The popular use of text summaries in business, science, education, and news, renders summary an attractive steganographic carrier and averts an adversary's suspicion. The steganalysis validation results demonstrate the effectiveness of Sumstega, as will be shown later in the book.

The remainder of this chapter is organized as follows: Section 6.1 and 6.2 briefly provide some background and related work discussion of the summarization field; Section 6.3 introduces and demonstrates the Sumstega methodology; finally, Section 6.4 concludes the chapter.

6.1 Automatic Summarization Overview

Automatic summarization is the scientific art of representing the essence of a long document(s) in a document(s) that is significantly smaller than its original by employing computer programs. The field is traced back to the 1950s [113], and in recent years has enjoyed significant progress and is still more promising in the future [77,80,109]. Automatic summarization systems employ a procedure that may be based on one or more of the following: statistical process, knowledge base, artificial intelligence, computational linguistics, and other related techniques to achieve its goal [77,80,109]. Examples of automatic summarization systems are AutoSummarize [81], SweSum [82], Inxight Summarizer [82], IBM Intelligent Miner [117], and DimSum [84,109]. Automatic summarization approaches may categorize into three types: high level, low level, and hybrid approaches [77,80,109].

High level approaches are also referred to as shallow approaches [77,80,109,119–121]. These depend mainly on extraction approaches and reordering techniques while they attempt to represent the extracted essence in as good a shape as possible. The majority of these approaches produce a summary that is entirely a subset of its original. These approaches employ techniques such as frequency and location weight of sentences and words. To illustrate, the resulting abstract is as if a set of important sentences is highlighted, copied, and then pasted in a desirable order to form a summary. From the point of view of implementation, these approaches are desirable because they are significantly easier and cost less than low-level approaches. Low-level approaches are also referred to as deep approaches [77,80,109,119], in which the need of a knowledge base and other related techniques, such as artificial intelligence and natural language generation, are essential to generate an abstract. Therefore, these approaches are sophisticated to implement, which makes the cost higher than the cost of high-level approaches. Low-level approaches employ techniques such as extraction, paraphrasing rules, reordering, semantic equivalency, and information equivalency to generate summaries. Hybrid approaches, which produce a compaction-based summary, are useful for handling multidocument input. Yet, hybrid approaches may use some reordering and discourse techniques for refining an output [77,80,109].

Note that Section 6.2 demonstrates some summarization techniques that can be used by Sumstega methodology to conceal data.

6.2 Sumstega Carriers

The aim of this section is to explore examples of automatic summarization techniques to demonstrate possible Steganographic

Summarization Carriers (SSC) that are capable of concealing data while retaining a summary cover to be plausible, ordinary, and legitimate. It is imperative to study automatic summarization techniques to explore these plausible SSC before implementing a Sumstega scheme. Investigating the manipulation of the Parameters and Factors of Automatic Summarization Techniques (PFAST) is necessary in order to generate plausible SSC, which practically comprise all possible different legitimate summaries for the same document. It is well-known that summarization systems naturally produce different legitimate summaries for the same document [77,109]. Examples of PFAST may be the weight (e.g., weight of frequency, location, semantics), paraphrasing, truncation, reordering, semantic, and information equivalency. Sumstega can then be tuned to exploit PFAST in order to generate adequate SSC that can camouflage a message without violating the pattern of a summary. Virtually, Sumstega embeds data by substituting a set of elements (e.g., sentences, words) of a particular summary with other legitimate elements from peer summaries in such a way that the summary cover looks like any other legitimate summary. The next sections are described from a steganographical point of view that can be used by Sumstega methodology to conceal data, rather than from an automatic summarizer point of view, which it is out of the scope of this book. Note that all of the following examples are confirmed by the experimental results and observations of both the literature of the automatic summarization field [77,80,109] and Sumstega experimental research work, as shown in this chapter and in Chapter 12.

6.2.1 Extraction

Extraction techniques [77,80,109,119–121,124–126] are mainly based on the sentence level to produce a summary that is entirely a subset of its original document(s). To illustrate, the summary is as if a set of important sentences were highlighted, copied, and then pasted in a desirable order to form a summary. Different implementations of the same extraction techniques can generate variations of a summary (different alterations). Similarly, different extraction techniques can also generate variations of a summary. Extraction techniques may use the weight of frequency or location of sentence or word to generate a summary. Obviously, different elements (e.g., words, sentences) may have the same or similar weights and, when a summarizer needs to select only one element out of these different elements, then selecting any one of these different elements can be legitimate. Thus, Sumstega can select legitimate elements that have the required steganographic code (encoded message) to generate a plausible summary cover. To emphasize, two automatic summarizers can extract different sentences while they summarize the same document(s). For instance, when requesting from AutoSummarize [81] and Automatic Text Summarizer [86] the summary of a document(s) from the news [87] in only one sentence, the output of both summarizers was different. AutoSummarize [81] extracted the sentence shown in Sample 6.1:

SAMPLE 6.1

Police, mistaking de Menezes for Osman, trailed him into Stockwell tube station and down the escalator onto a platform.

Sample 6.1 illustrates the output of AutoSummarize [81]. AutoSummarize is an extraction-based summarizer and some techniques such as superfluous terms, sentence truncation, text compaction, deletion macro-rule, and construction macro-rule may be involved in the extraction procedure.

However, Automatic Text Summarizer [86] extracted a different sentence as shown in Sample 6.2:

SAMPLE 6.2

London was on high alert on the morning that police surveillance teams stationed outside an apartment block in South London spotted de Menezes leaving his building on his way to work.

Sample 6.2 illustrates the output of Automatic Text Summarizer [86], which is different from Sample 6.1. Automatic Text Summarizer [86] is also an extraction-based summarizer, and some techniques such as superfluous terms, sentence truncation, text compaction, deletion macro-rule, and construction macro-rule may be involved in the extraction procedure.

From the point view of automatic summarization techniques both AutoSummarize [81] and Automatic Text Summarizer [86] are generally based on the same technique, which is extraction, but they are differently implemented. Note that these are just examples and are used to show the feasibility of Sumstega scheme to generate numerous different paths of legitimate virtual summaries to create a summary cover.

6.2.2 Abstraction

Summaries that are generated by abstraction techniques have different legitimate elements (e.g., words, sentences, partial sentences, etc.) from the original document(s) [77,80,109,126,129]. Steganographically, such elements along with others can obviously play an essential role in embedding a message in the generated legitimate summary using the Sumstega methodology. Abstraction techniques are most likely complemented by other summarization techniques to generate summaries such as:

- Extraction
- Paraphrasing rule
- Lexical substitution
- Wording prescription
- Superfluous terms
- Sentence truncation
- Text compaction

- Deletion macro-rule
- Construction macro-rule
- Generalization macro-rule
- Reordering sentence aggregation
- Latent semantic analysis
- Semantic equivalency
- Information equivalency

Some of these techniques are shown by virtual examples in Sample 6.3, 6.4, 6.5, 6.6, 6.7, and 6.8. For instance, the goal of revision techniques is to improve the generated summary. Revision techniques may accomplish their goal with or without referencing the source document(s) [77,80,109,129]. When revision techniques function without taking into account the original source document(s), they will alter the generated summary to improve it. This may be accomplished by adding some external elements to the generated summary. These external elements are neither from the summary nor from its original source document(s). On the other hand, when revision techniques function by taking into account original source document(s), they will also alter the generated summary to improve it, which may be accomplished by adding some internal elements to the generated summary. These internal elements may be from the summary, from its original source document(s), or both. In either case, such elements can definitely be employed to embed data in the generated summary. It is worth noting that the revision techniques are, most likely, used by abstraction-based summarizers, as shown by virtual example in Samples 6.5, 6.6, 6.7, and 6.8.

SAMPLE 6.3

~~Automatic summarization is the scientific art of representing the essence of a long document(s) in a significantly smaller document(s) than its original by employing computer programs. The field is traced back to the 1950's. However, the field of automatic summarization has enjoyed significant progress in recent years and is still promising more in the future.~~ Automatic summarization systems employ a procedure that may be based on one or more of the following: statistical process, knowledge base, artificial intelligence, computational linguistics, and other related techniques to achieve its goal. ~~Some examples of automatic summarization systems are AutoSummarize, SweSum, Inxight Summarizer, IBM Intelligent Miner, DimSum, and more.~~ Automatic summarization approaches may categorize into three types: high level, low level, and hybrid approaches.

Illustrates the original document during virtual extraction procedure. Some techniques such as superfluous terms, sentence truncation, text compaction, deletion macro-rule, construction macro-rule may be involved in the extraction procedure.

SAMPLE 6.4

Automatic summarization approaches may categorize into three types: high-level, low-level, and hybrid approaches. Automatic summarization systems employ a procedure that may be based on one or more of the following: statistical process, knowledge base, artificial intelligence, computational linguistics, and other related techniques to achieve its goal.

Sample 6.4 illustrates the abstract after virtual reorder procedure of the extracted text. The abstract started with the second extracted sentence and ends with the first extracted sentence.

SAMPLE 6.5

~~Automatic summarization~~ Summarizers ~~approaches may categorize into~~ are three types: ~~high level~~ shallow, deep ~~low level~~, and hybrid ~~approaches.~~ ~~Automatic summarization systems employ~~ They use ~~a procedure that may be based on one or more of the following:~~ statistical ~~process~~, knowledge base, artificial intelligence, and computational linguistics~~, and other related~~ techniques ~~to achieve its goal~~.

Illustrates the abstract (in Sample 6.4) during the virtual revision procedure. Some techniques such as paraphrasing rule, lexical substitution, wording prescription, superfluous terms, sentence truncation, text compaction, deletion macro-rule, construction macro-rule, generalization macro-rule, reordering sentence, discourse, aggregation, latent semantic analysis, semantic equivalency, information equivalency, and information retrieval may be involved to generate abstracts. All underlined words are added to the abstract during the revision procedure. Additionally, the highlighted words are external elements that did not exist in the original document input.

SAMPLE 6.6

Summarizers are *three types:* shallow, deep, *and* hybrid. They use *statistical, knowledge base, artificial intelligence,* and *computational linguistics techniques.*

Sample 6.6 illustrates the abstract (in Sample 6.4) after a virtual revision procedure. All italicized words are embedded in the abstract during the revision procedure. Additionally, the highlighted words are external elements that do not exist in the original document input.

SAMPLE 6.7

Automatic ~~summarization~~ Summarizers ~~approaches may categorize into~~ are three types: extractor, abstractor *~~high level, low level,~~ and* hybrid ~~approaches~~. ~~Automatic summarization systems employ a procedure that may be~~ They are *based* on ~~one or more of the following: statistical process, knowledge base,~~ artificial *intelligence, ~~computational linguistics, and other related~~* techniques ~~to achieve its goal~~.

Illustrates the abstract (in Sample 6.4) during a different virtual revision procedure other than that used in Samples 6.5 and 6.6. Some techniques such as paraphrasing rule, lexical substitution, wording prescription, superfluous terms, sentence truncation, text compaction, deletion macro-rule, construction macro-rule, generalization macro-rule, reordering sentence, discourse, aggregation, latent semantic analysis, semantic equivalency, information equivalency, and information retrieval may be involved to generate abstracts. All underlined words are added to the abstract during the revision procedure. Additionally, the highlighted words are external elements that do not exist in the original document input.

SAMPLE 6.8

> *Automatic* Summarizers *are three types:* extractor*,*
> abstractor*, and hybrid.* They *are based on*
> *artificial intelligence techniques.*

Sample 6.8 illustrates the abstract (in Sample 6.4) after a different virtual revision procedure other than Samples 6.5 and 6.6 is used. It is noted that both abstracts of Samples 6.6 and 6.8 are different in words, in sentences, and even slightly in meaning. All italicized words are embedded in the abstract during the revision procedure. Additionally, the highlighted words are external elements that do not exist in the original document input.

6.2.3 *Multi-document*

Multi-document summarization techniques [77,80,109,130–133] are capable of handling multiple documents to generate the required summary. The demands of the modern age, such as the World Wide Web and data mining, have rendered the field of multi-document summarization very active and imperative. From the point of view of Sumstega methodology, it is argued that multi-document input may play a critical role in easing the task of generating a mature summary. For example, the use of a domain-specific subject and knowledge base can be used for generating a summary in which linguistics that do not exist in the "original document input" may be used in the generated summary. However, from a linguistics point of view, it is most likely more accurate to use the linguistics of the input documents rather than other linguistics that do not exist in the original input documents. For instance, when a journalist is having a discussion with an author of a book and the journalist uses pieces from the author's text, it is called "using the same language" because he is using the author's words to prove a point in order to convince him. It is argued that the multi-document summarization techniques may play a role in resolving some of these problematic issues, e.g., linguistic flaws such as the flow of text cover of contemporary linguistic steganography approaches. This may be accomplished by employing the linguistics from the multi-document input to generate a mature text cover (summary-cover). Since multi-document summarization techniques are the extension of single document summarization techniques [77,80,109,130–132], the demonstrated samples and examples in this section are sufficient for understanding how multi-document summarization techniques can be used.

6.2.4 Cross-lingual

Summarization techniques are not only capable of handling monolingual-documents [77,80,109], but also of handling multilingual-documents. Cross-lingual summarization techniques [77,80,109] can handle several languages where the input and output documents are in different languages. Both cross-lingual summarization techniques and machine translation techniques may intersect. However, from the point view of Sumstega methodology, cross-lingual summarization techniques are employed differently than in the translation-based steganography approach. This is because the translation-based steganography approach is errors-based. In other words, it hides data in the errors (noise), and it generates more noise to hide data. On the other hand, Sumstega neither camouflages data in a noise nor generates noise when concealing data in summary cover. Instead, when Sumstega employs cross-lingual summarization techniques, it conceals the data in the natural varietal elements (e.g., words, sentences, partial sentences) that are produced by the natural and legitimate process of the summarization techniques. Obviously, cross-lingual techniques can increase the room for concealing data in Sumstega cover. An example of this technique will be similar to the demonstrated samples in this section.

6.3 Sumstega Methodology

Sumstega still follows the five modules of Nostega. The first module is concerned about the selection of a suitable subject, e.g., business, science, education, news, etc., for which a summary cover (text cover) is to be generated. The second module of Nostega identifies steganographic parameters (steganographic carriers) that are capable of concealing data without creating noise. Sumstega exploits variations among the outputs of auto-summarization techniques as steganographic carriers to conceal data. In the third module, the message is encoded in a way that neither raises suspicions nor constrains the generation of the steganographic cover. Sumstega is capable of employing authenticated data such as public news to generate a summary cover. Fourth, summary cover is generated using non-steganographical tools such as a group of contemporary summarizers, as detailed later in this chapter. Finally, the fifth module is concerned with the establishment of the covert communication channel. Sumstega requires the communicating parties to use justifiable documents for generating summary covers in order to legitimize the discernable interaction among communicating parties. The next section gives an overview of Sumstega and is then followed by a detailed discussion of the relevant Sumstega modules.

6.3.1 Sumstega Overview

The main idea of Sumstega methodology is to exploit the variations among the outputs of auto-summarization techniques to conceal data. Basically, Sumstega manipulates the parameters of automatic summarization tools (e.g., the word frequency weights in the sentence selection), and employs other contemporary techniques such as paraphrasing and reordering to generate summary cover that looks legitimate. The popular use of text summaries in business, science, education, and news renders summary an attractive steganographic carrier and averts an adversary's suspicion.

To illustrate Sumstega, consider the following scenario. Bob and Alice are on a spy mission. Before they start their mission, which requires them to reside in two different countries, they plot a strategic plan and set the rules for communicating covertly using their professions as a steganographic umbrella. To make this work, they develop a steganographic summarizer capable of generating various legitimate summaries. Then, the summarizer predetermines a particular single unique course of generating summaries to generate an original summary cover (unaltered), which contains no hidden message at this moment. Next, it embeds a message by performing a summarization substitution procedure on the original summary cover using the legitimate variations of the generated summaries. This process is done in such a way that the summary cover appears to be an ordinary summary.

Bob and Alice establish a business relationship: they are journalists working for the same corporation. They generate summaries of real news data to make their covert communications more legitimate. When Bob wants to send a covert message to Alice, Bob either posts summary cover online for authorized clients and staff to access, or he sends it via email. Covert messages transmitted in this manner will not look suspicious because Bob and Alice are journalists and their interaction is legitimate and innocent. The use of automatic summary in such a profession is natural given the space constraints and the time a reader may dedicate to reading. Moreover, Bob and Alice are not the sole recipients. There are other non-spy journalists, staff, and clients who send and receive such documents, further warding off suspicion. However, only Bob and Alice will be able unravel the hidden messages because they know the rules of the game. They reveal a message by comparing the summary cover that contains a hidden message to the unaltered original summary, which is agreed on in advance, and then decode all substituted pieces (e.g., sentences, words) according to the predetermined encoding system to be used.

The above scenario illustrates how Sumstega methodology can be used effectively. Sumstega methodology is demonstrated in detail in the remainder of this section.

6.3.2 Sumstega Architecture

The core idea of Sumstega methodology is that the camouflage process of data must be accomplished in the natural and legitimate variations produced by the process of the automatic summarization techniques. As demonstrated in Sections 6.1 and 6.2, different automatic summarization techniques, implementations, or both, generate output variations (different summaries) of the same input. This is like multiple summaries of the same document(s) generated by different people where everyone will summarize the document(s) differently regardless of similarities in the meaning [77,80,109]. Therefore, Sumstega methodology takes advantage of such variations to conceal data. As stated earlier, it manipulates the Parameters and Factors of Automatic Summarization Techniques (PFAST), as shown in Sections 6.1 and 6.2, in order to generate output variations that can be employed for embedding data in the generated summaries without violating the

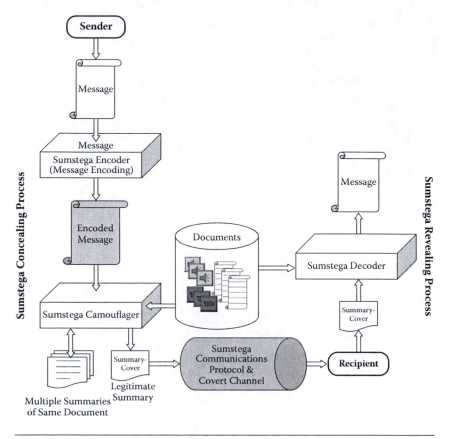

Figure 6.1   Sumstega architecture.

pattern of automated summaries. Sumstega generates summary cover that looks legitimate by exploiting PFAST such as the weight (e.g., weight of frequency, location, semantics), paraphrasing, truncation, reordering, semantic and information equivalency, etc. In addition, Sumstega methodology imposes on the communicating parties the necessity to establish a covert channel in order to transmit summary covers. The following is an overview of the Sumstega architecture, which consists of four modules, as shown in Figure 6.1:

1. **Sumstega Encoder** (Module 1): Encodes a message in an appropriate and required form for the camouflaging process (Module 2).
2. **Sumstega Camouflager** (Module 2): Generates a variety of legitimate summaries, as demonstrated in Section 6.1 and

6.2, to be employed by this camouflaging process to generate a summary cover in which data are embedded.

3. **Sumstega Communications Protocol** (Module 3): Configures the basic protocol of how a sender and recipient would communicate covertly. Obviously, it includes the covert channel for delivering a summary cover to the recipient and the decoder scheme to unravel a hidden message.

The above modules are detailed in the following sections.

6.3.3 Sumstega Encoder (Module 1)

The Sumstega encoder encodes a message in an appropriate and required form for the camouflaging process (Module 2). In general, Sumstega does not impose any constraint on the message encoder scheme as long as it generates a steganographic code that can be embedded in a summary cover. However, the selection and the implementation of the most appropriate encoding scheme are determined by other requirements such as the need for encryption and compression. Implementing the Sumstega encoder can be accomplished either by constructing the required encoder from scratch or by employing contemporary steganographic encoding techniques to encode messages. Given the availability of numerous steganographic encoding techniques, including encryption and compression techniques, in the literature [56,97–99,122,123] that can be employed by Sumstega methodology, the balance of the discussion in this chapter is focused on the generation of Sumstega cover (summary cover) rather than message encoding. In this chapter, the implementation of Sumstega encoder is mainly based on the number of different summaries and the type of different elements (e.g., words, sentences) that can be employed to generate steganographic code, regardless of whether or not other techniques may be included (e.g., encryption and compression). Since the focus of this chapter is steganography and the use of encryption and compression techniques are not part of the contribution, such techniques are neither discussed nor are used in this article.

In the implementation example shown in this chapter, a message is encoded as follows: A message is converted to a binary string. The binary string of a message can be a binary of ciphertext or compressed representation. The binary string is then partitioned into groups of m bits. The value of m is determined based on the number n of different summaries that can be produced, as specified by the Sumstega camouflager (Module 2). Basically, m is set to log n. If $n= 4$, i.e., four different summaries, the bit pattern 00, 01, 10, or 11 (as shown in Section 6.3.4 and in the implementation example in Section 6.3.5) will be applied to the first, second, third, and fourth internally generated summaries, respectively. Thus, if an element (e.g., word, sentence) is unique the internally generated summaries are unique. On the other hand, multiple matches imply null data bits (e.g., if an element and its index are the same in all generated summaries). Again, this encoding scheme is just for illustration and many more sophisticated alternatives can be employed.

6.3.4 Sumstega Camouflager (Module 2)

The Sumstega camouflager engine generates the summary cover that conceals data by employing Module 1 along with different implementations, techniques, etc. of automatic summarization. Technically, there are numerous ways, as expected, to implement the Sumstega camouflager engine. However, in this chapter the Sumstega camouflager engine is implemented based on the following algorithm, which consists of seven submodules:

Submodule 1 generates a variety of legitimate summaries by employing different implementations and techniques of automatic summarization, as demonstrated in Sections 6.1 and 6.2.

Submodule 2 predetermines one of the summaries generated by Submodule 1, which is a particular path of generating summaries, to be the mother summary (original summary). This step will ease the process of revealing the hidden message only for the legitimate recipient. Simply, it allows the decoder to compare the summary cover to the mother summary in order to determine all alterations, which represents the hidden message. These alterations will then be assigned the values of the steganographic code to unravel the hidden message. The steganographic code is the same set of values used by the sender to conceal data.

Submodule 3 maps the summaries generated by Submodule 1 into a matrix, which is called the Sumstega matrix, as shown in Figure 6.2. The Sumstega matrix is $m \times n$ where m is the number of rows and n is the number of columns. The number of columns is the number of different summaries that can be generated by Submodule 1. In other words, Submodule 3 maps one summary in each column of the Sumstega matrix. The number of rows is the number of how many elements in each summary. The value of m should be same for all generated summaries since it is possible to have such control, especially at the sentence level, e.g., sentence extraction summarization.

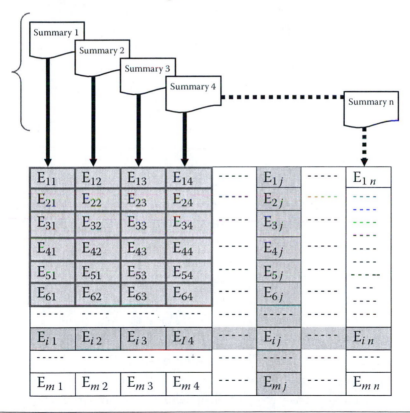

Figure 6.2 The Sumstega matrix contains all the elements of each summary as shown in the matrix. The gray part (shaded) shown in the Sumstega matrix represents the current implementation example and the sample example of summary cover which are described in Table 6.1 and Figure 6.3 as if only four different summaries can be generated.

However, if the value of m in some cases, as in the exception case, varies from one summary to another, then m can be the same for all generated summaries by assigning empty values for any summary that contains fewer elements than its peer summaries. This is necessary in order to render the same value of m for all summaries. The index of rows is denoted by i, while the index of columns is j. Note that a mother summary will be a particular column of the the Sumstega matrix in which the Sumstega system is configured by pre-agreeing upon it.

Submodule 4 compares only the peer elements of all summaries to determine the differences among the summaries. Mathematically, it compares only the peer elements of the same row to determine the differences among all elements of that row. In other words, it compares the elements that have the same value of i while the value of j is changing from its initial value, which is equal 1, to its maximum value, which is equal to n, in order to distinguish all different elements of the entire Sumstega matrix. For instance, the result of this step may be accomplished by marking all elements as follows: same elements, unique elements, and semi-unique elements.

Submodule 5 encodes the Sumstega matrix using the general steganographic code of the Sumstega encoder (Module 1). For example, Submodule 5 may encode the entire Sumstega matrix by general steganographic code values as follows. The elements that are the same in the entire row may be non-coded elements, which may be assigned a value of null. The elements that are unique may be assigned a full value of the steganographic code. Finally, some elements are semi-unique or partially different and may be assigned a partial value of the steganographic code. To emphasize, if Sumstega generates a maximum of four different summaries, then the full value of the steganographic code may be two bits, e.g., 00, 01, 10, or 11, and obviously the partial value of the steganographic code can be one bit, either 0 or 1.

Submodule 6 generates a summary cover by selecting the mandatory elements that may have null values and all elements that have the same steganographic values of the encoded message.

The mandatory elements, most likely, have null values which cannot conceal data because these elements along with their indices are the same in all generated summaries which do not have different elements.

Submodule 7 evaluates a summary cover by using the evaluation techniques [77,80,109] to assure that the summary cover appears normal.

6.3.5 *Implementation Example*

This section demonstrates an example of an actual implementation of Sumstega methodology, discusses important aspects of the implementation, and highlights possible directions for implementation. The purpose of the presented implementation in this chapter is to show Sumstega's capability of achieving the steganographic goal rather than making it difficult for the adversary to decode a message. Employing a hard encoding system or cryptosystem to protect a message is feasible and simple and can be accomplished by using any contemporary encoder or cryptosystem. Similarly, employing compression techniques to increase the bitrate can easily be accomplished by using the appropriate contemporary compression techniques. However, this is not the focus of the present chapter. Therefore, neither cryptosystem nor compression technique is used here. Given the availability of numerous encoding, encryption, and compression techniques in the literature [28,56,97–99,122,123] that can be employed by Sumstega methodology, the discussion in the balance of this section will focus on the generation of Sumstega cover rather than message encoding. Obviously, the technique presented in this chapter, as stated earlier, is just an example of possible implementation, but Sumstega methodology can be implemented in different ways. In this example, the Sumstega encoder (Module 1) converts a message to the binary string of its ASCII representation. Obviously, it is expected that the Sumstega encoder may be implemented differently and generally includes a procedure of both data compression and encryption during the generation of the steganographic code, as mentioned earlier. Applying such techniques is a trivial task. As mentioned in Section 6.3.4, the goal is to construct a Sumstega camouflager (Module 2) that is capable of applying the seven submodules in Section 6.3.4. In this example, as

Table 6.1   Sumstega Code Example That Will Be Employed by Sumstega Camouflager (the Camouflage Procedure) to Conceal A Message

| | | STEGANOGRAPHIC CODE | | | |
| | | SUMSTEGA CODE | | | |
NOTE	ELEMENT TYPE	SUMMARY 1	SUMMARY 2	SUMMARY 3	SUMMARY 4
	Unique	00	01	10	11
No overlap	Semi-unique	00	01	10	11
	Two options	0	1	1	1
Non coded	Same	Null	Null	Null	Null

Note that this is just an example.

illustrated in Figures 6.1 and 6.2, Sumstega employs several contemporary summarizers, in particular, four summarizers [81,82,85,86] that are capable of generating numerous variations of summaries. Obviously, the Sumstega methodology may employ more summarizers or build a Sumstega Summarizer from scratch without employing contemporary summarizers. Consequently and according to the algorithm of the Sumstega camouflager (Module 2), the presented Sumstega system maps the elements of the generated summaries in a table, called the Sumstega matrix, and compares them in order to assign Sumstega code from the Steganographic Code Table detailed in Table 6.1. The Sumstega system then selects all elements that match the encoded message, which is the binary code of a message in this chapter, along with the non-coded elements in order to generate a summary cover.

6.3.5.1 Sample of Sumstega Cover   The gray part shown in the Sumstega matrix in Figure 6.2, which is mapped to Figure 6.3, represents the current implementation example and Sample 6.9 of summary cover. The presented sample was generated by using an input public news article from *The New York Times* [135]. Sample 6.9, the presented summary cover, was generated from the four summaries that contain 5 to 6 elements in each summary path (the generated summary). This implementation example is based on sentence extraction summarization techniques. Therefore, in this example an element is referred to as the extracted sentence, as denoted by the letter E in the Sumstega matrix shown in Figure 6.2. The following example of Sumstega cover (Sample 6.9) conceals 8 bits of data that represent the letter "G" which, in binary, is 01000111.

Sumstega Code	All elements of Summaries			
	00	01	10	11
	Summary 1	Summary 2	Summary 3	Summary 4
01	E_{11}	E_{12}	E_{13}	E_{14}
	E_{21}	E_{22}	E_{23}	E_{24}
00 01	E_{31}	E_{32}	E_{33}	E_{34}
11	E_{41}	E_{42}	E_{43}	E_{44}
	E_{51}	E_{51}	E_{53}	E_{54}
	E_{61}	E_{62}	E_{63}	E_{64}

Figure 6.3 Sumstega matrix which shows the selected elements (the shaded squares) that conceal a message. These elements form the summary path of Sample 6.9 of Sumstega cover. This is an actual process of generating summary cover.

SAMPLE 6.9

Although the ministry did not confirm that the drawdown would begin in March, it confirmed that the ministry was "expecting to see a fundamental change of mission in early 2009." The plans by Britain — and its talks with Washington — have been complicated by pressure from the Bush administration to couple the British drawdown in Iraq with an increase in British forces in Afghanistan. The leaking of the British withdrawal plan appeared to have been prompted, at least in part, by President-elect Barack Obama's victory in the election last month and his plans to draw up a timetable for the withdrawal of American troops from Iraq. Within 18 months of the invasion, British commanders were complaining privately that the Americans lacked Britain's colonial experience in countries like Iraq, and that the heavy use of firepower against Mr. Sadr was counterproductive.

Sample 6.9 illustrates the summary cover by employing only extraction-based summarization techniques. As shown, the presented sample of Sumstega cover has the same qualities of comparable summaries that contain no hidden data.

6.3.6 Sumstega Communications Protocol (Module 3)

The communicating parties configure the communications protocol of the Sumstega system, as shown in Figure 6.1, in order to communicate covertly by predetermining the particular specifications of Sumstega system used. These include the decoder and the input used to generate the steganographic cover which is already available to the public, e.g., the news article. The communicating parties then determine the covert channel for securely transmitting summary covers. Once the communications protocol is agreed upon, the intended parties are ready to communicate covertly with each other using Sumstega. The first item is addressed by Modules 1 and 2, which are discussed in the previous sections. The second item is a particular covert channel that mainly defines how the cover will be delivered to the recipient without raising suspicion. Covert transmittal of the steganographic cover is crucial to the success of steganography. At the core of the cover transmittal issue is how to prevent the association between the sender and recipient from attracting suspicion. For example, exchanging email messages would automatically imply a relationship between the communicating parties. Similarly, downloading files from a web site indicates an interest in the accessed material. With advances in monitoring tools for network and Internet traffic, profiles of a user's access pattern can be easily established. An adversary most probably will suspect the presence of a hidden message, even if the content does not look suspicious, because of the observed traffic pattern if there is a lack of a justification for the interest in the contents of such traffic. For example, if the pretended profession of a sender or recipient is as an online-journalist who sends or receives documents such as nuclear specifications, suspicions can easily be aroused. Someone working in an online-news field may send or receive only documents that are justifiable as news reports. Therefore, it is very important to legitimize the sending and receiving of steganographic cover to avoid attracting any attention that may trigger an attack. Sumstega enables an effective solution. The use of a particular domain allows establishing a covert channel in a form that legitimizes the association among communicating parties. Thus, sharing a summary cover would appear to be an ordinary practice. The use of summaries is very popular all over the world such as was described in the example of Bob and Alice, Section 6.3.1. Thus, the transmission of the summary covers via email or posting them on web pages is natural and does not raise suspicion.

6.3.7 Bitrate

The presented implementation of the Sumstega scheme may achieve a bitrate from roughly 0.064% up to 0.20%, with an approximate average of 0.12%. This bitrate is limited to the current implementation example, which employs only one type of summarization technique, namely an extraction technique. However, there are numerous summarization techniques [77,80,109], as detailed in Sections 6.1 and 6.2, that can be employed by Sumstega such as: abstraction, revision, discourse, paraphrasing rule, lexical substitution, semantic equivalency, and information equivalency. Obviously, employing such techniques can easily increase the bitrate. Unfortunately, there is no free or affordable summarizer that uses these techniques, which is why the current implementation example uses extraction-based summarizers [81,82,85,86] which are either affordable or free. Therefore, improving Sumstega's bitrate is feasible and will be investigated in future work. In regard to the message size, the size of a message is a concern for most, if not all, steganography approaches. However, in the presented implementation example of the Sumstega scheme, Sumstega provides the ability to camouflage a long message. Note that if a particular steganographic system achieves low bitrate, it does not imply that a long message cannot be concealed by such a scheme. For example, the low bitrate of the text cover will require a long text cover to camouflage a long message. Generally, text files do not burden a network like image or audio files, which are huge compared to text files. Obviously, Sumstega is capable of concealing a long message but due to space constraints, an example of this could not be shown here.

6.4 Conclusion

In this chapter, Sumstega, a novel methodology for steganography, has been presented. Sumstega achieves legitimacy by basing the camouflaging of a message on auto-summarization of documents. Messages are neither concealed as noise (errors) nor cause a detectable noise. Instead, Sumstega pursues the variations among the auto-summarization techniques to conceal the desired data. The popularity of automatic summarization has been on the rise in business, science, the World Wide Web, education, and news, rendering document summaries as attractive steganographic carriers.

7

MATLIST

Mature Linguistic Steganography Methodology

The text generated by Natural Language Generation (NLG) and template systems is meaningful and looks legitimate. Therefore, the **Mature Linguistic Steganography (Matlist) Methodology** employs NLG and template techniques along with Random Series (RS) values (e.g., binary, decimal, hexadecimal, octal, alphabetic, alphanumeric, etc.) of a Domain-Specific Subject (DSS) to generate noiseless text-cover [27]. This type of DSS, e.g., financial, medical, mathematical, scientific, and economical, has plenty of room to conceal data and allows communicating parties to establish a covert channel, such as a relationship based on the profession of the communicating parties, to transmit a text cover. Matlist embeds data in a form of RS values, functions of RS, related semantics of RS, or a combination of these. Unlike synonym-based approaches, Matlist does not preserve the meaning of text cover every time it is used. Instead, Matlist cover employes a different legitimate meaning for each message while it remains semantically coherent and rhetorically sound. Matlist is based on the Nostega paradigm; therefore, it conceals data in a noiseless (flawless) manner. The presented implementation, validation, and experimental results demonstrate that Matlist is capable of accomplishing the steganographic goal with a higher bitrate than all other linguistic steganography approaches. Note that Chapter 12 provides a comprehensive steganalysis validation that confirms the robustness not only of Matlist, but also of all other Nostega-based methodologies as well.

The remainder of this chapter is organized as follows: Section 7.1 briefly highlights some background of NLG-related work. Then, it discusses Matlist versus all other contemporary approaches. Section 7.2 introduces Matlist methodology in detail, Section 7.3 demonstrates the implementation of Matlist schemes, and finally, Section 7.4 concludes the chapter.

7.1 Introduction

The output of both linguistic steganographical schemes and NLG systems is text. However, their goals are totally different. The goal of linguistic steganographical schemes is to conceal information in non-legitimate text to communicate covertly. On the other hand, the goal of NLG systems is to represent legitimate text either through an on-line-display or audio speech [9]. In the following sections, a brief review of prior work on NLG systems and Matlist versus previous work is presented.

7.1.1 Natural Language Generation and Template

NLG is the process of employing a nonlinguistc data input to produce an understandable text for both humans and machines. NLG employs knowledge bases, artificial intelligence, computational linguistics, and other related techniques to achieve its goal [9,17]. Contemporary NLG techniques employ the knowledge of a domain-specific subject (DSS) [9] and its linguistics to generate texts in the form of reports, help messages, documents, and other desirable text. Note that contemporary NLG and template systems generate mature linguistic text [9,17]. The field of NLG systems has enjoyed significant progress in recent years and is still promising more in the future [9].

Examples of NLG systems are WeatherReporter [9,142], FoG [9,142], and StockReporter [17,143]. WeatherReporter and FoG generate textual weather descriptions. The data input to these schemes is a numerical random series [9,17] and the DSS is the weather. This numerical random series represents the numerical weather data, and the text generated by these systems describes the changes in weather. However, FoG is more advanced than WeatherReporter and it can generate a textual weather description in two different languages—English and French. Another example of an NLG system is the StockReporter, which was formerly known as the Ana scheme. The data input to the StockReporter scheme is a numerical random series and the DSS is stock prices. The numerical random series represents the values of key stocks, and the generated text describes the fluctuations in stock market prices.

The template techniques were formerly known as mail-merge technology [9]. Mail-merge techniques have been employed in software packages including Microsoft Word and others. The core idea of mail-merge is as simple as "fill in the blank" by employing a predetermined template. Generic mail-merge can generate various text based on its input. Theoretically, NLG and mail-merge are equivalent in terms of functionality. To emphasize, any task that can be done by NLG systems can also be achieved by mail-merge systems and vice versa. It is argued that mail-merge techniques are NLG techniques [9]. However, from a complexity point of view, the NLG systems are a step ahead of mail-merge. Thus, in this chapter the NLG system is also referred to as the template system.

7.1.2 Matlist Versus Previous Work

The text cover of contemporary linguistic steganography approaches may contain numerous flaws such as incorrect syntax, lexicon, rhetoric, and grammar. In addition, the content of text cover may be meaningless and semantically incoherent. These unusual patterns can easily raise suspicion in covert communications, which obviously defeats the steganographic goal. For example, in synonyms-based approaches suspicion can be easily raised because not all synonyms are semantically compatible. Linguistically, this is because not many synonyms can be generally used in various pieces of text. A synonym may be perfect in one piece of text, but can be incorrect in another because of the different context. Even if the text cover of the synonym-based approach looks legitimate from a linguistics point of view given the adequate accuracy of the chosen synonyms, reusing the same piece of text to hide a message is a steganographic concern. If an adversary intercepts the communications and sees a piece of text with the same meaning being reused over and over again between communicating parties with just a different group of synonyms, he will question such use. The solution is to avoid reusing the same piece of text. Yet, the source of the original text that is used to hide data has to be kept secret.

Matlist avoids these issues by taking advantage of NLG and template techniques to generate a text cover that naturally has a different legitimate meaning for concealing different messages while it remains semantically coherent and rhetorically sound. In addition, Matlist neither depends on the secrecy of a particular source of text, as a steganographic cover, nor its NLG system. Obviously, what is not made public is only the encoding system, including a cryptosystem and other related security procedures, if used. Matlist does not depend on synonym substitutions for concealing data. Instead, Matlist employs NLG and template techniques to generate a text cover in which a message is embedded in a form of RS values (e.g., random series of binary, decimal, hexadecimal, octal, alphabetic, or alphanumeric), functions of RS, related semantics of RS, or a combination of these.

Unlike synonym-based steganography, linguistic flaws in noise-based approach are not a concern unless they appear excessively. For instance, machine translations (MT) commonly produce translations that contain numerous errors (noise). For an adversary to suspect a covert communication, he has to detect an unusual frequency of flaws, or odd patterns other than those generated by the use of MT. However, Grothoff et al. state that one concern is that the continual improvement of machine translation may narrow the margin of hiding data [13–15]. On the contrary, an improvement in NLG is in fact beneficial to Matlist, as demonstrated later in Sections 7.2, 7.3, and 7.4.

Similar to the translation-based approach, both the confusing approach [50] and the SMS-based approach [51] hide data in noise (errors), and as long as the noise looks ordinary, they can fool an adversary. Unlike the translation-based approach, these approaches are not concerned with the margin of hiding data, which is the amount of noise (errors) that occurs due to human error in a noisy text, e.g., emails, forums, blogs, and SMS, because it is not expected that natural errors will decrease. Conversely, Matlist neither employs errors nor uses noisy text to conceal data. Instead, it generates flawless text cover, as demonstrated later in this chapter.

Note that the presented samples in this book are just examples to show the applicability of employing a wide variety of Domain Specific Subjects (DSS). Unlike the Edustega methodology (presented in Chapter 5), Matlist is based on a DSS that regularly uses RS values (e.g., binary, decimal, hexadecimal, octal, alphabetic, or alphanumeric [27]).

7.2 Matlist Methodology

Bob and Alice are on a spy mission. Bob is a medical practitioner and Alice is a market analyst consultant. Before they go on their mission, which requires them to reside in two different countries, they set the rules for communicating covertly using their professions as a steganographic umbrella. Basically, they agree they will conceal messages through numerical data and the semantics often used in their professions. They make sure that every time the text cover is generated, it has a different meaning and it remains legitimate to avoid suspicion of being a steganographic tool. To make this work, they establish a business relationship as follows: Bob is Alice's medical doctor and Alice is Bob's market analyst consultant. When Bob wants to send a covert message to Alice, Bob either posts medically related documents online for authorized patients to access, or he can send medically related documents via email to the intended patients. These documents conceal messages. Covert messages transmitted in this manner will not look suspicious because of Bob's profession. Furthermore, Alice is not the sole recipient of Bob's messages; other non-spy patients also receive medical documents, further warding off suspicion.

When Alice sends Bob a message, she does it in the same manner except that she uses her profession. She either posts market analysis reports that Bob or anyone else can access, or sends market analysis-related documents via email to a set of clients that includes Bob. These market analysis reports conceal hidden messages. However, only Bob will be able to unravel the hidden message because he knows the rules of the game. Alice's communications look legitimate and nothing is suspicious because she is a market analyst and has a business relationship with both Bob and other non-spy clients. Alice or Bob can use real data from their professions and their established business relationship to make their covert communications legitimate. If real data is not used, then untraceable data can be fabricated to avoid comparison attack if an adversary should attempt to trace and compare data to an original. In addition, Bob and Alice are using their professions as linguistic domain-specific subjects (DSS) for concealing messages.

The above scenario demonstrates how Matlist methodology can be used. Matlist methodology is demonstrated in the remainder of this chapter.

7.2.1 Matlist Architecture Overview

Matlist achieves legitimacy by basing the camouflage of both a message and its transmittal on a particular DSS. As stated earlier in the above example of Bob and Alice, using the DSS of the intended users gives legitimacy for camouflaging both the message and its transmittal. The following is an overview of the Matlist architecture, which consists of five modules that are based on the Nostega paradigm, as shown in Figure 7.1:

1. *DSS determination* (Module 1) determines a DSS, such as financial, medical, mathematical, scientific, or economic, that is appropriate for achieving the steganographic goal. The major factor is the use of random series values in the DSS. Examples include the use of binary, hexadecimal, octal, alphabetic, and alphanumeric series in computer science subjects such as discrete math, digital circuits and data structure, and decimal values in financial documents.

2. *DSS specifications* (Module 2) explores the properties and criteria of the DSS selected by Module 1 and its RS to define DSS specifications, which include but are not limited to, the appropriate linguistics for concealing data. Next, Module 3 and 4 will construct the Matlist encoder and NLG system based on the defined DSS specifications.

3. *Building the Matlist encoder* (Module 3) implements an encoder by employing the DSS specifications from Module 2 to encode messages. For example, based on the properties of the RS, the encoder may represent the message as random numerical values (e.g., 43, 93, 109, 83, 4, etc.), a function of RS values, the linguistics used (e.g., increased, decrease, subset, not subset, etc.), or a combination of these.

4. *Building Matlist NLG* (Module 4) implements an NLG or template system by employing the process of building an NLG system [9] (outlined in Section 7.2.5) along with the outputs of

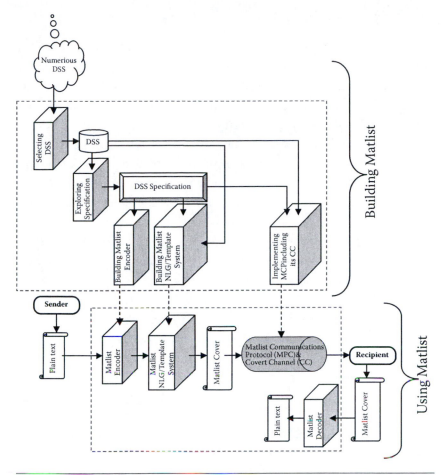

Figure 7.1 The architecture and the use of Matlist. The schematic shows the interaction of various Matlist modules utilized to build Matlist. Next, it shows the use of a Matlist scheme by the communicating parties.

all previous modules. The constructed NLG or template system must be capable of accepting the encoded message from the Matlist encoder as an input to generate a text cover.

5. *Implementing Matlist Communications Protocol* (Module 5). As mentioned earlier, Matlist averts the suspicion during the transmittal of a hidden message by basing the camouflage of both a message and its transmittal on the same DSS. This module defines how the sender would deliver the text-cover covertly to the recipient.

The following sections explain these modules in detail.

7.2.2 DSS Determination (Module 1)

The communicating parties must first agree on a DSS that they will use to conceal a message. For example, legitimate users may employ a financial, medical, mathematical, scientific, or economical report as the DSS. To enable usage of the Matlist methodology, the selected DSS must involve a random sequence of recognizable tokens (e.g., binary, decimal, hexadecimal, octal, alphabetic, alphanumeric, or any other form). To illustrate, changes in prices can be one form of a random series. Other selection criteria include the suitability of the chosen DSS for concealing a message without raising suspicion. Moreover, Matlist narrows the scope of the DSS in order to limit the linguistics used in a text cover. For instance, Matlist favors the stock market as a DSS over the general economy. Such a limitation will ease the text generation process and enhance its maturity [9].

The following elaborate on key criteria for selecting the DSS.

Random Series-Based: Randomness in this context means that the members of the series do not exhibit patterns like the time series (e.g., 2, 4, 6, 8, etc.) where the increase and decrease are predicted. A DSS based on a random series allows Matlist to conceal a message in text without violating any pattern. For example, if the message is encoded using numbers, it should be possible to blend these numbers in the cover text without exhibiting inconsistency, e.g., decreasing a value when an increase is expected. As will be demonstrated in Section 7.3, a DSS that is based on a random series has plenty of room for concealing messages. Nonetheless, this process requires careful manipulation. For instance, while prices in the stock market, foreign exchange rates, or temperatures are considered random, they are still somewhat controlled. In other words, there are limitations placed on a random series by its DSS, and thus it is imperative to pick a DSS that suits a particular steganographic encoder scheme. One could argue that the selection of the DSS and the encoder scheme are interrelated, and thus it is hard to decide which one should be established first. However, determining the DSS is influenced by other factors and criteria and would need to be selected first. In addition, the specifications of the DSS can be exploited in order to ensure the feasibility of the camouflaging process as elaborated later.

Appropriateness of DSS: The chosen DSS must fit the communicating parties and provide some grounds for justifying the communications. It is also recommended that the chosen DSS suit the desired frequency of communications. With some domain-specific subjects, it may be possible to send messages every hour or so. As an example, it is customary for a stockbroker to receive a market update every half-hour. On the other hand, some domain-specific subjects may not justify more than one message per month, per season, or even per year. For example, someone would not very often receive an e-mail message from a utility company about the rate of energy consumption or payment history. It is also worth noting that multiple domain-specific subjects may also be employed to enable periodic and sporadic communications. In this case, the sender may need to have multiple scenarios in order to avoid potential suspicion concerning the sender-receiver association.

7.2.3 DSS Specifications (Module 2)

This module studies the properties and criteria of the selected DSS in order to generate its specifications. These specifications will be the base for constructing the Matlist encoder and NLG system to conceal messages. The specifications include two main aspects: the linguistics and the random series.

Linguistics Properties and Criteria: In order to generate an appropriate text cover, the text has to be derived from the DSS specifications. In other words, the linguistics of the text cover have to be compatible with the DSS. The linguistic properties and criteria include, but are not limited to, the following:

- The factors and inference of speech, text, or report, in other words, the reasons that motivate a topic or event to be reported.
- The linguistic structure of a DSS. For example, the linguistic structure of a DSS such as the stock market is mainly a description of the fluctuation in stock market prices.
- The vocabulary, phrases, and technical terms that are popularly used in the chosen subject.

- The style of the presentation. This usually depends on the target reader or audience, e.g., general public, academics, professionals, or students.
- The text structure, e.g., documentary, report, or email.

Properties and Criteria of Random Series: The properties and criteria of random series are critical for concealing a message because they directly affect the way a message is encoded and how a linguistic cover is generated. These specifications of RS may include, but are not limited to, the following:

- Types of RS members, e.g., binary, decimal, hexadecimal, octal, alphabetic, or alphanumeric.
- The ways the RS are used. For example, numbers are used in the medical field to represent measurements, e.g., when measuring blood pressure.
- The causes of the differences among RS values. For example, the numbers reported about the stock market may represent the fluctuations in stock market prices.
- Constraints imposed on the RS values, e.g., numbers may have to be greater than a particular value. For instance, the numbers that usually appear in a medical report for blood pressure will have to be within the normal range of living human beings, and thus the message encoding scheme will have to cope with such a constraint.
- Relationships among a subset of the members of an RS. For example, one member may be the average of a few other members or a set may be a subset of another.

The specifications of an RS and its related linguistics are fully integrated together and can be used to generate a text cover, as elaborated below from a linguistics point of view.

Attributes: Investigating and studying each member of the RS as if it is alone and not in a series. After investigating each member of the RS and its nature, the result of the study will be defined as the criteria for the next stage of generating the Matlist cover (linguistic cover). For example, a member of an RS can be a number integer (real, even, odd, prime, floating point), or in any other form other than numbers. This criterion can ease the task of forming the Matlist code which will be used for generating the Matlist cover, as will be demonstrated in the implementation section. For example, in a DSS such as the stock market, the price of a particular stock dropped or rose to a particular value that is an integer type not a real number or vice versa. This value as an integer or a real type can drive a sentence such as "rose up to twenty dollars even" or "dropped by twenty-one dollars and five cents."

One-to-One Relationship: In a one-to-one relationship, the first and last members of an RS set are studied. Excluding the first and last members, each member of an RS (set) has two neighbors. Investigation based on both the DSS and general relationships is conducted by studying each member of the RS and its relationships in the series (set). In more detail, the first member (N_1) of the RS is studied in conjunction with the member immediately succeeding it (N_2), and the last member (N_k) of the RS is studied in conjunction with the member immediately preceding it (N_{k-1}). The study of the first and last members of the RS, is a one-to-one relationship. A one-to-one relationship can play a role in generating the mature linguistic-cover, as will be demonstrated in the implementation section. For instance, in a DSS such as the stock market, the price of a particular stock dropped or rose to a particular value on the first day or the last day of a month. This event can drive a sentence such as "the stock rose twenty monetary units" or "the stock dropped by twenty-one monetary units."

One-to-Two Relationship: In a one-to-two relationship, each member of the RS, excluding the first and last members, are studied with the members of the RS succeeding and preceding it. This type of relationship is one-to-two. A one-to-two relationship can play a role for generating the Matlist cover, as will be demonstrated in the implementation section. For example, in a DSS such as the stock market, the price of a particular stock dropped or rose to a particular value during a month. This event can drive a sentence such as "the stock rose twenty monetary units after dropping by twenty-one monetary units last week."

One-to-Many Relationship (Classes): In a one-to-many relationship, every aspect and the nature of each member of the RS (set) and its relationship to the entire series (set) or subset are investigated and studied based on a DSS and general relationships. Defining the results of this investigation can play a role for generating the mature linguistic-cover as will be demonstrated in the implementation section. For instance, in a DSS such as the stock market, the price of a particular stock dropped or rose to a particular value during a month. This event can drive a sentence such as "the price rose up to its highest value during the month."

Note that the presented properties and criteria in this section are just examples and other optimized specifications and criteria can be integrated with Matlist.

7.2.4 Building Matlist Encoder (Module 3)

Coding is a very well researched technical area and there are numerous published techniques that can be employed to generate steganographic code [3,8,25,56,97–99,107]. Therefore, this section only focuses on key issues that affect the implementation of the Matlist encoder. The Matlist encoder generates a steganographic code (Matlist code) in the form of a random series (RS), linguistics of a RS, or a combination of these based on the specifications of the chosen DSS. Then, Matlist code (encoded message) serves as an input to the Matlist NLG system to generate the text cover.

Mathematically, defining relationships in a random series is relatively more difficult than defining it in a time series. This is not the case in Matlist. For example, prices in the stock market, foreign exchange rates, and temperatures are not controlled but random. Furthermore, there are limitations placed on the random series by its DSS. However, generating a steganographic code that preserves similar specifications of the DSS is feasible. If a message is in a form of an RS, then the relationships to itself (in terms of its attributes), its neighbor(s), a subset of the series, or the entire set (series), can be used when generating artificial properties that look legitimate. The process in this module is similar to the process of Module 2 (DSS Specifications).

Examples: As mentioned earlier, properties derived from relationships such as one-to-one, one-to-two, and one-to-many can be employed by the Matlist encoder to generate a steganographic code. For instance, a set of values in the form of a random series as similar as possible to the random series of the chosen DSS can form Matlist code (an encoded message). If the Matlist code is fully represented by the random series, then it may take a numeric form such as an integer, real, even, odd, prime, or floating point number, or any form other than numbers. The fluctuations in random series values can be described using the linguistic properties of a DSS through the Matlist NLG system. Matlist code can be represented in the Matlist cover using forms other than a random series, such as the linguistics that are related to the RS. To emphasize, in the stock market, the price of a particular stock dropped or rose to a particular value on the first day or the last day of a month. This can be described as a one-to-one or one-to-two relationship in a random series. The specifications of this DSS are the base for describing the fluctuation in stock market prices. For instance, encoding words like events of dropped, rose, etc., can conceal a message. Matlist code will be demonstrated in Section 7.3. Note that the Matlist decoder will simply be the inverse mode of the Matlist encoder.

7.2.5 Building Matlist NLG or Template System (Module 4)

In this module, an NLG system or a template will be implemented to conceal messages. However, employing or modifying an existing NLG system or template is feasible as long as the generated text cover will not raise suspicion. A Matlist NLG/template employs the encoded message (Matlist code), generated by the Matlist encoder, to create a text cover. Obviously, the NLG systems or templates must be examined linguistically, steganographically, and technically by both humans and computers before using them. This provides an advantage and added robustness to Matlist in passing both human and machine examinations because it has already passed these examinations by legitimate examiners. Furthermore, Matlist can employ either unaltered authenticated data or fabricated untraceable data to generate Matlist cover, thereby avoiding the comparison attacks. It is worth noting that from the Matlist point of view, both NLG systems and templates are the same, as stated by Reiter and Dale [9]. Both are capable of generating the Matlist cover, as will be demonstrated in Section 6.3. Thus, in this chapter NLG system is also referred to template system. In general, the implementation of templates based on an NLG is relatively easy and inexpensive. An NLG system or template can be implemented in any language. However, in this chapter, the implementation is only in English. Building a Matlist NLG/template system is mainly based on the DSS specifications generated by

Module 2, the Matlist encoder and its code constructed by Module 3, and the process of building NLG systems.

The process of building NLG systems, including templates, may be summarized, as Reiter and Dale state, in seven procedures [9] as follows:

1. *Content determination* determines the required information to be presented in the generated text. In a DSS such as weather reporting, the needed information may include temperatures, rainfall, rainy days, rain quantity, mist, fog, etc.

2. *Document structuring* determines the required informational classes (e.g., classification, grouping, ordering of content) and relates each class to its rhetorical terms. This informational classification can be in a form of an informational tree (categorization) as shown in Figure 7.2.

3. *Lexicalization* determines the required linguistics, such as specific words and syntaxes, to be used in the output.

4. *Referring expression generation* involves the determination of the required expressions that correlate entities. The relationship among these entities, e.g., fluctuation of market prices, temperatures, etc., can be used to generate informative text.

5. *Aggregation* determines the details of mapping the informational tree from a document structuring procedure into linguistic structures such as sentences, paragraphs, etc.

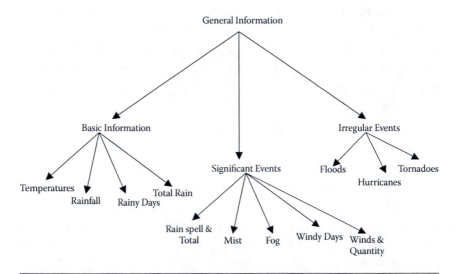

Figure 7.2 A possible structure of an informational tree of a weather report.

6. *Linguistics realization* transforms the abstract representations of a sentence level collected from previous procedure(s) (the output of the previous procedure(s) is unordered text) into the required readable text.

7. *Structure realization* transforms the linguistic structures, e.g., paragraphs, sections, etc., into the required encoding sequence that generates the actual text. This step is analogous to converting a pseudo code, algorithm, or flowchart, into a particular programming language.

The above was just a brief overview of the process of building NLG and template systems. Since the focus of this chapter is the linguistic steganography, for more details refer to [9].

Once the Matlist scheme is implemented, camouflaging a message will be done in two steps. The first is generating the required Matlist code. In the second, Matlist code will serve as input to the Matlist NLG system or the Matlist template to generate the Matlist cover, which will be demonstrated in the implementation section.

7.2.6 Implementing Matlist Communications Protocol (Module 5)

Covert communication is done through two steps, concealing the message and then transmitting the hidden message. Contemporary steganography approaches are focused on how to hide a message and not on how to hide the transmittal of a hidden message. Concealing the transmittal of a hidden message is as important as concealing a message. Consider the following scenario: a sender when communicating covertly always uses the same steganographic technique and the same steganographic cover type (e.g., translation-based, image-based, or audio-based). Furthermore, the sender always uses email to deliver a hidden message. Covert communications using the same steganographic technique, cover type, and email transmission all the time will raise suspicion. The suspicions of an adversary monitoring these communications will be raised and the communications will be flagged. Suspicion is raised because the adversary will wonder why the emails always contain one of the following: a translated document, an image, or an audio file. It is unusual for someone to send such content by email all the time. If the sender has no legitimate reason for sending an email containing one of the mentioned items, suspicion can be raised even if the content does not look suspicious and nothing is detected. Suspicion is raised because of the method of delivering the hidden message, not because of a vulnerable hiding technique used. However, it is more convincing when a sender has a website and posts a hidden message on it, for a recipient to retrieve rather than sending the message through email all the time. As another example, a sender in the financial industry has a legitimate reason for distributing a price analysis graph. Suspicion will not be raised if a message is concealed in the graph because of the legitimacy of distributing financial graphs. On the other hand, if the graph is a medical report, suspicion will be raised because the sender has no legitimate reason for sending a medical report. To emphasize, the way of delivering the hidden message can raise suspicion even if using a secure hiding technique.

Matlist averts the suspicion that may arise during the transmittal of a hidden message by basing the camouflage of both a message and its transmittal on a DSS. In addition, it should be required that the intended users employ the appropriate arrangements, techniques, policy, rules, and any other related requirements for achieving the steganographical goal.

Matlist Communications Protocol (MCP) works as shown in Figure 7.1. A sender and a recipient communicate covertly using Matlist, and they agree to the following:

1. The particular specifications and configurations of the Matlist scheme and its decoder
2. The particular specifications, configurations, policy, arrangements, and techniques of establishing a covert channel for the legitimate users to communicate covertly

Once an MCP is agreed upon, the intended users are ready to communicate covertly with each other using Matlist.

7.3 Matlist Implementation

This section demonstrates possible implementation examples for five different DSS: Consumer Price Index (CPI), elementary math, selling books, chemistry, and discrete math. It discusses some important aspects of the implementation, and highlights possible directions for future implementation. Note that these are just a few examples and they are expected to be implemented differently to achieve better results. The purpose of the presented implementation is to show Matlist's capability of achieving the steganographical goal rather than making the adversary's task difficult to decode a message. Employing a hard encoding system or cryptosystem to protect a message is obviously recommended, feasible, and simple using any contemporary encoder or cryptosystem. Similarly, employing compression techniques to increase the bitrate can easily be accomplished by using the appropriate contemporary compression techniques. However, this is not the focus of this chapter. Thus, for simplicity neither cryptosystem nor compression technique is used in this chapter. Given the availability of numerous encoding, encryption, and compression techniques in the literature [25,56], the discussion in the balance of this section will focus on the generation of Matlist cover rather than the message encoding.

7.3.1 DSS of Consumer Price Index

A text example of the DSS of Consumer Price Index (CPI) is presented in Sample 7.1. This sample is authenticated and was written by a human and the source was the U.S. Bureau of Labor Statistics [144]. Obviously, this sample of CPI was written for CPI purposes, not for concealing a message. Sample 7.1 is provided to show how the DSS of CPI looks. Obviously, collecting the numerical values in this sample will form a random series (RS) that is constrained by its domain, as indicated before in Section 7.2. However, the values are still in the form of an RS. The text is just a linguistic description of the fluctuations among the values and shows that CPI is an appropriate DSS to be employed by Matlist methodology as demonstrated next.

SAMPLE 7.1

CONSUMER PRICE INDEX: DECEMBER 2006

The Consumer Price Index for All Urban Consumers (CPI-U) increased 0.1 percent in December, before seasonal adjustment, the Bureau of Labor Statistics of the U.S. Department of Labor reported today. The December level of 201.8 (1982-84 = 100) was 2.5 percent higher than in December 2005.

The Consumer Price Index for Urban Wage Earners and Clerical Workers (CPI-W) increased 0.2 percent in December, prior to seasonal adjustment. The December level of 197.2 (1982-84 = 100) was 2.4 percent higher than in December 2005.

The Chained Consumer Price Index for All Urban Consumers (C-CPI-U) increased 0.1 percent in December on a not seasonally adjusted basis. The December level of 117.1 (December 1999 = 100) was 2.4 percent higher than in December 2005. Please note that the indexes for the post-2004 period are subject to revision. On a seasonally adjusted basis, the CPI-U increased 0.5 percent in December, the first advance since August. Energy prices, which had declined in each of the preceding three months, rose 4.6…

7.3.1.1 First Implementation Example of CPI   In this implementation example, Matlist predetermines the Matlist encoder to encode a message based on the DSS specifications of the CPI. The Matlist encoder employs a PSM Encoder [25,27,107] without encryption to assist in generating the Matlist code. Note that the PSM Encoder is not a part of the contribution and it is just used as an example. Matlist code is generated as follows: Matlist employs a PSM Encoder to convert the plain text message to a binary message, then group the message's binary in lengths of 7 digits. The grouping in lengths of 7 digits will result in a value of 0 up to 127 in decimal. In other words, changing the value from 0000000 up to 1111111 in binary. The Matlist encoder employs an index that starts from 1 referring to 0 in integers (in binary 0000000) to 128 referring to 127 in integers (in binary 1111111). The Matlist encoder uses this index technique to avoid the occurrence of the value of zero in the encoded messages (the Matlist code, which is in an RS form). This index plays a role as if the Matlist encoder adds 1 to each value after PSM encodes the message. To illustrate, the Matlist encoder encodes the message as follows:

- The plain text of the message is *"Use my secret key"*.
- The concatenated binary string of the ASCII representation of this message is:

0101010101110011011001010010000001101101011110010010000001110011011100101011000110111001001100101011101000010000001101011011001010101111001

- Slicing this string (from the previous step) into 7 bits each will result in:

  0101010 1011100 1101100 1010010 0000011 0110101
  1110010 0100000 0111001 1011001 0101100 0110111
  0010011 0010101 1101000 0100000 0110101 1011001
  0101111 001

- Converting the individual slices (from the previous step) into decimals results in:

  42 92 108 82 3 53 114 32 57 89 44 55 19 21 104 32 53 89 47 1

Matlist then explores the feasible criteria that are compatible with the criteria of the selected DSS.

If Matlist will use numerical values in the Matlist cover, then the value of zero should not be used or should be used only rarely. Therefore, in this example Matlist manipulates its code (Matlist code), which is the RS, by adding 1 to each value in order to avoid the occurrence of a zero value, as stated before. As a result, the Matlist Code of the message in the form of integer values is as follows:

  43 93 109 83 4 54 115 33 58 90 45 56 20 22 105 33 54 90 48 2

In addition, the distribution of an RS that is generated in this manner would not raise suspicion because using the index of the RS values by adding 1 to each of the RS values plays a partial role in randomizing the message. For instance, a real value of "101", which is the ASCII of lowercase "e", would be mapped to a different value by adding 1. Then, the new value will become "102", which is the ASCII of lowercase "f". Obviously, the letter "e" and "f" have totally different frequency. Also, a value of "90", which is the ASCII value of uppercase "Z", would be mapped to a different value by adding 1. Hence, the new value will become "91", which is the ASCII of character "[". The letter "Z" and character "[" also have totally different frequency. Similarly, the entire message is randomized. In reality, both the steganography and cryptography are complementing each other. Therefore, it is not only strongly recommended but essential to conceal a ciphertext instead of plain text. Note that Matlist code is also referred to as the "encoded message" or the "steganographic code."

Attributes
- A member of an RS can be an in the numeric form of an integer or real number, and it is constrained by the DSS of CPI.

Inter-Member Relationship
- One-to-one relationship between a member and its neighbor. The first number of the Matlist code is "43" and the next number is "93". The following properties can be tabulated:
  - The first number is less than the second number (its neighbor) or the second number is greater than the first number.
  - The difference between the two numbers is 50.
  - The noticeable trend is "Rose".
- One-to-two relationship between a member and its neighbors in the Matlist code. The following properties can be tabulated for the second number and its neighbors (43 **93** 109):
  - The 2nd number is greater than the 1st number by 50
  - The 2nd number is less than the 3rd number by 16
  - The noticeable trend is " Rose" and "Rose again".

These would be repeated for all values of the Matlist Code.

- One-to-many relationship (classes) between each member and the entire or subset of the Matlist code. For example, the range of the numbers in the RS can be sliced into three sub-ranges and the numbers then grouped according to their values. In other words, a Matlist code, such as "*43* **93 109** *83* 4 54 **115** 33 58 **90** *45 56* 20 22 **105** 33 *54* **90** *48* 2 ", can be categorized in classes using the following procedure.
  - The highest members of the above Matlist code (the RS) are indexed as follows 7, 3, 15, 2, 10, 18, and 4 with their values as 115, 109, 105, 93, 90, 90, and 83, respectively (as marked in bold above and also shown in Table 7.1).
  - The medium members, marked in italics, are indexed as follows 9, 12, 17, 6, 19, 11, and 1 with their values as 58, 56, 54, 54, 48, 45, and 43, respectively, and also shown in Table 7.1.
  - The lowest members are underlined and indexed as follows 20, 5, 13, 14, 8, and 16 with their values as 2, 4, 20, 22, 33, and 33, respectively, and also shown in Table 7.1.

Table 7.1 Example of the Relationship of One-to-Many (Classes)

HIGHEST (H)		MEDIUM (M)		LOWEST (L)	
INDEX	VALUE	INDEX	VALUE	INDEX	VALUE
7	115	9	58	20	2
3	109	12	56	5	4
15	105	17	54	13	20
2	93	6	54	14	22
10	90	19	48	8	33
18	909	11	45	16	33
4	83	1	43		

The relationship of one-to-many can drive a sentence such as "The price rose up to its highest value during the month."

The Matlist encoder encodes Matlist code in the form of real numbers:

0.43 0.93 0.109 0.83 0.4 0.54 0.115 0.33 0.58 0.90 0.45 0.56 0.20 0.22 0.105 0.33 0.54 0.90 0.48 0.2

The above Matlist code is embedded directly in the Matlist template, as shown in Sample 7.2.

SAMPLE 7.2

CONSUMER PRICE INDEX: QUARTERLY REPORT

As recently reported by our department, the consumer price index for the first product lost 0.43 percent in the second period. However, the second period level increased 0.93 percent higher than last year's second period.

The consumer price index for the second product elevated 0.109 percent in the second period. The second period level ascended 0.83 percent higher than last year's second period.

The consumer price index for the third product sank 0.4 percent in the second period. However, the second period level barely budged 0.54 percent higher than last year's second period. The consumer price index for the fourth product augmented 0.115 percent in the second period, following a 0.33 percent depressed value in the first period. The fifth product costs held 0.58 percent in the first period while increasing 0.90 percent in the second period. The index for the seventh product retained 0.45 percent and the consumer price index for the eighth product held 0.56 percent. The ninth product fell 0.20

```
percent in the second period after falling 0.22 percent
in the first period. The index for the tenth product
elevated 0.105 percent, after being depressed by 0.33
percent in five of the six major subgroups. The consumer
index for all goods and services not including the
eighth product and the ninth product barely budged 0.54
percent in the second period, following a 0.90 percent
increase in the first period.

The consumer price index for the eleventh product
retained 0.48 percent in the second period. However,
the second period level sank 0.2 percent lower than
last year's second period.

In summation, the CPI rose during this study period.
However, in the next quarter, the price trend is
forecasted to drop.
```

7.3.1.2 Second Implementation Example of CPI   The technique in this implementation example, as shown in Table 7.2, is to define distinct code-words for the various ranges of values in the RS (Matlist code). In order to allow decoding of the message, a qualifier is used with the individual code words to identify the particular number in the designated range. For example, the Matlist code word "*lost*" is equal to a value range from 40 to 44. When using the text "*lost 0.4 percent*" in the linguistic cover to determine the exact value, simply look up the index from 40 to 44 so that the index value will be from 1 to 5. The index value 4 is equal to 43 and so on. Note that 0.4 refers to the index 4. Table 7.3 shows the code words of the Matlist code for the message "*Use my secret key*". Unlike the synonym-based approach, the code words in this example are not synonyms. To emphasize, the code word "*lost*" in a particular position in the Matlist template may be substituted by another code word "*increase*", which is the antonym. As a result, the entire Matlist cover will retain different legitimate semantically coherent meanings every time it is used for concealing different messages. The code words are used naturally because they are a subset of the linguistics of the DSS used, which are defined by the DSS specifications. Furthermore, the use of NLG or a template provides and maintains correct text generation. Therefore, code words in Matlist methodology do not cause any noise in its text cover, as shown in Sample 7.3.

Table 7.2 An Example Message
Encoding Scheme Using Value Range

RANGE	CODE-WORDS
125–127	Mounting
120–124	Leap
115–119	Augment
110–114	Escalated
105–109	Elevated
100–104	Jump
95–99	Boost
90–94	Increase
85–89	Climbed
80–84	Ascend
75–79	Inflate
70–74	Equate low/high
65–69	Cling low/high
60–64	Move up/down
55–59	Hold low/high
50–54	Budge up/down
45–49	Retain up/down
40–44	Lose
35–39	Dip
30–34	Depress
25–29	Flop
20–24	Fall
15–19	Decreased
10–14	Deflate
5–9	Decline
0–4	Sink

SAMPLE 7.3

CONSUMER PRICE INDEX: QUARTERLY REPORT

As recently reported by our department, the consumer
price index for the first product lost 0.4 percent in
the second period. However, the second period increased
0.4 percent higher than last year's second period.

The consumer price index for the second product
elevated 0.5 percent in the second period. However, the
second period level ascended 0.4 percent higher than
last year's second period.

Table 7.3   Details of Encoding the Message
"Use my secret key" By Using the Value-Range
Scheme of Table 7.2

INITIAL MATLIST CODE	CORRESPONDING CODE WORDS	QUALIFIER
43	Lose	3
93	Increase	3
109	Elevated	4
83	Ascend	3
4	Sink	4
54	Budge	4
115	Escalated	5
33	Depress	3
58	Hold	3
90	Climbed	5
45	Lose	5
56	Hold	1
20	Decreased	5
22	Fell	2
105	Jump	5
33	Depress	3
54	Budge	4
90	Climbed	5
48	Retain	3
2	Sank	2

Note: The qualifier field indicates the order of the coded number in the corresponding range so that the receiver can decode the message.

The consumer price index for the third product sank 0.5 percent in the second period. However, the second period level barely budged 0.5 percent higher than last year's second period. The consumer price index for the fourth product augmented 0.5 percent in the second period, following a 0.4 percent depressed value in the first period. The consumer price index for the fifth product held at 0.4 percent in the first period after increasing 0.1 percent in the second period. The consumer price index for the seventh product retained 0.1 percent and the index for the eighth product held at 0.2 percent. The consumer price index for the ninth product fell 0.1 percent in the second period after falling 0.3 percent in the first period. The consumer price index for the tenth product elevated 0.1 percent, after being depressed by 0.4 percent in five of the six major subgroups. The consumer index for all goods and services, not including the eighth product and the ninth product, barely budged 0.5 percent in the second period, following a 0.1 percent increase in the first period.

The consumer price index for the eleventh product retained 0.4 percent in the second period. However, the second period level sank 0.3 percent lower than last year's second period.

In summation, the CPI rose during this study period. However, in the next quarter, the price trend is forecasted to drop.

7.3.1.3 Text Substitution   The previous examples are given in the form of a generic report. Alternatively, words or a combination of words can be substituted with other words or combinations of words, such as the format of a "wizard form and fill in the blank" [9]. This technique is simple. Unlike synonym-based methods, in Matlist the text substitution procedure may not preserve the same meaning of text and can result in another meaning. For example, *increased* can be substituted by an antonym such as *decreased*; *As recently* can be substituted by a specific date or month such as *February*; *our department* can be substituted with a corporate name such as the *Department of Labor*; *"the first product"* can be substituted with an actual item like *fuel*; *lost 0.2 percent* can be substituted with other numerical values; *in the second period* can be substituted with a date, month or any other time including *in the second quarter, in the second month, or in February;* and so on. These examples represent only a few samples of what text can be substituted. Matlist does not cause any errors when it employs any text substitution techniques. Obviously, the Matlist methodology is based on natural language generation or template techniques where these techniques ensure the production of legitimate text. Matlist Text Substitution (MTS) is a feature that gives Matlist the advantage of being flexible in generating the Matlist cover and it can be used to increase the bitrate. This technique is discussed in more detail in the next section.

7.3.1.4 Third Implementation Example of CPI   In this implementation example, the technique used directly maps code words to an exact value. First of all, the entire data represented in the Matlist cover in Sample 7.4 are valid and authenticated data (the information not the text). The source of the authenticated data (not text) used in this example is the U.S. Bureau of Labor Statistics [145]. These data are collected and embedded along with Matlist code to generate Matlist cover. Tremendous amounts of authenticated data which can be used to generate Matlist cover are available, especially by employing the World Wide Web (Internet). Note that the use of the authenticated data is totally different from using an existing text. The use of an existing text is vulnerable to comparison attack. Therefore, Matlist uses the authenticated data, but not existing text. In other words, the use of authenticated data refers only to the use of the informational facts, not their existing text. Furthermore, this technique does not embed a message in the form of numerical values of Matlist code. Instead, it embeds a message in the linguistics of the generated text. This technique is similar to the previous one (Sections 7.3.1.2 and 7.3.1.3), except that the code words are assigned to exact values. The idea is simply to define an implicit mapping of code words used naturally in the DSS to represent the fluctuations in its RS. As stated earlier, this is unlike the synonym-based approach because the code words are not synonyms. For instance, a code word "*lost*" in a particular position in the Matlist template may be substituted by another code word "*increase*", which is not only different in meaning, but is in fact an antonym. Yet, Matlist cover remains semantically coherent and rhetorically sound. The receiver will collect the words in the text cover (Matlist cover), convert them to the corresponding numbers, and decode the numbers to form the hidden message. Table 7.4 shows the code words that can be used to conceal a message, as shown in Sample 7.4. The Matlist encoder encodes the message "*Use my secret key*" as follows. The Matlist encoder employs a PSM encoder to convert the plain text message to a binary string and then slice the string into groups of 5 digits. Grouping in lengths of 5 digits yields numbers in the range of 0 to 31 (in binary from 00000 to 11111). Table 7.5 shows the code words that need to be used and the order of their appearance in the Matlist cover. Since no values of the RS will conceal data, there is no need for using an index such as adding 1 to each value of the PSM code. To emphasize, the value of zero was avoided in all previous techniques by using the index. This technique can produce text cover like the one that is shown in Sample 7.4.

Table 7.4 Directly Mapped Code Word to Exact Values

VALUE	CODE WORD	VALUE	CODE WORD
31	Mounting	15	Hold low/high
30	Leap	14	Budge up/down
29	Augment	13	Retain up/down
28	Escalated	12	Devalue
27	Elevated	11	Reduce
26	Jump	10	Lose
25	Boost	9	Dip
24	Gain	8	Depress
23	Increase	7	Flop
22	Climbed	6	Fall
21	Ascend	5	Shrink
20	Inflate	4	Decreased
19	Check	3	Deflate
18	Equate low/high	2	Decline
17	Cling low/high	1	Droop
16	Move up/down	0	Sink

SAMPLE 7.4

CONSUMER PRICE INDEX: OCTOBER'S AND NOVEMBER'S REPORT
OF 2006

As recently reported by our department, the CPI for food and beverages lost 0.1 percent in the period of October to November. The CPI for food ascended 0.3 percent in the period of September to October, higher than the period of October to November. The CPI for food at home boosted 0.3 percent in the period of September to October. The CPI for cereals and bakery products climbed 0.4 percent in the period of October to November, higher than the period of September to October.

The CPI for fruits and vegetables lost 2.2 percent in the period of October to November. The CPI for dairy and related products depressed 0.6 percent in the period of October to November. The CPI for other food at home deflated 0.3 percent in the period of October to November, after a 0.2 percent retention in the period of September to October. The CPI for other foods held at 0.1 percent in the period of September to October, while decreasing 0.6 percent in the period of October to November. The CPI for other miscellaneous foods moved up 0.1 percent in the period of October to November, after flopping 0.4 percent in the period of

Table 7.5   Message Encoding Using Directly Mapped Code Words to Exact Value of the Sliced Binary Representation of Message from Table 7.4

ORDER	PSM SLICED BINARY STRING	GROUP VALUE IN INTEGER	MATLIST CODE WORD
1	01010	10	Lose
2	10101	21	Ascend
3	11001	25	Boost
4	10110	22	Climbed
5	01010	10	Lose
6	01000	8	Depress
7	00011	3	Deflate
8	01101	13	Retain Up/Down
9	01111	15	Hold Low/High
10	00100	4	Decreased
11	10000	16	Move Up/Down
12	00111	7	Flop
13	00110	6	Fall
14	11001	25	Boost
15	01011	11	Reduce
16	00011	3	Deflate
17	01110	14	Budge Up/Down
18	01001	9	Dip
19	10010	18	Equate Low/High
20	10111	23	Increase
21	01000	8	Depress
22	01000	8	Depress
23	00011	3	Deflate
24	01011	11	Reduce
25	01100	12	Devalue
26	10101	21	Ascend
27	11100	28	Escalated

September to October. CPI for alcoholic beverages fell 0.1 percent in the period of October to November, after boosting 0.2 percent in the period of September to October.

The CPI for apparel reduced 0.3 percent in the period of October to November, after deflating 0.7 percent in the period of September to October. The CPI for infants' and toddlers' apparel barely budged 0.1 percent down in the period of October to November, after a 1.4 percent rise in the period of September to October. The CPI for men's and boys' apparel dipped 1.0 percent in the period of September to October. However, the period of October to November equated 0.9 percent lower than the previous month. The CPI for footwear increased 0.5 percent in the period of September to October. However, CPI for footwear in the period of October to November depressed to 0.0 percent lower than last month. The CPI for women's and girls' apparel depressed 1.2 percent in the period of September to October. However, the period of October to November deflated 0.3 percent lower than last month.

The CPI for transportation reduced 3.1 percent in the period of September to October. However, CPI for transportation in the period of October to November devalued 0.9 percent less than the previous month. The CPI for motor vehicle parts and equipment ascended 0.2 percent in the period of September to October, following a 0.5 percent escalation in the period of October to November. Finally, the CPI for public transportation dropped 1.0 percent in the period of September to October. However, the period of October to November dropped 1.9 percent more than last month.

The upcoming Quarterly Report will include the period of November to December with a summarization of the entire quarter.

7.3.2 Other DSS

The aim of this section is to demonstrate that Matlist can be applied to a wide variety of DSS. In other words, the limitation of using DSS is an advantage and not a disadvantage because it not only legitimizes the communications between Bob and Alice, but also eases the process of generating a better quality of text cover. The following are some examples of different DSS using Matlist.

7.3.2.1 DSS of Elementary Math

A text example of the DSS of elementary math is presented in Sample 7.5. This sample, which was picked from [146,147], is authenticated and was written solely for teaching purposes and obviously not for concealing data. It is provided to show how the DSS of elementary math looks. Apparently, the text is just a normal question in elementary math that contains a real RS and its value almost has no constraint. Thus, the DSS of elementary math is an appropriate DSS to be employed by Matlist methodology, as demonstrated by the implementation example. Obviously, Sample 7.5 shows that a simple NLG or template system can be employed by Matlist to generate text cover. This fact is confirmed by Sample 7.6. Sample 7.6 is generated to conceal the message *"Use my secret key"* and its Matlist code is generated in the same way as shown in Section 7.3.1.1. The message is directly embedded in the form of an RS, as shown in Sample 7.6. Obviously, a bitrate for such domain will be very high.

SAMPLE 7.5

Example 2:
Look at these numbers:

3, 7, 5, 13, 20, 23, 39, 23, 40, 23, 14, 12, 56, 23, 29

The sum of these numbers is equal to 330.
There are fifteen numbers.
The mean is equal to 330 ÷ 15 = 22.
The mean of the above numbers is 22.

SAMPLE 7.6

Find the mean of the following numbers:

43 93 109 83 4 54 115 33 58 90 45 56 20 22 105 33 54 90 48 2

As indicated earlier, these presented samples are just examples to demonstrate the applicability of employing a wide variety of DSS. Unlike Edustega [ref], Matlist is based on DSS that commonly use RS (e.g., binary, decimal, hexadecimal, octal, alphabetic, alphanumeric, etc.).

7.3.2.2 DSS of Selling Books   Given the growing online businesses nowadays, there are many people selling new and used books. The DSS of selling books allows communicating parties to send and receive legitimate book prices, averting suspicion in covert communications. To see a legitimate sample of book prices, which do not conceal messages, refer to the website of any online bookseller (e.g., amazon.com, ebay.com, yahoo stores, etc.). Apparently, any individual that is selling books online can post prices for books on unrelated subjects. This is because most sellers are also buyers for both new and used books. The text in this DSS is just a linguistic description of book titles, author names, prices, etc., and either the fluctuations among book prices or their alphabetic string (e.g., different book titles, different author names, etc.) can be the steganographic carrier used to conceal data. Matlist code will be represented by different prices, as shown in Sample 7.7. Yet, different book titles or author names can form alphabetic strings of RS (Matlist code). Sample 7.7 conceals the message *"Use my secret key"* and its Matlist code is generated in the same way as shown in Section 7.3.1.1. It employs true and authenticated data (not text) to form the text cover. The data, not the text, were collected on May 6, 2008 from www.amazon.com using Internet search engines. If an adversary looks at the data of the Matlist cover, he will conclude that the book titles, author names, and prices are valid data. Thus, this technique justifies the use of Matlist.

SAMPLE 7.7

BOOK TITLE	AUTHOR	PRICE
Memoirs of Halide Edib	Halide Adivar Edib	$43.00
Mandeville's Used Book Price Guide	Richard L. Collins	$93.00
Conclog: A Methodological Approach to Concurrent Logic Programming	Jean-Marie Jacquet	$109.00
From Paris to Peoria: How European Piano Virtuosos Brought Classical Music to the American Heartland	R. Allen Lott	$83.00
Bank Shots (Kindle Edition)	Jim Strahle	$4.00
Grad Guides Book 3: Biological Sciences 2007	Peterson's	$54.00
Elements of Chemical Reaction Engineering (3rd Ed.)	H. Scott Fogler	$115.00
Good Practice Teacher's Book	Marie McCullagh, Ros Wright	$33.00
DDC Learning Macromedia Flash 5	Suzanne Weixel	$58.00
Frontiers of Combining Systems 2 (Studies in Logic and Computation)	Dov M. Gabbay	$90.00
THE SPIDER—Master of Men—Volume 6, number 1—June 1935	John Howitt; J. Fleming	$45.00
Murder In The Dark	Kerry Greenwood	$56.00
Hands-On Celebrations	Yvonne Y. Merrill	$20.00
Ramayana Book Two: Ayodhya	Valmiki, Sheldon Pollock	$22.00
Black History	Mary Ellen Snodgrass	$105.00
The Trail of Tears	John P. Bowes	$33.00
The Celebrity Black Book 2008	Jordan McAuley	$54.00
Nonlinear Dynamics and Chaos	J. M. T. Thompson, H. B. Stewart	$90.00
How to Establish a Unique Brand in the Consulting Profession	Alan Weiss	$48.00
Good and Evil Coloring Book #1	Michael Pearl	$2.00

7.3.2.3 DSS of Chemistry   A text example of the DSS of chemistry is presented in Sample 7.8. Sample 7.8 is authenticated and was written by members of the Department of Chemistry at Ohio State University only for teaching purposes and obviously not for concealing data [147]. It is provided to show how the DSS of chemistry looks. Apparently, the text is a normal question in chemistry that contains numerical values that can form an RS. Since the question is multiple-choice, most likely only one choice is correct and the others must be wrong. Thus, concealing data in the incorrect answers is easy and the text is still legitimate. Topics in chemistry are appropriate DSS to be employed by Matlist methodology as demonstrated next. Sample 7.8 shows that a simple NLG or template can easily be employed by Matlist to generate text cover, as confirmed by the example in Sample 7.9. Sample 7.9 conceals the message *"stop"* and its Matlist code (the encoded message) is generated in the same way as shown in Section 7.3.1.1. The question in Sample 7.9 is similar to other questions in the DSS of chemistry. For more authenticated samples, which do not conceal messages, refer to [147].

SAMPLE 7.8

```
Assume that the freezing point and melting point of
antifreeze, which are -45°C and 115°C, respectively,
are defined as 0°A and 100°A respectively. What is the
boiling point of water in °A?

      a) 83  b) 95    c) 78    d) 105  e) 91
```

SAMPLE 7.9

```
The ultimate temperature is _____ if the exact heat
of Al is 0.21 cal/g °C when 152 g of Al at 75.0°C in
145 g of H2O at 23.5°C.

      a) 58  b) 94  c) 14  d) 120.1   e) 32.8
```

As stated earlier, these presented samples are just examples to show the applicability of employing a wide variety of DSS for use with Matlist. Obviously, Matlist is unlike Edustega because Matlist is based on a DSS that regularly uses RS.

7.3.2.4 DSS of Discrete Math   The DSS of discrete math is a well-known topic in the field of computer science. The use of binary,

Table 7.6 Matlist Code Using the Alphabetic Letters

STEGANOGRAPHIC VALUES	CODED LETTERS	NON-CODED LETTERS
0000	A	Q
0001	B	R
0010	C	S
0011	D	T
0100	E	U
0101	F	V
0110	G	W
0111	H	X
1000	I	Y
1001	J	Z
1010	K	
1011	L	
1100	M	
1101	N	
1110	O	
1111	P	

Note: Other symbols can be included such as numerical values. However, these are just for showing the feasibility of the discrete math domain.

decimal, hexadecimal, octal, alphabetic, or alphanumeric in this DSS is an ordinary practice. For more detail about the DSS of discrete math, refer to [148]. Sample 7.10 conceals the message *"stop"*. The Matlist code of a message is generated in a similar way to that shown in Sections 7.3.1.1 and 7.3.1.3. Tables 7.6 and 7.7 detail the Matlist code that is used in Sample 7.10. The bitrate for this domain will be superior without raising suspicion which helps to achieve the steganographical goal. This is because of the excessive use of random values and strings of binary, decimal, hexadecimal, octal, alphabetic, alphanumeric, etc., in the discrete math domain.

SAMPLE 7.10

$q \notin r$ True [ ] or False [ ] if q = {J,L,K} and r = {D,H,L,I,A}

This presented sample is just an example to show the feasibility of employing wide variety of DSS, which is obvious that Matlist is differ from Edustega because Matlist is based on a DSS that uses excessively RS.

Table 7.7 Shows the Matlist Code Using Some Notations of Discrete Math

STEGANOGRAPHIC VALUES	SYMBOLS	CODE WORD
000	⊈ ⊈	Subsets
001	⊂ ⊃	Proper subset
010	⊄	Not subset
011	⊄	Not proper subset
100	∩	Intersection of sets
101	∪	Union of sets
110	∈	Element a member of a set
111	∉	Element is not a member of a set

Note: Other notations can be also included, these are simply examples. The values of the symbols are circulated. For example, the notation for "subset" is equal to "000" the first time it is used, the second time it will be equal to "001", the third time it will be equal to "010", and so on. In other words, after the first time a notation is used, its value increases by 1 every time it is used thereafter. Note, the code words are not synonyms.

7.3.3 Matlist Bitrate

The aim of this section is to show the bitrate of Matlist. The linguistics experiment of Matlist investigated the bitrate of different DSS with different implementations versus all other contemporary approaches. Matlist, based on experimental observation, achieves a bitrate superior to all contemporary approaches, as shown in Table 7.8. The bitrate of Matlist may differ from one DSS to another and from one implementation to another, as observed. Generally, the size of messages is a concern of most if not all steganography approaches. However, in the Matlist scheme presented here, Matlist is capable of camouflaging long messages. For example, in the presented implementation

Table 7.8 Shows the Bitrate of the Presented Matlist Scheme Current

DSS	BITRATE OF MATLIST
CPI	0.58%–1.02%
Elementary math	19.09%–21.51%
Bookseller	1.35%–2.16%
Chemistry	2.424%
Discrete math	18.4%

example, if a message does not fit within a single report of a CPI, elementary math quiz, book price list, chemistry question, or discrete math problem, Matlist will distribute it on multiple pieces of text without decreasing the bitrate.

For more detail about the experimental bitrate results of Nostega-based methodologies and all other contemporary approaches, refer to Chapter 13.

7.4 Conclusion

Matlist achieves the steganographical goal by basing the text cover generation and its transmittal on a DSS. The qualified DSS is the domain that is an RS based on any value type including binary, decimal, hexadecimal, octal, alphabetic, alphanumeric, etc. This type of DSS, e.g., financial, medical, mathematical, scientific, economical, etc., has adequate room for concealing data and allows communicating parties to establish a covert channel, such as a relationship based on their professions to transmit a text cover. Since the text generated by NLG and template techniques is meaningful, rhetorically sound, semantically coherent, and legitimate, Matlist takes advantage of these techniques to generate noiseless text cover. A message can be embedded in a form of RS values, as a function of RS values, the related semantics of RS, or a combination of these. The experimental results confirmed that Matlist cover is capable of fooling both human and machine examinations. The presented implementation achieves a superior bitrate to all other contemporary linguistic steganography approaches. Matlist is truly a public methodology that does not rely on the secrecy of its technique.

8

NORMALS

Normal Linguistic Steganography Methodology

Since the twentieth century, the progress and development of linguistic steganography have been minimal. Academically, roughly five major approaches were introduced before Nostega-based methodologies were invented: null cipher, mimic functions, NICETEXT, and the noise-based approach which included translation-based, confusing, and SMS-based approaches. Text cover of these approaches has numerous flaws such as incorrect syntax, lexicon, rhetoric, and grammar. Additionally, the content of such text cover is often meaningless and semantically incoherent. Such detectable noise (flaws) can easily raise suspicion during examinations by both humans and machines. These deficiencies render contemporary approaches (the non-Nostega-based) highly vulnerable. Unlike all other approaches, the **Normal** Linguistic **S**teganography (NORMALS) Methodology neither generates noise nor uses noisy text to camouflage data [26]. This is because NORMALS methodology is based on the Nostega paradigm. NORMALS employs Natural Language Generation (NLG) techniques to generate noiseless (flawless) and legitimate text cover by manipulating the non-random series input parameters of an NLG system in order to camouflage data in the generated text. As a result, NORMALS is capable of fooling both human and machine examinations. To emphasize, NORMALS is unlike Matlist methodology because NORMALS is capable of handling non-random series domains, as demonstrated in this chapter. The implementation validation of NORMALS demonstrates that there is room for clever concealing of data within adequate bitrates. The steganalysis validation confirms the robustness of achieving the steganographic goal as shown later in the steganalysis chapter of this book.

The remainder of this chapter is organized as follows: Section 8.1 introduces the NORMALS methodology; Section 8.2 demonstrates

NORMALS implementation; Section 8.3 discusses NORMALS performance; and Section 8.4 concludes the chapter and highlights directions for future research.

8.1 NORMALS Methodology

Bob and Alice are on a spy mission. Before they go on their mission, which requires them to reside in two different countries, they set the rules for communicating covertly using their professions as a stegano-graphic tool. To make this work, they establish a business relationship as follows. Bob and Alice are smoking cessation consultants working for the same corporation, and they agree to use a steganographic text cover. When Bob wants to send a covert message to Alice, Bob either posts counseling-related documents online for authorized clients and staff to access, or he sends counseling-related documents via email to the intended clients and staff. These counseling-related documents conceal a message. Covert messages transmitted in this manner will not look suspicious because both Bob and Alice are smoking cessation consul-tants. Everything looks legitimate. Furthermore, Bob and Alice are not the sole recipients. Other non-spy smoking cessation consultants and clients send and receive such documents, further warding off suspicion. However, only Bob and Alice are able to unravel the hidden message because they know the rules of the game. When Alice and Bob commu-nicate, they can use real data from their professions and their established business relationship to make their covert communications legitimate. If real data is not used, then untraceable data can be fabricated to avoid a comparison attack if an adversary should attempt to trace data and compare them to authenticated data. This will avert suspicion.

The above scenario demonstrates how NORMALS methodology can be used. NORMALS methodology is demonstrated in detail in the remainder of this chapter.

8.1.1 NORMALS Overview

The text generated by a Natural Language Generation (NLGS) system is meaningful, syntactically correct, lexically valid, rhetorically sound, semantically coherent, and legitimate [25–27,35,140]. Therefore, NORMALS takes advantage of the NLG techniques to generate the NORMALS cover (text cover) by employing an NLGS. Briefly, NORMALS employs NLG techniques to generate flawless and legitimate linguistic cover by manipulating the input parameters of the NLG system in order to camouflage data in the generated text. Linguistically, NORMALS cover inherits the same qualities of the text generated by NLGS, rendering NORMALS cover noiseless and legitimate. As a result, NORMALS is capable of fooling both human and machine examinations. The NLGS has plenty of room to conceal a message and allows the communicating parties to establish a covert channel to transmit the hidden message. NORMALS achieves the steganographic goal through three major components, as shown in Figure 8.1: the NLGS, the steganographic encoder, and the communication protocol. NORMALS' components are detailed in the following sections.

Once the NORMALS scheme is constructed, steganographic communication will be accomplished in three steps: first, NORMALS generates the required NORMALS code; second, NORMALS code will serve as input to the NORMALS NLGS to generate the NORMALS cover; and third, NORMALS covertly transmits the hidden message through a covert channel.

The following briefly describes an overview of NORMALS components. As stated above, each component will be elaborated on in the following sections.

NORMALS consists of three major components, as shown in Figure 8.1:

1. **NORMALS NLGS** is responsible for generating NORMALS cover.
2. **NORMALS encoder** encodes the message in the form of NLGS inputs.
3. **NORMALS Communications Protocol (NCP)** is responsible for how the intended users will communicate covertly to achieve the steganographic goal.

8.1.2 NORMALS NLGS

Legitimate users have to predetermine the NORMALS NLGS, as shown in Figure 8.1. Predetermining a particular NLGS is the initial

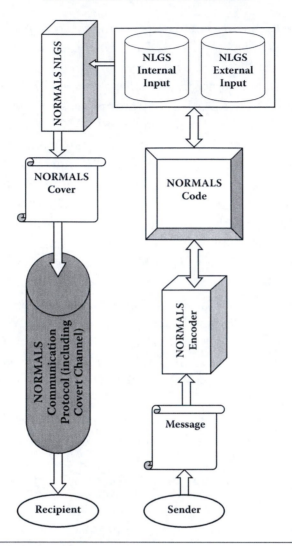

Figure 8.1 NORMALS architecture.

stage of constructing a NORMALS scheme. From the steganographic viewpoint, a major criterion for either selecting or implementing an NLGS to be used by NORMALS is that the output (the generated text) of the NLGS must be free of contradictions with itself, with old data from the communicating parties, and with publicly authenticated data. For example, weather reports and stock reports cannot be used because they depend on public data that may cause a detectable noise. The noise can be contradictions in the content of a single output (the same text cover contradicts itself), the output versus the accessible authenticated data, or the output versus the old data from the same communicating parties. Unlike Matlist [27], NORMALS does not depend on a random series. Therefore, if a particular domain-specific subject is not based on a random series, then Matlist cannot be applied. Conversely, NORMALS can be applied on domains that are not based on a random series.

There is no need to keep the NORMALS NLGS secret, and a contemporary public NLGS can also be employed, as will be demonstrated in the implementation section. Furthermore, there is no need to alter or modify the NORMALS NLGS if a contemporary NLGS is employed. This will make an adversary's job horrendous because the NORMALS NLGS is well-known as a non-steganographic scheme. Because there is no need to alter the generated text to conceal a message, the fact that the generated text is unaltered and linguistically flawless will never arouse suspicion. To emphasize, a particular text generated for one non-legitimate user or recipient means precisely whatever the content of the plain text states. On the other hand, the identical generated text for a legitimate recipient means there is a hidden message. In such a case, it is unlikely that an adversary will suspect or detect a hidden message. Nonetheless, implementing or modifying a contemporary NLGS is feasible, and as long as the use of the NORMALS NLGS among legitimate users is well planned, the adversary neither will suspect nor detect a hidden message. Modifying a contemporary NLGS to be used by NORMALS should appear as a non-steganographic scheme. This can be accomplished by fabricating a scenario that avoids the conception of suspicion in covert communications. For example, if a NORMALS NLGS is used by both public and legitimate users, such a scenario can convince an adversary that the NORMALS cover (text cover) is innocent because it is generated by a non-steganographic scheme. Since the focus of this chapter is the linguistic steganography, the details and the approaches of how to build an NLGS are not detailed here.

8.1.3 NORMALS Encoder

Based on the predetermined NLGS, the legitimate users have to construct the NORMALS encoder. The initial step of constructing the NORMALS encoder requires implementing a NORMALS code that can be used to encode a message, as shown in Figure 8.1. Normal code is implemented by encoding all possible factors and parameters that can generate a text through the predetermined NLGS. In other words, encoding all possible inputs of the NORMALS NLGS that can generate text will form NORMALS code. NORMALS code will serve as the input of the NORMALS NLGS. In this chapter, NORMALS code will refer to the encoded message and vice versa. When a legitimate user wants to conceal a message, the NORMALS encoder will encode a message using NORMALS code, then use the encoded message to feed the NLGS in order to generate the NORMALS cover. There are effective ways to construct a NORMALS encoder and its code that will make the adversary's job extremely difficult.

8.1.4 NLGS Inputs

There are two types of NLGS inputs, as shown in Figure 8.1: internal inputs, such as a knowledge base; and external inputs, such as user inputs or machine inputs. Machine inputs, such as those from an electronic device (e.g., sensors), can feed the NLGS the required data inputs. The external inputs may become internal inputs for future use. For example, an updateable NLGS such as FOG or WeatherReporter collects weather information and saves it in a knowledge base for future use to be compared to its current data inputs. Rather than abstract explanations, answering the following question can clarify the picture of an NLGS. The question is: what and how is the generated text produced? Briefly, the NLG system employs knowledge bases, artificial intelligence, computational linguistics, and other related techniques to achieve its goal [25–27,140]. Contemporary NLG techniques employ the knowledge of a domain-specific subject and its linguistics to generate text in the form of reports, assistance messages, documents, and other desirable text. Contemporary NLG systems generate a mature linguistic text [25–27,140]. This process of generating text is based on both internal inputs and external inputs, as stated earlier. For example, letter-generator [59], STOP [59,60], and Chessmaster [154] are NLGS. Chessmaster is a software program for playing and teaching chess. It has internal inputs such as the knowledge base of most professional games and their analyses. If a user runs a particular game and asks Chessmaster about a move that is not an authenticated move, Chessmaster will respond with both text and audio feedback. The audio is a voice reading the generated text. This generated text is the Chessmaster's response to the user's question, explaining the analysis of a particular move. This example of Chessmaster represents both an internal input, which is the authenticated game, and an external input, which is a different move rather than an authenticated move. The other example, letter-generator, also has both internal inputs and external inputs similar to Chessmaster. However, the external inputs are obtained through a questionnaire or a selector. A particular user will either answer the questionnaire or select the desirable answer or parameters. Based on the user's response, letter generator will produce the desirable letter (text). For more examples of NLG systems, refer to [9]. From the steganographic point of view, internal inputs, external inputs, or both can be encoded to generate NORMALS code. However, one of the major criteria for implementing NORMALS code is that the text generated (text cover) by NORMALS code has to be free of contradictions with itself, with old data (used by the communicating parties in the past), and with publicly authenticated data.

8.1.5 NORMALS Communications Protocol

Steganography is a Greek word which means "cover writing" [25,27]. When defining "steganography science" as the scientific art of hiding a message, suspicion can still be raised and the goal of steganography will be defeated. Covert communication is done through two steps: concealing a message and then transmitting the hidden message. Contemporary steganography approaches are focused on how to hide a message and not on how to hide the transmittal of a hidden message. Concealing the transmittal of a hidden message is as important as concealing the message.

Consider the following scenario: a sender, when communicating covertly, always uses the same steganographic technique and the same steganographic cover type (e.g., mimic functions, translation-based, image-based, or audio-based). Furthermore, the sender always uses email to deliver a hidden message. Covert communications consistently using the same steganographic technique, cover type, and email for transmission will raise suspicion. Suspicion is raised because an adversary will wonder why the emails always contain one of the following: a fingerprint of mimic functions, a translated document, an image, or an audio file. If the sender has no legitimate reason for sending an email containing one of the mentioned items, suspicion can be raised even if the content does not look suspicious and nothing is detected because it is unusual for someone to send such content by email all the time. Suspicion is raised because of the way of delivering the hidden message not because a vulnerable hiding technique was used. However, it is more convincing when a sender has a website and posts a hidden message on it for a recipient to retrieve rather than sending the message through frequent emails.

Another example: a sender in the financial industry has a legitimate reason for distributing a price analysis graph. Suspicion will not be raised if a message is concealed in the graph because of the legitimacy of distributing financial graphs. On the other hand, if the graph is a medical report, suspicion will be raised because the sender has no legitimate reason for sending a medical report. To emphasize, the method of delivering the hidden message can raise suspicion even if using a secure hiding technique. NORMALS averts the suspicion that may arise during the transmittal of a hidden message by camouflaging the transmittal. Therefore, NORMALS methodology requires that the intended users agree on the appropriate arrangements, techniques, policy, rules and any other related specifications for achieving the steganographic goal.

NORMALS Communications Protocol (NCP) works in the following way, as shown in Figure 8.2. A sender and a recipient communicate covertly using NORMALS, and they agree to the following:

1. The particular specifications and configurations of the NORMALS scheme and its decoder.
2. The particular specifications, configurations, policy, arrangements, and techniques of establishing the channel for the users to communicate covertly.

Based on the agreed upon NCP, the intended users are ready to communicate covertly with each other using NORMALS.

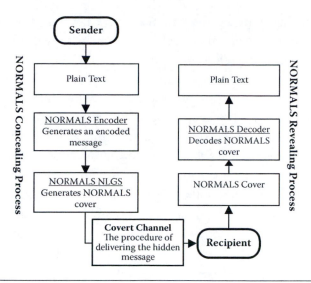

Figure 8.2   Illustrates NORMALS Communications Protocol (NCP) between sender and recipient.

8.2 NORMALS Implementation

According to the Nostega paradigm, five essential modules must be applied in order to implement a successful steganographic system. The first module determines a particular field (domain) that can be employed and is capable of achieving the steganographic goal. For NORMALS, this module concerns the selection procedure of an appropriate context for which a NORMALS cover is to be generated. In the current implementation in this chapter smoking cessation is the employed domain. The second module identifies steganographic parameters (steganographic carriers) capable of concealing data without creating noise. NORMALS exploits Natural Language Generation (NLG) techniques to generate noiseless (flawless) and legitimate text cover by manipulating the non-random series input parameters of the NLG system in order to camouflage data in the generated text. Unlike Matlist, NORMALS is capable of handling non-random series domains. In the third module of the Nostega paradigm, a message is encoded that neither raises suspicions nor constrains the generation of the steganographic cover. NORMALS employs either authenticated data or untraceable data (private data). Fourth, if there are contemporary non-steganographic tools that can be employed to generate the steganographic cover so that it appears legitimate and innocent, then such tools—such as the one used in this chapter—should be preferred. In this chapter, the text cover example is generated using a non-steganographic tool called STOP, which was designed to help people to quit smoking. Finally, the fifth module is the communications protocol which deals with the way a sender and a recipient communicate covertly to transmit a hidden message. In other words, it establishes the covert communications channel.

The following section demonstrates an actual implementation of the NORMALS methodology. Note that the techniques presented in this chapter are just examples of possible implementations, but NORMALS methodology can be implemented in different ways. Obviously, NORMALS can easily employ systems other than the NLG system used. In other words, NORMALS can employ other NLG systems for domains other than the smoking cessation domain [9]. Nonetheless, the presented demonstration shows the capability and flexibility of achieving the steganographic goal while employing the NORMALS methodology. To emphasize, the purpose of the presented implementation is to show the NORMALS capability for achieving the steganographic goal rather than making it difficult for the adversary to decode a message. Employing a hard encoding system or cryptosystem to protect a message is feasible and simple using any contemporary encoder or cryptosystem [54,93]. However, that is not the focus of this chapter and no cryptosystem was used in this chapter. The implementation of the NORMALS scheme can be achieved through three stages to predetermine the following modules: first, NORMALS NLGS; second, NORMALS encoder; and third, NORMALS Communications Protocol (NCP). These stages are detailed in following sections (Sections 8.2.1 to 8.2.3).

8.2.1 Determining NORMALS NLGS (Stage 1)

Legitimate users employ a contemporary public NLGS called STOP [59,60], as shown in Figures 8.3, 8.4, and 8.6 (Figure 8.6 is the entire NLGS input). STOP, an NLG system, was created to help people stop smoking. The output (the generated text) of STOP is free of contradictions with itself, with the publicly authenticated data.

Smoking Information Questionnaire

Note: The online version of STOP is a simplified version of the main STOP system, and does not perform certain computationally time-consuming types of tailoring.

Name: [   ]
Age: [   ]   Male: ⊙ Female: ○

(If you don't fill in your name and age the program cannot produce a letter for you!)

How many cigarettes do you smoke in a day?

Less than 5 ○   5 - 10 ○   11 - 15 ○   16 - 20 ⊙   21 - 30 ○   31 or more ○

Do you smoke your first cigarette within 30 minutes of waking?   Yes ○   No ⊙

Are you intending to stop smoking in the next 6 months?   Yes ○   No ⊙

If Yes,   Are you intending to stop within the next month?   Yes ○   No ⊙

If NO,   Would you like to stop if it was easy?   Yes ○   No ○   Not Sure ○

Figure 8.3   A screenshot [60] of STOP, which illustrates a piece of the NORMALS NLGS. The NLGS is called Stop Smoking and is made public to help people stop smoking. The Stop Smoking scheme (the NLGS) is neither modified nor is its output (the generated text) altered. This will render an adversary's job extremely difficult by making it unfeasible to suspect or detect a hidden message.

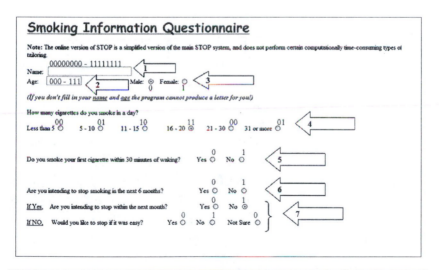

Figure 8.4   A screenshot [60] of STOP, which illustrates a piece of the NORMALS encoder where all external inputs are encoded to predetermine the NORMALS code. Unlike Matlist, NORMALS does not depend on a random series as shown in the figure. The legitimate user generates a NORMALS cover (text-cover) by answering questions that represent the message, and then the user generates the text based on the encoded message. The entire scheme is demonstrated in Figure 8.6.

NORMALS is capable of employing the STOP NLGS although it is not based on a random series.

Not only is there no need to keep the NORMALS NLGS (STOP NLGS) secret, but, as demonstrated, it is a contemporary public NLGS. Additionally, the NORMALS NLGS presented in this section is not a steganographic scheme as shown in Figure 8.3. Furthermore, the NORMALS NLGS is neither altered nor modified, which will make an adversary's task much more difficult because the NORMALS NLGS is well known to the public as a non-steganographic scheme. Moreover, because the text generated by the NORMALS NLGS is unaltered and linguistically flawless, suspicion will never be raised.

To emphasize again, a particular text generated for a non-legitimate user/recipient means precisely what the content of plain text states. On the other hand, the same generated text for another recipient that is a legitimate user means there is a hidden message. In such a case, it is unlikely an adversary will suspect or detect a hidden message. As stated earlier, because linguistic steganography is the focus of this chapter, details and methods for building an NLGS are not detailed.

8.2.2 Determining NORMALS Encoder (Stage 2)

Based on the predetermined NLGS (STOP NLGS), the legitimate users have to construct the NORMALS encoder [26]. As stated earlier, the initial step of constructing the NORMALS encoder is implementing a NORMALS code that can be used to encode a message. The NORMALS encoder employs a NORMALS code to encode a message simply by encoding all possible factors that can generate a text using the predetermined NLGS. In other words, encoding all possible inputs of the NORMALS NLGS that can generate text will form NORMALS code. There are two types of inputs in the NORMALS NLGS: internal inputs and external inputs. Internal inputs are those such as a knowledge base, while external inputs include user inputs or machine inputs. In this chapter, the NORMALS scheme employs only external inputs to implement NORMALS code and to construct the NORMALS encoder, as shown in Figure 8.4. The external inputs of the NORMALS NLGS, as shown in Figure 8.4, are done through a questionnaire. Obviously, it is a trivial task to modify the STOP

NLGS to automate the input process (encoding message) without a questionnaire and to appear as if a user answered the questionnaire.

The implementation presented in this chapter of constructing both the NORMALS encoder and NORMALS code has no effect on the generated text. Therefore, the generated text is free of contradictions with itself, old data that was used by the communicating parties in the past, and publicly authenticated data. Additionally, the generated text is identical for both cases whether STOP NLGS is used for smoker's counseling or for steganographic proposes by NORMALS. In other words, the generated text is identical both when STOP NLGS is used to help smokers quit smoking, and when it is used for steganographic purposes.

8.2.3 NORMALS Cover

The NORMALS concealment process is as follows. The NORMALS encoder will encode a message using NORMALS code then use the encoded message to feed the NLGS to generate the NORMALS cover (text cover), as shown in Figure 8.5. To emphasize, the NORMALS encoder implements NORMALS code by encoding each answer (input) in the STOP NLGS questionnaire as shown in Figure 8.4. Encoding each answer (input) can be done using any encoding technique. In this chapter, each answer (input) in the STOP NLGS questionnaire is encoded in binary to construct the NORMALS code as shown in Figure 8.4. When a legitimate user wants to conceal a message, the NORMALS encoder will convert the message (plain text) in a concatenated binary string of the ASCII representation of message. Then, the NORMALS encoder will divide this binary message in each answer. As a result, each answer will conceal a part of the message as shown in Figure 8.4. The NORMALS encoder simply selects the answers that represent the same binary string of the message. Finally, the NORMALS NLGS, which in this implementation example is the STOP NLGS, will generate a text cover (NORMALS cover) based on the selected answers (inputs of the STOP NLGS), as shown in Figures 8.4 and 8.5. Note that there are numerous ways of constructing the NORMALS encoder and its code, which makes the adversary's job extremely difficult.

SMOKING INFORMATION FOR HAYMAN LATHAM

Dear Hayman Latham

Thank you for taking the trouble to return the smoking questionnaire that we sent you. In it you said that you're not planning to stop smoking in the next six months. However, you would like to be a nonsmoker if it was easy to stop. Many people like you have been able to stop and you could too if you really wanted to. We hope this information will be of interest to you.

It's easier to stop if you WANT to...

You like to smoke because:
- It helps to break up your working time.
- It stops you from putting on weight.
- It helps you to relax.
- It helps you cope with stress.
- It is something you do when you are bored.
- It is something to do with friends and family.
- It stops you from getting withdrawal symptoms.

You don't like smoking because:
- It is bad for your health.
- It makes you less fit.
- It is expensive.
- It is bad for the health of those near you.
- It is unpleasant for people near you.
- It makes your clothes and breath smell.

You said you don't like smoking because it is *bad for your health*. You are right to think this.

You are less likely to have another stroke if you stop smoking. Stopping smoking for the sake of your health really does make sense. Stopping smoking would prevent your lungs getting any worse. Ex-smokers notice an improvement in their health and fitness when their lungs begin to recover. This may take a few weeks.

If you stop smoking you are less likely to get circulation problems in the future. There is no safe number of cigarettes to smoke. Even if you only smoke occasionally it is still worth giving up. You also dislike smoking because it *affects your fitness*. Giving up smoking improves your physical and mental fitness. It also increases your stamina. Another bad thing about smoking for you is that it is a *bad example to children*. This is true. Children are far more likely to smoke if those around them smoke. Stopping smoking sets a good example.

You could do it... You are right to think that if you tried to stop smoking you would have a good chance of succeeding. You have several things in your favor.

- You have stopped before for more than a month.
- You are a light smoker.
- You have good reasons for stopping smoking.
- You expect support from your workmates.

We know that all of these make it more likely that you will be able to stop. Most people who stop smoking for good have made more than one attempt.

Figure 8.5 NORMALS cover after camouflaging the message "*{Come 8pm}*". As shown, it is meaningful, syntactically correct, lexically valid, rhetorically sound, semantically coherent, and looks legitimate. These are some of the advantages that enable NORMALS to fool both human and computer examinations.

It's often easier than you think... You said in your questionnaire that you might find it difficult to stop because you would *put on weight*. A few people do put on some weight. If you did stop smoking, your appetite would improve and you would taste your food much better. Because of this it would be wise to plan in advance so that you're not reaching for the biscuit tin all the time. Remember that putting on weight is an overeating problem, not a no-smoking one. You can tackle it later with diet and exercise. You also said that you might find it difficult to stop because *your partner and a lot of your friends smoke*. When lots of people around you are smoking it can be more difficult to stop, but not impossible. Many people have managed. If you decide to stop, tell your family and friends. Some of them might want to stop as well and you can help each other. If not, think what they could do to help and ask for their support. They might decide to stop when they see that you have succeeded. For you, another difficulty with stopping is that smoking helps you cope with stress. Many people think that cigarettes help them cope with stress. Taking a cigarette only makes you feel better for a short while. Most ex-smokers feel calmer and more in control than they did when they were smoking.

And finally... We hope this letter will help you to think more about the benefits of stopping smoking tobacco. Many people who feel like you do now, do eventually stop smoking. Although it might be hard, if you really want to stop you will be able to do it.

With best wishes,
The STOP Team.

SMOKELINE is the Scottish helpline for stopping smoking. Calls are free and there is someone to speak to between 12 noon and 12 midnight. The phone number is: **0800 84 84 84**

Figure 8.5 (continued).

Example of NORMALS cover

- The plain text is: "*{Come 8pm}*"
- In this chapter the NORMALS encoder converts the plain text into a concatenated binary string of the ASCII representation of the message as follows:

  0111101101000011011011110110110101100101001000
  0000111000011100000110110101111101

- The NORMALS encoder will divide the above binary message on each answer. As a result, each answer will conceal a part of the message, as shown in Figure 8.4, simply by selecting the answers that represent the same

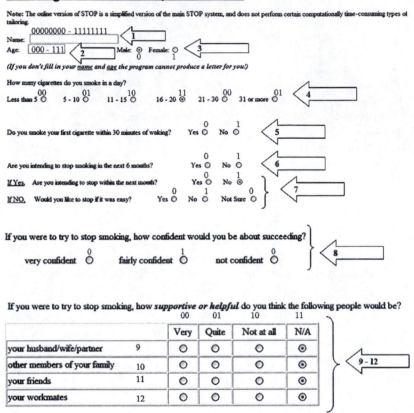

Figure 8.6 Screenshot [60] from the questionnaire that illustrates all the inputs of the NORMALS scheme employing STOP NLGS [59,60].

binary string of the message, as shown in Figure 8.4 and in Tables 8.1 and 8.2.

- Finally, the STOP NLGS will generate a text cover (NORMALS cover) based on the selected answers (inputs of the STOP NLGS), as shown in Figure 8.4.

8.2.4 Determining NORMALS Communications Protocol (Stage 3)

Legitimate users prearrange and plot the required scenario to avert suspicion in covert communications. Simply, the legitimate users are a counseling group helping smokers quit. The clients are required to answer an online questionnaire and to submit it.

What are the things you *don't like* about your smoking? 21 - 29

		Very important	Quite important	Not important
		0	1	0
it is expensive	21	○	○	◉
it is bad for my health	22	○	○	◉
I don't like feeling dependent on cigarettes	23	○	○	◉
it makes my clothes and breath smell	24	○	○	◉
it is a bad example for children	25	○	○	◉
it is unpleasant for people near me	26	○	○	◉
it makes me less fit	27	○	○	◉
people around me disapprove of my smoking	28	○	○	◉
it is bad for the health of people near me	29	○	○	◉

What might make it *difficult* for you to stop smoking? 30 - 40

		Very important	Quite important	Not important
		0	1	0
I enjoy smoking too much	30	○	○	◉
I don't think I have enough willpower	31	○	○	◉
I think I would put on weight	32	○	○	◉
I would be too stressed	33	○	○	◉
I think I am too addicted to cigarettes	34	○	○	◉
my partner smokes	35	○	○	◉
I would miss smoking with friends	36	○	○	◉
I can't resist the craving for a cigarette	37	○	○	◉
I don't really want to stop	38	○	○	◉
I would be bored	39	○	○	◉
I would miss smoking breaks at work	40	○	○	◉

Figure 8.6 (continued).

Consequently, based on the answers of each client, the NLG system generates a letter for each client. Obviously, the legitimate users are required to submit the entire records for each client. This legitimizes the procedure of sending a group of records to headquarters. Transmitting a hidden message in this manner will avoid raising suspicion. Briefly, a sender and a recipient communicate covertly using NORMALS, and they agree to the following: the particular specifications, configurations, policy, arrangements, and techniques of the NORMALS scheme, and its covert channel for delivering the hidden message.

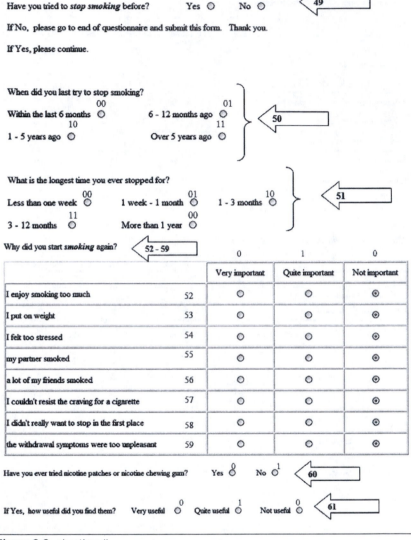

Figure 8.6   (continued).

8.3 Performance

In NORMALS, the bitrate may differ from one NLG system to another; however, the NORMALS scheme presented achieves a bitrate of 0.20% by encoding only the external inputs. Obviously, by encoding both internal and external inputs of the NORMALS NLGS, the bitrate will be increased. This bitrate is lower than the bitrate of other approaches. However, linguistically NORMALS is superior

Thank you for filling this in, please SUBMIT the form now by pressing the 'Submit' button.

Submit

Return to STOP homepage

Figure 8.6 (continued).

Table 8.1 The Steganographic Code of the Message "*(Come 8pm)*" Which Also Is Shown in Figures 8.4 and 8.6 (Figure 8.6 Represents the Entire NLGS Input)

INPUT ORDER NUMBER AS APPEARS IN THE NLGS USED IN FIGURE 8.6	NUMBER OF DIGIT THAT CAN BE CONCEALED IN A SINGLE INPUT IN THE NLG SYSTEM USED, AS SHOWN IN FIGURE 8.6	TOTAL OF DIGITS THAT CAN CONCEAL DATA, AS SHOWN IN FIGURE 8.6	THE CONCATENATED BINARY STRING OF THE ASCII REPRESENTATION OF THE MESSAGE
1	8	8	0111 1011 (from Table 8.2)
2	3	3	010 (2nd #, e.g., for age 62, 2 is the string represented in binary)
3	1	1	0
4	2	2	00
5-8	1 (for each input)	4	1101
9–12	2 (for each input)	8	10111101
13–40	1 (for each input)	28	1011010110010100100000001110
41–44	2 (for each input)	8	00011100
45–49	1 (for each input)	5	00011
50–51	2 (for each input)	4	0110
52–60	1 (for each input)	9	101111101
61	1	1	None
Total	81	81	80 digit

to mimic functions and NICETEXT. Continual improvement of machine translation will soon make the use of the translation-based approach to steganography obsolete [13–15]. Inversely, improvements in natural language generation systems will make NORMALS stable and attractive for future use [26,140].

Improving NORMALS' bitrate can be accomplished. As stated above, by encoding both internal and external inputs of the

Table 8.2   The Steganographic Code for the First Letter of the First or Last Name

FIRST/LAST LETTER OF THE FIRST OR LAST NAME		NORMALS CODE FOR THE FIRST NLGS SYSTEM'S INPUT[a]
A	Q	0000 (Note, A or Q takes same value which is "0000")
B	R	0001 (Note, B or R takes same value which is "0001")
C	S	0010 (Note, C or S takes same value which is "0010")
D	T	0011 (Note, D or T takes same value which is "0011")
E	U	0100 (Note, E or U takes same value which is "0100")
F	V	0101 (Note, F or V takes same value which is "0101")
G	W	0110 (Note, G or W takes same value which is "0110")
H	**X**	**0111 (Note, H or X takes same value which is "0111")**
I	Y	1000 (Note, I or Y takes same value which is "1000")
J	Z	1001 (Note, J or Z takes same value which is "1001")
	K	1010 (Unique letter, which means that the value of "1010" assigned to only "K")
	L	**1011 (Unique letter, which means that the value of "1011" assigned to only "L")**
	M	1100 (Unique letter, which means that the value of "1100" assigned to only "M")
	N	1101 (Unique letter, which means that the value of "1101" assigned to only "N")
	O	1110 (Unique letter, which means that the value of "1110" assigned to only "O")
	P	1111 (Unique letter, which means that the value of "1111" assigned to only "P")

Note: The highlighted rows represent the encoded message.
[a] This encoding is done by selecting names that start or end with a particular letter according to this table.

NORMALS NLGS, the bitrate definitely will be increased. In the presented NORMALS scheme, the bitrate achieved was based on encoding only the external inputs. Encoding the internal inputs and increasing the amount of linguistics used will greatly improve the bitrate. For instance, a technique such as text substitution can be employed by NORMALS where words or a combination of words can be substituted for other words or combinations of words. Maximizing the amount of linguistics and using text substitution (e.g., words, sentences, etc.) will obviously increase the bitrate.

The technique of text substitution is similar to the semantic substitution of NICETEXT [9–11]. However, semantic substitution has been used by other steganographic approaches. Unfortunately, they create detectable noise which causes their approaches to fail [9–15].

Unlike all other steganographic approaches in which the use of text substitution causes semantic errors, NORMALS does not cause any errors when it employs text substitution techniques. NORMALS methodology is based on natural language generation techniques where these techniques ensure the production of legitimate text. NORMALS Text Substitution (NTS) is a feature in NORMALS that gives it the advantage of being flexible in generating the NORMALS cover as well as increasing the NORMALS bitrate.

Message Size: Generally, the size of a message is a concern for most if not all steganography approaches. However, in the presented NORMALS scheme, NORMALS camouflages a long message. When a message is long, then NORMALS generates a longer text cover and distributes it in a set of client records (the generated text covers) using either single or multiple transmissions. In the presented implementation example, sending a set of client records is a common procedure in the counseling profession. On the other hand, short messages can be a bit tricky. However, NORMALS supports the camouflage of short messages by using any end of message symbols such as delimiters or null characters.

8.4 Conclusion

The text generated by NLG techniques is meaningful, syntactically correct, lexically valid, rhetorically sound, semantically coherent, and legitimate. Therefore, NORMALS takes advantage of NLG techniques to generate NORMALS cover, rendering it linguistically flawless (noiseless) and legitimate by manipulating the input parameters of the NLG system in order to camouflage data in the generated text. As a result, NORMALS is capable of fooling both human and machine examinations. NORMALS is a truly public methodology that does not rely on the secrecy of its approach. An NLGS has plenty of room to conceal a message as demonstrated in this chapter. To date, the NORMALS scheme presented achieves a bitrate of 0.20% by encoding only the external inputs where the bitrate may differ from one NLG system to another. Obviously, by encoding both internal and external inputs of the NORMALS NLGS, the NORMALS bitrate will definitely be increased. In Matlist, the use of NLG techniques is applied to a domain-specific subject that is based on a random series (e.g., a random series of binary, decimal, hexadecimal, octal, alphabetic, alphanumeric, or any other form). Inversely, NORMALS is capable of handling a non-random series domain. Regarding the translation-based approach, the continual improvement of machine translation will eliminate and ban the use of the translation-based approach. Conversely, improvement in natural language generation is promising and will make NORMALS more stable for future use. Unlike the translation-based approach, NORMALS can be applied to all known languages without any exceptions, while the generated text cover will remain linguistically legitimate.

9

HEADSTEGA

Steganography Methodology

The frequent exchange of emails is widely popular and generates a high volume of traffic that allows communicating parties to establish a covert channel without a suspicious pattern. Thus, emails are an attractive steganographic carrier to transmit hidden messages. This was the motive for developing the Email-**Head**ers-Based **Stega**nography (Headstega) Methodology [24]. Headstega encodes a message then assigns it to steganographic carriers, e.g., recipient's email addresses, names, or subject fields, to camouflage data. For example, Headstega can conceal a message in the primary and secondary message recipients' addresses that are the "To" and "Cc" fields of an email respectively. In addition, the generated text cover can be embedded among other legitimate non-coded elements. For instance, if a message is concealed using a recipient's email address then this email address can be combined with other email addresses that are not used to camouflage data for more protection. Thus, Headstega neither hides data in noise (errors) nor produces noise when a message is concealed in the textual email headers. The email contents (the body of emails) are completely legitimate and do not conceal data. Headstega establishes a covert channel among communicating parties by employing justifiable reasons based on a legitimate exchange of emails in order to achieve unsuspicious transmission of covers. The presented implementation, validation, and steganalysis of Headstega demonstrate its robust capabilities for achieving the steganographic goal, the adequate room for concealing data, and a bitrate which is roughly 3.38%, and up to 7.67%, superior to all contemporary text steganography of non-Nostega approaches.

The remainder of this chapter is organized as follows. Section 9.1 explains the Headstega methodology in detail. Section 9.2 demonstrates the Headstega implementation. Finally, Section 9.3 concludes the chapter.

9.1 Headstega Methodology

Since Headstega is based on the Nostega paradigm, Headstega addresses the requirements of the five Nostega modules. However, when explaining Headstega in the next section, the contents of the modules are combined in order to avoid as much repetition as possible. In brief detail, the following shows how Headstega obeys these five modules of Nostega paradigm. Headstega predetermines a particular field (domain) that can be used as a profile of all legitimate users and that matches the content domain of emails in order to achieve the steganographic goal. The second module of the Nostega paradigm identifies steganographic parameters (steganographic carriers) that are capable of concealing data without creating noise. Headstega exploits email header fields such recipients' email addresses, names, and subject fields to camouflage data. These fields are employed as steganographic carriers. For example, Headstega can conceal a message in the primary and secondary message recipients' addresses, that is the "To" and "Cc" fields of an email, respectively. In the third module of Nostega, the message is encoded in a way that does not raise suspicions or constrain the generation of the steganographic cover. Headstega may employ either authenticated email headers that are publicly available, e.g., email lists, or untraceable email headers such as made-up email headers, without raising suspicion. Fourth, Headstega generates the steganographic cover so that it appears legitimate and innocent. In Headstega, a head cover (text cover) will be generated in the form of email headers. Finally, the fifth module is concerned with the communications protocol that includes the covert channel. This determines how a sender and recipient will communicate covertly. Obviously, in Headstega a steganographic cover (head cover) is sent as regular email. Again, Headstega follows the five modules of Nostega, as detailed in this section. However, Headstega is presented in this book in the form of two modules in order to avoid repetition.

The next section provides an overview of Headstega.

9.1.1 Headstega Overview

To illustrate Headstega, consider the following scenario. Bob and Alice are on a spy mission. Bob and Alice, like other ordinary people, each own an email account. Before they go on their mission, which requires them to reside in two different countries, they set the rules for communicating covertly using their friendship as a steganographic umbrella to justify sending and receiving emails. Basically, they agree on concealing messages only in email headers by embedding data in the form of email addresses, names, individual titles, and abbreviations that look innocent, while the content of the emails (the body) is fully legitimate and has nothing concealed within it. To make this work, Bob and Alice have a legitimate reason to send, receive, and forward emails, e.g., personal, advertising, business, and invitations, to either an individual or a group of friends. Covert messages transmitted in this manner will not look suspicious because the relationship between Bob and Alice is legitimate. Furthermore, Alice is not always the sole recipient of Bob's email and vice versa. Other non-spy people also receive these emails, further warding off suspicion. As mentioned earlier, these emails conceal data only in the headers while the contents (bodies) are fully legitimate and do not camouflage any message. However, only Bob and Alice are able to unravel the hidden messages because they know the rules of the game.

The above scenario demonstrates how Headstega methodology takes advantage of the common frequent exchange of emails, which is a popular practice worldwide and generates a high volume of traffic. The core idea of Headstega methodology is basically camouflaging data in the natural and legitimate email headers such as recipients' email addresses, names, and subject lines. Obviously, such steganographic cover is linguistically and logically legitimate. Headstega's algorithm works as follows.

Mainly, the Headstega system architecture consists of two modules, as shown in Figure 9.1. The first module is the message encoding, which encodes a message in an appropriate and required form for the camouflaging process (the second module). The process of generating a head cover, by Module 2, may influence the process of how a message should be encoded. For example, a message may be encoded by slicing its binary string into a particular length of bits such as four bits, seven bits, or any required bit length. For instance, a message: *"no more"* can be converted to its binary: *011011100110111100100000011011011 0111101110010011001010101*. Then, slicing this binary string into lengths

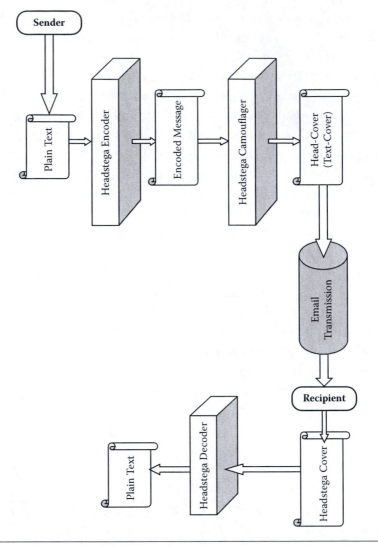

Figure 9.1   Architecture of the Headstega system.

of four bits: *0110 1110 0110 1111 0010 0000 0110 1101 0110 1111 0111 0010 0110 0101*. The second module is the message camouflager that generates the head cover (text cover), which conceals the encoded message. The head cover may be in a form of recipients' email addresses, recipients' names, or subjects. Implementing such camouflage schemes may involve employing other components such as the following in order to ease the automation process of generating head cover:

- Email generator systems such as iContact [155]
- Internet search engines such as the free search engines of Google [156], Yahoo [157], Live Search [158], etc.
- Email account providers such as the free Yahoo Mail [159], Gmail [160], MSN Hotmail [161], etc.

Once the Headstega system is implemented, the covert communications will be accomplished in three steps. First, a message is encoded using the predetermined steganographic encoder from Module 1. Second, Module 2 camouflages the steganographic code (encoded message), which was generated by Module 1. Finally, the message is emailed to its legitimate recipient. The above modules are detailed in the following sections.

9.1.2 Message Encoding (Module 1)

Implementing the message encoder follows a two-steps process. The first step is to determine the encoding parameters that will serve as steganographic carriers. The second is to define a steganographic coding based on those parameters. A parameter (steganographic carrier) in this context means some aspects of text used that can be referred to steganographic values throughout a head cover (text cover). In other words, the steganographic carriers used by Headstega are the textual elements that are commonly used in the email headers such as recipients' email addresses, names, and subjects and these will be assigned steganographic code values such as a particular binary bit string (e.g., 0000, 0001, 0010) to conceal data. The definition of the steganographic code will depend on the selected parameters. For example, encoding a message by using a recipient's email address is different from encoding it using a recipient's name or an email subject. The coding module of Headstega exploits theses types of options and determines the parameters that will be employed to conceal messages. The popularity of certain parameters is an important factor in the selection. Nonetheless, the appearance of certain types of elements may draw suspicion. For example, if a husband sends emails to his wife containing private communication, that email will be sent only to her and not to a group of people. If such an email, containing private content from a husband to his wife was Cc'd to a group of people, that might raise suspicion. Headstega methodology counters all of these concerns by simply requiring that the implementation of Headstega system be made aware of such issues or possible attacks. In addition, it is also crucial to justify the interaction among the communicating parties to establish a covert channel for delivering the steganographic cover (head cover), which is done using the communication protocol (Module 3). Note that the encoding parameters may influence the covert channel or vice versa, which is responsible for justifying the interaction among the communicating parties.

Headstega does not impose any constraint on the message encoder scheme as long as it generates a set of data values that can be embedded in a head cover. Given the availability of numerous encoding techniques in the literature that fit [25], the balance of this section will focus on an example that will be used in Section 9.2 to demonstrate the applicability of Headstega. In the presented examples in Section 9.2, the encoding is done as follows. A message is first converted to a binary string. The string can be a binary of cipher text or a compressed representation. The binary string is then partitioned into groups of m bits. The value of m is determined based on the encoding parameters that Headstega exploits. The text of email headers such as the recipients' email addresses, recipients' names, subject fields, etc., may be exploited for concealing data. For example, if the head cover will contain four possible elements (steganographic carriers), the binary message is partitioned into groups of two bits, e.g., 00, 01, 10, and 11, corresponding to the possible options. Again, this encoding scheme is just for illustration and many alternate and more sophisticated schemes can be employed, as demonstrated in Section 9.2.

9.1.3 Message Camouflager (Module 2)

As mentioned earlier, the high demand and popularity of the use of email by a wide variety of people render emails attractive steganographic carriers. Headstega takes advantage of such demand and popularity to camouflage data only in email headers and not in the body of emails. These headers include recipients' email addresses, names, abbreviations, and subject, in order to embed messages without generating any suspicious pattern. From a steganographic point of view, reusing or altering an existing text to hide data is not a recommended practice because an adversary can reference the original text and detect the differences. In addition, reusing the same piece of text may increase the vulnerability of the covert communications. If an adversary intercepts the communications between communicating parties and notices a similar piece of text used over and over, the overuse may raise his suspicions. However, this is not a concern in Headstega methodology because reuse of recipients' email addresses, names, abbreviations, and subject lines are common practice. This strong feature of the Headstega system eases the automation of a text cover (head cover). Note that Headstega system utilizes all aspects that can ensure the success for the covert communications and avoids those aspects that can cause failure. The following is the fundamental idea of the Headstega camouflager algorithm that automates the generation process of the head cover (text cover). Simply, the Headstega system generates text cover such as email addresses, names, individual titles, and abbreviations by either fabricating the textual email headers or generating them from an actual collection of legitimate email headers. For example, a steganographic carrier may look as follows:

- "Individual Titles" <USER_ID@DOMAIN_NAME. Extension>

  Individual titles such as Prof., Dr., CEO, etc. can be employed to conceal data.
- "Abbreviations" <USER_ID@DOMAIN_NAME.Extension>

  Abbreviations of labs, division, groups, teams, etc., can be employed to conceal data.
- "Names" <USER_ID@DOMAIN_NAME.Extension>

  Names such as First Name, Middle Name, Last Name, Nicknames, etc., can be employed to conceal data.
- USER_ID@DOMAIN_NAME.Extension

  The USER ID such as particular alphabet character or numerical representation can be embedded to conceal data in available email addresses such as X_mary_23@ DOMAIN_NAME.Extension.
- And any other legitimate text may also be used.

  START HERE

A huge collection of textual email headers may be employed to conceal data. Implementing this bank of email headers is accomplished by collecting the required text. Initially, the texts, like any actual (existing) email address, are generated by humans. The texts can be collected in an application that manages textual email headers and allows fast storage and retrieval of that data, e.g., a database. The head cover is then formed from the updateable collection, which provides more robustness with the ability to choose email headers that are capable of concealing the encoded messages. In addition, if an email address is to be used for concealing data, then available email addresses (ones not yet taken) can be generated in order to employ it by Headstega. This is like creating a new email account and the system indicates the availability of the email address [159–161]. Text generated in this manner, along with the way it is often used (embedded in the email headers, e.g., email address in the "To" or "Cc" fields), is linguistically legitimate because there are no textual structures to be obeyed. The reuse of such text, which is a common practice as is re-emailing, further legitimizes the text reusability. For instance, if a message will be concealed by using numerical values in email addresses, a set of authenticated email addresses that matches the symbols (bit string) used in the encoded message have to be selected. Embedding the picked steganographic carriers (email headers) in the head cover is handled based on a protocol predetermined by the communicating parties. It is worth noting that justifying the head cover for sending emails is essential. For example, if someone is advertising for a product by email, the scope of the target market will vary. Other styles may require a higher level of sophistication in order to generate a head cover that a sender may use to mix steganographic carriers (encoded email addresses) in among other legitimate non-encoded email addresses. This can be accomplished by following a particular sequence, such as odd number, even number, every other 3, or any other method that is pre-agreed upon between sender and receiver. Obviously, the basic configuration of the communication protocol should include how a recipient can decode only the right covers.

9.2 Headstega Implementation

This section demonstrates the feasibility of the Headstega methodology and its distinct capability of achieving the steganographic goal with a higher bitrate than contemporary textual steganography approaches. Note that this section is focused on showing how Headstega achieves the steganographic goal rather than making it difficult for an adversary to decode an encoded message. Employing a hard encoding system or cryptosystem to increase the protection of a message is obviously recommended and straightforward using any contemporary encoder or cryptosystem. Similarly, employing compression to boost the bitrate can easily be accomplished by using the contemporary techniques in the literature. This section shows just few examples of possible implementations following the steps outlined in the previous section.

9.2.1 Headstega Configuration

This section explains how Headstega modules are employed and configured to construct the overall Headstega system used by the communicating parties. In this chapter, Headstega encodes a message in a form that suits the camouflaging process. The steganographic code in this Headstega configuration works as follows. Each element (e.g., recipients' email addresses, names, or subject fields) of head cover conceals m bits according to the steganographic code defined. In the presented examples, the length of the bit string (m bits) that can be concealed in a particular element is four or/and seven bits. However, the coding is not dependent on the element. Instead, the first letter of an element in the head cover contains a steganographic value according to Table 9.1, which is illustrated later in this section. For example, when an element starts with the letter "B," the element conceals "0001." On the other hand, the coding that uses seven bits for the length of the bit string camouflages data. Numerical values in the elements such as a binary value of "0000100" can be concealed in the email address like love4u@yahoo.com. The grouping in lengths of 7 digits will result in a value of 0 up to 127 in decimal; in other words, changing the value from 0000000 up to 1111111 in binary.

In the Headstega system presented in this chapter, head cover is mainly textual data of email headers. The camouflage module generates a text cover that may employ Internet search engines such as google.com, an email generator [155], and/or free email account providers [159–161] to conceal data. The elements chosen to camouflage data are picked or generated based on either the first letter of the

Table 9.1 The Steganographic Code for Camouflaging Four Bits for the Elements That Are Employed in Email Headers

INDEX	BINARY	LETTERS	INDEX	BINARY	LETTERS
1	0000	A	14	1101	N
2	0001	B	15	1110	O
3	0010	C	16	1111	P
4	0011	D	17	0000	Q
5	0100	E	18	0001	R
6	0101	F	19	0010	S
7	0110	G	20	0011	T
8	0111	H	21	0100	U
9	1000	I	22	0101	V
10	1001	J	23	0110	W
11	1010	K	24	0111	X
12	1011	L	25	1000	Y
13	1100	M	26	1001	Z

element, the numerical values that match the steganographic code value of an encoded message (the bit string of a message), or both. As will be shown in the examples below, the use of first letters or numerical values does not impose constraints on the employed implementation. Based on the presented Headstega configuration, each element (steganographic carrier) may conceal four to eleven bits. Once the communicating parties have agreed upon the Headstega system configuration, they are ready to communicate covertly with each other using Headstega. The following demonstrates examples of head cover.

9.2.2 Headstega Example

This section shows how the Headstega system can be used to conceal messages, including the actual process of encoding a message and concealing the encoded message in the generated text-cover (head-cover). It also demonstrates samples of head-cover. Note that for two reasons the presented implementation uses the domain "www.test.xyz," which is a nonexistent domain. First, it is used to avoid breaching a provider's email policy. Second, it is used to avoid any liability arising from someone using such emails for spamming. Obviously, email addresses from any existing email provider such as free Yahoo Mail [159], Gmail [160], or MSN Hotmail [161] can be used. Obviously, the email in Figure 9.2 does not contain a hidden message and is

Figure 9.2 Shows the common practice of sending emails to a group of people. Obviously, the email in this figure does not contain a hidden message and was just an innocent and common practice by people who are interested in marketing and promoting business.

simply an example of an innocent and common practice by people interested in marketing and promoting their business.

9.2.2.1 Sample Head Cover   The sample in this chapter conceals up to 11 bits in the examples of email addresses. This is accomplished by concealing 4 bits in the email addresses according to the first letter of each as detailed in the steganographic code shown in Table 9.1. In addition, 7 bits are concealed in each email address by selecting or generating addresses that contain the required numerical values in order to embed a message. The presented sample is demonstrated in Table 9.2 and Figure 9.3.

For more protection, after a message is concealed using the recipients' email addresses, these email addresses can be combined with other non-coded email addresses that are not being used to camouflage data. In this case, a predetermined protocol can be employed among communicating parties, such as read every other email address, every fifth email address, or any other method in order to ease the process of unraveling a hidden message while making it harder on an adversary.

9.2.3 Bitrate

The aim of this section is to compare the bitrate of contemporary textual steganography approaches to the bitrate achieved by Headstega.

Table 9.2   Encoding of the Message *"2night@8AM Use My Secret Key"* Employing Email Addresses Based on Figure 9.3 Along With Embedding Numerical Values

	THE PLAIN TEXT OF THE MESSAGE IS: "2NIGHT@8PM USE MY SECRET KEY"							
	THE PLAIN TEXT OF 1ST PART OF THE MESSAGE IS: "2NIGHT@8PM"				THE PLAIN TEXT OF 2ND PART THE MESSAGE IS: "USE MY SECRET KEY"			
INDEX	BINARY STRING OF THE ASCII REPRESENTATION OF A MESSAGE SLICED IN 4 BIT LENGTHS	DECIMAL	1ST LETTER OF EMAIL ADDRESS	INDEX OF THE RAW USED FROM TABLE 3	BINARY STRING OF THE ASCII REPRESENTATION OF A MESSAGE SLICED IN 7 BIT LENGTHS	DECIMAL	VALUE TO BE EMBEDDED IN EMAIL ADDRESS	HEADSTEGA COVER USING BOTH THE FIRST LETTERS AND NUMERICAL VALUES IN THE EMAIL ADDRESSES
1	0011	3	D or T	1	0101010	42	dream42@test.xyz
2	0010	2	D or T	2	1011100	92	tarak92@test.xyz
3	0110	6	I or Y	3	1101100	108	yvonne108@test.xyz
4	1110	14	R	4	1010010	82	rob82@test.xyz
5	0110	6	K or A	5	0000011	3	adam3@test.xyz
6	1001	6	L or B	6	0110101	53	lawrence53@test.xyz
7	0110	6	M or C	7	1110010	114	mariya114@test.xyz
8	0111	7	O or E	8	0100000	32	omar32@test.xyz
9	0110	6	O or E	9	0111001	57	edward57@test.xyz
10	1000	8	R or H	10	1011001	89	harry89@test.xyz
11	0111	7	R or H	11	0101100	44	honey44@test.xyz
12	0100	4	P or F	12	0110111	55	paula55@test.xyz
13	0100	4	Q or G	13	0010011	19	qhelp19@test.xyz
14	0000	0	N or D	14	0010101	21	nancy21@test.xyz
15	0011	3	R or H	15	1101000	104	rashama104@test.xyz
16	1000	8	X or N	16	0100000	32	xrob32@test.xyz
17	0100	4	U or K	17	0110101	53	kennedy53@test.xyz
18	0001	1	S or I	18	1011001	89	sam89@test.xyz
19	0100	4	W or M	19	0101111	47	william47@test.xyz
20	1101	13	G	20	001	1	george1@test.xyz

Note: Note that the presented implementation uses the domain "www.test.xyz", which is a nonexisting domain, for two reasons. First, it is to avoid breaching a provider's email policy. Second, it is to avoid any liability of someone using such emails for spamming. Obviously, email addresses from an existing email provider such as free Yahoo Mail [159], Gmail [160], MSN Hotmail [161], etc., can be used.

Figure 9.3 Illustrates head cover concealed in first letter of each email address and numerical values. Note that the presented implementation uses the domain "www.test.xyz," a non-existent domain, for two reasons. First, it is to avoid breaching a provider's email policy. Second, it is to avoid any liability of someone using such emails for spamming. Obviously, email addresses from an existing email provider such as free Yahoo Mail [159], Gmail [160], or MSN Hotmail [161] can be used.

The bitrate is defined as the size of the hidden message relative to the size of the cover. The average bitrate of the Headstega system used in this chapter is roughly between 3.38% and 7.67%, and differs from one element to another and from one implementation to another as observed. To put this bitrate figure in perspective, the bitrate of contemporary textual steganography approaches has been investigated. Headstega achieves a bitrate superior to all comparable approaches, making it a very effective steganography approach. For more detail about the experimental bitrate results of Nostega-based methodologies and all other contemporary approaches, refer to Chapter 13.

9.3 Conclusion

The use of emails by a wide variety of people allows the communicating parties to establish a covert channel to transmit hidden messages (head cover) rendering emails an attractive steganographic carrier. Such features motivate the development of the Email-**Head**ers-Based **Stega**nography (Headstega) Methodology. Headstega conceals data only in textual email headers. Headstega neither hides data in a noise (errors) nor produces noise. Instead, it camouflages data in legitimate elements of textual email headers mainly by exploiting elements such as recipients' email addresses, names, subject, and abbreviations in order to embed data without generating any suspicious patterns. The presented implementation achieves bitrates up to 7.67%. This is superior to contemporary text steganography approaches found in the literature, confirming the effectiveness of the Headstega methodology. The steganalysis validation has shown the Headstega methodology is capable of achieving the steganographic goal.

10

JOKESTEGA

Automatic Joke Generation-Based Steganography Methodology

This chapter presents a novel steganography methodology, namely Automatic **Joke** Generation-Based **Stega**nography (**Jokestega**) Methodology that pursues textual jokes in order to hide messages [28]. Basically, Jokestega methodology takes advantage of recent advances in Automatic Joke Generation (AJG) techniques to automate the generation of textual steganographic cover. In a corpus of jokes, one may judge a number of documents to be the same joke although letters, locations, and other details are different. Generally, jokes and puns can be retold with totally different vocabularies, while still retaining their identities. Therefore, Jokestega pursues the common variations among jokes to conceal data. Examples of ordinary variations among textual jokes may include different texts of the same joke, altering some words without changing the joke's core, and taking advantage of unnecessary variations to follow the classic linguistic rules of writing. However, when a trivial question such as why is employing jokes useful in steganography is asked, another trivial question pops up, i.e., who does not joke? The obvious answer is no one. Furthermore, when someone is joking, anything may be said, which legitimizes the use of joke-based steganography. This makes employing textual jokes very attractive as a steganographic carrier for camouflaging data. In addition, Jokestega allows communicating parties to establish a covert channel to deliver a steganographic joke-cover without raising suspicion. It is worth noting that Jokestega follows the Nostega paradigm, which implies that a joke-cover is noiseless. The validation results demonstrate the effectiveness of Jokestega.

The remainder of this chapter is organized as follows. Section 10.1 briefly provides background and discussion of related work about the field of Automatic Joke Generation. Section 10.2 introduces the

Jokestega methodology. Section 10.3 demonstrates implementation of Jokestega. Finally, Section 10.4 concludes the chapter.

10.1 Automatic Joke Generation Systems

A joke is a fabricated short story or expression with a humorous twist [28,140,162–166]. Jokes can be in many different forms, e.g., short stories or questions and answers. Jokes may employ mockery, sarcasm, or wordplay, and they are different than either regular slang linguistics or classic linguistics. As a result, when jokes are represented in text the structural linguistics of a particular language won't be obeyed, yet textual jokes are still recognized as legitimate text because jokes have their own linguistics. The purpose of using jokes is to entertain friends, relatives, colleagues, or an audience. The expected response is laughter, but if this does not occur the jokester has a fallen-flat or bombed. Jokes are part of human culture and can be traced back to the ancient civilizations.

The field of Automatic Joke Generation systems (AJGS) has enjoyed significant advances in recent years and is promising more in the near future [162–168]. AJGS employ a procedure that may be based on one or more of the following: knowledge bases, artificial intelligence, computational linguistics, natural language generation, and other related techniques to achieve their goal [169–171]. Some famous examples of AJG systems are Joke Analysis and Production Engine (JAPE) and System To Augment Non-speakers' Dialog Using Puns (STANDUP). JAPE generates question–answer based jokes and puns [162,163], while STANDUP is an improved system to generate jokes. STANDUP is implemented in the JAVA language [172–176]. It was created for children with communication disabilities resulting from cerebral palsy.

Since the focus of this chapter is linguistic steganography, not the field of AJG, and also because of space constraints, the work covered in this chapter focuses on linguistic steganography.

10.2 Jokestega Methodology

Jokes are very popular and are enjoyed worldwide by people of all ages, which creates a high volume of electronic traffic. As a result, it

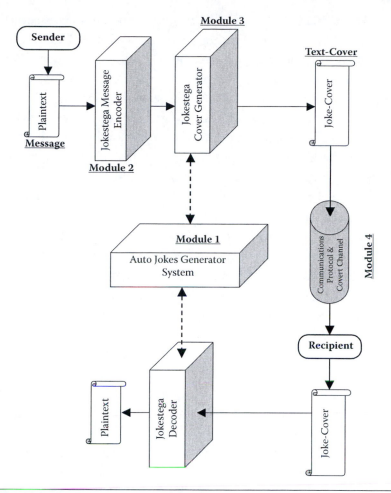

Figure 10.1   This figure demonstrates interaction of the various Jokestega modules and how the outputs of the individual modules are used for covert communications between two parties.

is impractical for an adversary to investigate all jokes. The normal and frequent exchange of jokes in electronic, printed, and audio formats, allows communicating parties to establish a covert channel to transmit hidden messages (see Figure 10.1). Yet, textual jokes are not only capable of concealing messages, but also have adequate room to conceal data; so much room, in fact, that joke cover (text cover) provides bitrate superior to contemporary linguistic steganography approaches, as will be shown later. Jokestega can also be applied to all languages.

Consequently, textual jokes are an attractive steganographic carrier. Therefore, the novel AJG-Based Steganography (Jokestega) Methodology, which is presented in this chapter, takes advantage of recent advances in the field of AJG to securely communicate covertly. Jokestega is based on the Nostega paradigm [25,28,32,35], which implies that it neither hides data in a noise (errors) nor produces noise. Instead, it camouflages data in textual jokes primarily by manipulating words, letters, nonlinguistcs, and elements (symbols) in order to embed data without generating any suspicious patterns. Since the core notion of Jokestega is based on Nostega paradigm modules, the correlation between both is not covered in this chapter because it is adequately detailed in previous chapters. Note that if a particular Nostega-based methodology is represented in a number of modules different than the five modules of the Nostega paradigm, it will still retain the core fundamentals of the Nostega paradigm.

The fundamental algorithm of the Jokestega system consists of four modules: the AJG system, message encoder, camouflager, and a covert channel. The ultimate goal of these modules is to define a Jokestega system configuration for the communicating parties to use. The four modules are utilized as follows. First, the communicating parties opt to either implement the AJG system or to use one that is already built. Module 1 is only involved in constructing the configuration of the Jokestega system. Second, a message encoder is involved in encoding a message in an appropriate form for the camouflaging process (Module 3).

For simplicity, in this chapter encoding a message may be done by converting a message into a binary representation of its ASCII code and slicing it into a particular length of digits, e.g., 3, 4, 5. For instance, a message after encoding may look like the following: 00011, 10101, 00000, 11110, 11111, and so on. Note that any other technique of encoding may be used and the employed encoding technique in this module is just an example to make it simple for illustration.

Third, the camouflager (Module 3) conceals messages in the generated textual jokes (original text that contains no hidden data) by embedding data that represent the message to be camouflaged. This process can be accomplished in numerous ways. However, the chosen technique in this chapter for embedding data pursues the common variations among the outputs of AJGS to conceal data. Examples of ordinary variations among textual jokes may include: different text of same joke, altering some words without changing the core of a joke, taking advantage of unnecessary to follow the classic linguistic rules of writing, etc. Fourth, communicating parties opt to establish a covert channel (Module 4) which is the means for hidden delivery of steganographic cover. These modules are elaborated in the following sections.

10.2.1 Automatic Jokes Generator System (Module 1)

The aim of this section is to discuss the AJGS (Module 1). The AJGS produces an original text (textual joke) that contains no hidden messages. The output of this module is generated by the request of the camouflager (Module 3), which is capable of embedding the steganographic code (the encoded message) in the text generated by the AJGS (Module 1) in order to conceal a message. The output of this procedure is in the form of legitimate jokes. Obviously, the fact about textual jokes known to everyone is that they are untrue, funny, and legitimate. From a steganography point of view, untrue content of text may raise suspicions. However, when using textual jokes, this is not a concern because it is the legitimate to use untrue information when someone is joking. Furthermore, reusing or altering an existing text to hide data is not generally a recommended practice since an adversary can reference the original text and detect the differences. In addition, the reuse of the same piece of text more than once may increase the vulnerability of the covert communications. If an adversary intercepts the communications and sees a similar piece of text being exchanged between communicating parties over and over again, suspicion may be raised because the adversary will wonder at such use. However, these are not concerns for Jokestega, because reusing and modifying textual jokes is common practice because it is not a serious text such as medical or court documents. Jokestega's strong feature eases the automation of a joke cover (steganographic textual cover). In addition, it is a trivial task for communicating parties to use contemporary AJGS as demonstrated in Section 10.4. Examples of AJGS include:

- MIT Project, Chuck Norris Joke Generator [182]
- Jokes2000 [183]
- The Joke Generator dot Com [184]
- Online Joke Generator System (pickuplinegen) [185]

10.2.2 *Message Encoder (Module 2)*

Implementing a steganographic message encoder (Module 2) follows a two-steps process: first, determining the encoding parameters in the topic picked by Module 1; second, defining a steganographic code based on these parameters. A parameter in this context means those aspects of textual jokes that can refer to steganographic values throughout a joke cover (text cover). In textual jokes, the common variations among the outputs of AJGS can be used to conceal data. Examples include different texts of the same joke, altering some words without changing the core of a joke, taking advantage of unnecessary variations to follow the classic linguistic rules of writing, inserting symbols, etc., all of which can be exploited for camouflaging data. The definition of the steganographic code would depend on the selected parameters. For example, encoding a message using symbols ("☺" = 00, ":-)" = 01, "☹" = 10, ":-(" = 11, etc.) is different from encoding it using the order in which the various jokes appear and so on. The coding module of Jokestega exploits these options and determines the parameter(s) that will be employed for concealing data. The selection criteria may be driven by the size of the message, the popular joke styles, the availability of existing jokes, and many other factors.

Jokestega, like any other Nostega-based methodology, does not impose any constraint on the message encoding scheme, as long as it generates a set of data values that can be embedded in a joke cover. Given the availability of numerous encoding techniques in the literature that fit [25], the balance of this section will focus on an example that will be used in Section 10.3 to demonstrate the applicability of Jokestega. In the example, the encoding is done as follows: A message is first converted to a binary string. The string can be a binary of cipher text or a compressed representation. The binary string is then partitioned into groups of m bits. The value of m is determined based on the encoding parameters that Jokestega exploits. For instance, if the joke cover will be in a form of a group of jokes, the binary message is partitioned into groups of four bits, e.g., "0000", "0001", "0010", "0011," and so on up to "1111" corresponding to the possible choices. Again, this encoding scheme is just for illustration and many alternatives and more sophisticated schemes can be employed, as stated earlier and demonstrated in Section 10.3.

10.2.3 Camouflager (Module 3)

The aim of this section is to discuss and describe the camouflager (Module 3). Once a message is encoded using Module 2 (the message encoder), a camouflager (Module 3) produces first an original text (textual joke) that contains no hidden messages, and then embeds the steganographic code (encoded message) The output of this procedure is in the form of legitimate textual jokes such as those demonstrated in the implementation section. Such text can be in the form of family jokes, adult jokes, academic jokes, etc., in order to embed data without generating any suspicious patterns.

As stated earlier, reusing or altering an existing text to hide data is not a recommended practice from a steganographic point of view because an adversary may reference the original text and detect the differences, which easily may raise suspicions. In addition, the reuse of the same piece of text more than once may increase the vulnerability of the covert communications. If an adversary intercepts the communications and sees a similar piece of text being exchanged between communicating parties over and over again, suspicion may be raised because the adversary will wonder about such use. However, these are not concerns with Jokestega, because reusing and modifying jokes are common practices and, after all, it is just for fun and nothing is serious. For example, the common variations among the outputs of AJGS or imposing natural alterations can be used to conceal data by a text substitution procedure without generating detectable noise and thereby avoiding raising suspicion. Some examples of jokes that are generated by an AJG system called STANDUP, are shown in Table 10.1.

In a corpus of jokes, one may judge a number of documents to be the same joke although letters, locations, and other details are different

Table 10.1 Virtual Variations That Can Be Used to Camouflage Data

NO	ORIGINAL TEXTUAL JOKES CONTAIN NO HIDDEN DATA BY STANDUP SYSTEM		EMBEDDING DATA MAY USE
1	What do you get when you cross a car with a sandwich?	A traffic jam→	Subway is faster or, Subway eat fresh
2	What do you call a strange rabbit?	A funny bunny→	Rob it, honey bunny, happy bunny
3	What do you call a frog road?	A main toad→	A fake road
4	What do you call an artist who is a minister?	A pastor master→	A pastor toaster

[162–165]. Generally, jokes and puns could be retold with totally different vocabulary, while still retaining their identities. Linguistically, there are published systems whose task is identifying the "same joke." For more information, refer to [162–165]. Such features are capable of concealing data without raising suspicion.

In regard to message size, concealing long messages is generally a challenge for most known steganography approaches. Jokestega can hide long messages simply by employing more jokes and splitting the message over multiple jokes in a joke cover. When someone tells a joke, it initiates and legitimizes the others to joke back. Joking back is a common human behavior, which allows the communicating parties to repeatedly transmit joke covers back and forth that conceal hidden messages using Jokestega.

10.2.4 Establishing Covert Channel (Module 4)

Jokestega naturally camouflages the delivery of a hidden message in a way that makes it appear legitimate and innocent. To employ Jokestega, the communicating parties first need to define and agree on the basic configuration of the covert channel. This step includes determining the following: (1) a legitimate relationship among or between the communicating parties that justifies their interaction with each other, and (2) how the cover will be delivered from the sender to the recipient. Plotting a suitable scenario can play an essential role for securing the steganographic communications by establishing an appropriate covert channel for delivering a hidden message. The chosen scenario must facilitate the process of embedding data without generating noise in order to achieve the steganographic goal. Since Jokestega mainly manipulates jokes to camouflage messages, any relationship among the communicating parties (e.g., colleagues of a particular profession) that allows the employing of jokes can be used. The second important configuration parameter is how the cover will be delivered to the recipient without raising suspicion. Covert transmittal of the steganographic cover is very crucial to the success of steganography. The fact that Jokestega employs noiseless-based means for hiding data enables great flexibility in delivering the steganographic cover to its recipient.

Options may include web post and download, email transmission, etc. A sender may mix a joke cover among other legitimate documents; obviously, the basic configuration of the covert channel should include how a recipient can decode only the right covers. For instance, the communicating parties may agree on putting joke covers among other similar documents by designating a particular sequence such as odd number, even number, every other 3, or any other order. The core of covert channels is how to prevent the association between a sender and recipient from drawing suspicion and to render it an innocent communication. For example, exchanging emails would automatically imply a relationship between the communicating parties. Similarly, downloading files from a website indicates an interest in the accessed material. Due to the advances in monitoring tools for network and Internet traffic, profiles of a user's access pattern can be easily established. An adversary most probably would suspect the presence of a hidden message, even if the content does not look suspicious, because of the observed traffic pattern and the lack of a justification for the interest in the contents of the transmitted materials. For example, if a profession for one of the communicating parties is an elementary English teacher, and yet he sends or receives college-level chemistry exams, then suspicion will likely be raised. Therefore, it is very important to rationalize the exchange of steganographic cover in order to avoid attracting any attention that may trigger an attack. The communicating parties need to agree on how to justify their interest in the education documents of the selected topic. This may include defining a role, such as mentoring or tutoring that a sender plays, a profession, or simple an interest that justify a peer relationship.

10.3 Jokestega Implementation

The aim of this section is to demonstrate how Jokestega methodology can be used. It is worth noting that this section shows just a few examples of possible implementations following the steps outlined in the previous section. Jokestega implementation examples ae provided in the remainder of this section.

10.3.1 Jokestega System

This section contains an implementation example showing how Jokestega modules are employed and configured to construct the overall Jokestega system used by the communicating parties in this chapter.

AJGS and Camouflager (Modules 1 and 3): The reason that these modules are described in the same section is because both modules are closely interrelated. The AJGS Module 1 produces an original text that contains no hidden messages. Then, in order to conceal a message, the Jokestega camouflager (Module 3) embeds the steganographic code (encoded message) that is generated by the message encoder (Module 2), in the joke generated by the AJGS (Module 1). The output of this procedure is in a form of legitimate and ordinary jokes. Such text embeds data without generating any suspicious pattern and is capable of fooling an adversary. In this Jokestega configuration example, the Jokestega camouflager module employs online AJGS [162,163,173,174,176–178], online samples [182–185], online dictionaries [186–189], and Microsoft Thesaurus (built into Microsoft Word 97) [77] to embed the data and generate the joke cover.

The dictionaries and thesaurus are mainly exploited in order to pick the appropriate vocabulary for the chosen joke. Since one of the options is to conceal data in a keyword of a joke, the first letter of the keyword in a given joke would conceal data in a length of 4 bits using values from "0000" up to "1111," representing the letters from "A" to "Z" [25]. For instance, using Table 10.2, if the steganographic value that needs to be embedded is "0000," then the correct keyword of a joke will start with the letter "A" or the letter "Q". Classifying the jokes by the joke's keywords (e.g., vampire, teacher, hamburger, etc.) may ease both the process of hiding and revealing. However, if the steganographic value that needs to be embedded is equal to "0011" then the correct keyword of a joke will start with either the letter "D" or the letter "T", and so on. Furthermore, the use of first letters by the Jokestega system does not impose constraints on the employed vocabulary. Based on this Jokestega configuration, each joke may conceal at least four bits. Obviously, more bits of data may be concealed by simply embedding symbols such as the common symbols that are used by users nowadays (e.g., "☺", ":-)", "☹", ":-(", etc.). Such symbols can also conceal data; the length of bits would depend on the maximum number of symbols used. For example, if the maximum number of symbols is 16, then the maximum length of bits is 4, which is from "0000" up to "1111." On the other hand, if the maximum number of symbols is 64, then the maximum length of bits is 7, which is from "0000000" up to "1111111," and so on.

Jokestega Encoder (Module 2): It is worth noting that the focus of this chapter is on showing how Jokestega achieves the steganographic goal rather than making it difficult for an adversary to decode an encoded message. Employing a hard encoding system or cryptosystem to increase the protection of a message is obviously recommended and straightforward using any contemporary encoder or cryptosystem. Similarly, employing compression to boost the bitrate can easily be accomplished by using the contemporary techniques in the literature. Nonetheless, Jokestega encodes a message in a form that suits the camouflaging process. Encoding a message may be achieved by converting into a binary representation of its ASCII code and slicing it into a particular length of digits (e.g., 3, 4, 5, etc.). For instance, a message after encoding may look like the following: 00011, 10101, 00000, 11110, 11111, and so on. In this implementation example, a message is converted into the binary representation of its ASCII code and sliced into lengths of 4 digits. This will be assigned to the first letter of the joke's keyword according to Table 10.2. For example, when the joke's keyword starts with the letter "B," it is concluded that the joke conceals "0001," as shown in Table 10.2. However, when the joke's keyword starts with the letter "C," it is concluded that the joke conceals "0010," as shown in Table 10.2.

To increase the resistance to attacks, Jokestega introduces some randomness to the steganographic coding through the use of combinatorics operations to define the mapping of symbols to bit strings. The steganographic code in this Jokestega configuration works as follows. Based on a predetermined protocol, the presented implementation example of the Jokestega system in this section adds a counter value like an index value i to each steganographic bit string (e.g., 0000+ i, 0001+ i, 0101+ i, etc). To emphasize, it adds the value of "0" the first time, "1" the second time, "2" the third time, and so on. To illustrate, when using Table 10.2, to conceal data in a joke's keyword starting with the letter "A" implies "0000" the first time used, "0001" the second time, and so on. The auto-receiver used to reveal

Table 10.2   The Steganographic Code for Camouflaging Four Bits in the Joke's Keyword

STEGANOGRAPHIC CODE VALUES	
BINARY VALUES	FIRST LETTER OF THE JOKE'S KEYWORD
0000	A
0001	B
0010	C
0011	D
0100	E
0101	F
0110	G
0111	H
1000	I
1001	J
1010	K
1011	L
1100	M
1101	N
1110	O
1111	P
0000	Q
0001	R
0010	S
0011	T
0100	U
0101	V
0110	W
0111	X
1001	Z

the hidden message will check the joke's keyword against Table 10.2 and its index value i to find out the steganographic code values. The use of these tables is illustrated later in this section. Again, the encoding used in this book is just an example of a simple implementation to make it easy for the reader to follow and understand. However, more sophisticated encoding techniques can be used.

The Covert Channel (Module 4): As indicated earlier, the configuration of the covert channel includes the convincing scenario of the relationship between the sender and receiver and how a joke cover can be delivered. A scenario that makes it easy for the communicating parties to legitimize their communications in order to deliver joke cover that contains hidden messages in this chapter.

10.3.2 Joke Cover Example

This section shows a few examples of how the Jokestega configuration discussed above can be used by the communicating parties to conceal messages. The following describes how a message is encoded and processed by the Jokestega system prior to generating the joke cover. The following shows a joke cover sample that conceals data.

The plain text is: *"Stop"*.

- The Jokestega Encoder converts the message to a concatenated binary string using the ASCII representation of the individual characters, as follows: 01010011011101000110111101110000.
- The encoder will then divide the above binary message into slices of sizes that matches those supported by the steganographic coding. The result is shown as follows: 0101 0011 0111 0100 0110 1111 0111 0000. It should be noted that the binary string could have been encrypted or compressed prior to this step.
- The Jokestega camouflager then will generate the joke cover (text cover) that conceals the binary of the message. For simplicity for the reader, a joke cover is generated by selecting a group of jokes that contains the joke's keywords starting with the first letters according to Table 10.2 and shown in Table 10.3.

Table 10.3 Encoded Message Using First Letter of Joke's Keyword

BINARY	LETTER	JOKE'S KEYWORD
0101	F or V	**V**ampire
0011	D or T	**T**eacher
0111	H or X	**h**amburger
0100	E or U	**u**gly
0110	G or W	**w**ww.square.com
1111	P	**P**ublic
0111	H or X	**H**ogwash
0000	A or Q	**q**uarters

> - Where is Dracula's American office? The Vampire State Building.
> - Teacher: When do astronauts eat? Pupil: At launch time!
> - Can a hamburger marry a hot dog? Only if they have a very frank relationship!
> - I'm not ugly. I could marry anyone I pleased! But that's the problem—you don't please anyone.
> - Have you seen www.square.com? No, I haven't got around to it.
> - What do you call 4 blondes laying on the beach? Public access.
> - Why did the little pig hide the soap? He heard the farmer yell, "Hogwash!"
> - Why is the moon like a dollar? It has four quarters.

Figure 10.2   Virtual joke cover containing eight jokes that conceal 32 bits.

- Figure 10.2 shows a sample of a virtual joke cover that contains eight jokes, which conceal 32 bits.
- Figure 10.3 shows a sample of a virtual joke cover that contains five jokes, which conceal 32 bits by using both the jokes' keywords and symbols (see Tables 10.4 and 10.5).

Another plain text example is: "*war*".

- The Jokestega encoder converts the message to a concatenated binary string using the ASCII representation of the individual characters, as follows: 0111011101100001011100010.
- The encoder will then divide the above binary message into slices of sizes that match those supported by the steganographic coding. The result is shown as follows: 0111 0111 0110 0001 0111 0010. It should be noted that the binary string could have been encrypted or compressed prior to this step.
- Figures 10.4 and 10.5 show a sample of a virtual joke cover that contains four jokes concealing 24 bits by using semantic embedding and substitutions. These are illustrated in the transformation from Figure 10.4 to Figure 10.5.

- Where is Dracula's American office? The Vampire State Building. ☺
- Teacher: When do astronauts eat? Pupil: At launch time! :-)
- Can a hamburger marry a hot dog? Only if they have a very frank relationship! :0)
- I'm not ugly. I could marry anyone I pleased!
  But that's the problem—you don't please anyone. :-) ☺
- Have you seen www.square.com? No, I haven't got around to it. ☺

Figure 10.3 Virtual joke cover contains five jokes that conceal 32 bits by using symbols.

- Where is Dracula's American ~~house office~~? The Vampire State Building.
- Teacher: When do astronauts eat? Pupil: Hmm. At launch time!
- ~~Can~~ Would a hamburger marry a hot dog? Only if they ~~have~~ retain a very frank relationship!
- I'm not ~~ugly~~ hideous. I ~~could~~ can marry anyone I pleased! But that's the problem—you don't please anyone.

s.

Figure 10.4 Virtual joke cover that contains four jokes that conceal 24 bits by using joke substitutions.

Obviously, a joke-cover can be sent as group of jokes, can be among other text in emails, can be posted in a particular website blog, or be transmitted by any method that the communicating parties would agree upon as a legitimate scenario for transmitting hidden messages.

10.3.3 Jokestega Performance

The bitrate for this implementation example may achieve up to 8 bits per a short joke. In this chapter, a short joke can be determined by the

- Where is Dracula's American house? The Vampire State Building.
- Teacher: When do astronauts eat? Pupil: Hmm at hunger time!
- Would a hamburger marry a hot dog? Only if they retain a very frank relationship!

- I'm not homely. I can marry anyone I pleased! But that's the problem—you don't please anyone.

Figure 10.5   The final transformation of the virtual joke cover from Figure 10.4 containing four jokes that conceal 24 bits.

Table 10.4   Steganographic Code Values of Symbols

BINARY	SYMBOLS	
00	☺	☹
01	:0)	:0(
10	:0))	:0((
11	:-) or !	:-(or !

Table 10.5   Encoded Message Using First Letter of Joke's Keyword and Symbols

BINARY CODE	LETTER	JOKE'S KEYWORDS	BINARY CODE	SYMBOLS
0101	F or V	**V**ampire	00	☺
1101	D or T	**T**eacher	11	:-)
0100	H or X	**h**amburger	01	:0)
1011	E or U	**u**gly	11	:-)
0111	G or W	**w**ww.square.com	00	☺

length of sentences, questions and answers, expressions (e.g., funny bunny), and so on. This implies that the bitrate of Jokestega would vary from one particular joke to another, because the bitrate would depend on the size of jokes used, and from one implementation to another. In this chapter, the achieved bitrate of the implementation example is accomplished by encoding one keyword per joke, common nonlinguistic elements (e.g., symbols), or minor alterations of a few words (i.e., one or two words) as a natural version of a joke.

Obviously, the more steganographic carriers are employed, the higher bitrate that will be achieved. In regard to message size, the size of a message is a concern for most if not all steganography approaches. However, in the presented Jokestega scheme, Jokestega camouflages a long message. When a message is long, then Jokestega generates a longer text cover (joke cover). Jokestega simply distributes the required message to be camouflaged in a group of jokes using either single or multiple transmissions, posts them somewhere, or whatever the predetermined scenario is. The following shows some examples of Jokestega carriers that can be to conceal data and legitimize the use of this steganographic technique.

- *Joking Behavior:* Obviously, joking behaviors are intrinsic in humans. It is something that is inborn in all people, regardless of their nations. Note that joking is a normal behavior where someone does or tells something totally untrue and funny. Such behavior legitimizes the use of steganography where the need of fabricated text (untrue text) may be essential to conceal data.
- *Embedding Nonlinguistc Elements:* The use of nonlinguistc symbols such as ☺, ☻, !, :), :-), etc., is popular in textual jokes, which legitimately allows a steganographic system to conceal data by embedding such symbols.
- *Rhyme Substitution:* In jokes, the use of rhyming words is a common practice. Examples, funny bunny can be cutie bunny, sweetie bunny, honey bunny, and so on. The joking behaviors of human can legitimize such use of rhyming, which can be used to conceal data. In jokes, the use of a rhyme-substitution-based steganographic technique is different from other techniques, such as the use of a synonym-substitution-based technique. The rhyme-substitution-based steganographic technique does not attempt to preserve the same linguistic meaning like in synonym substitution.
- *Antonyms Substitution:* A joke is a joke! In other words, textual jokes are not considered serious text and are just for fun. This legitimizes the use of an antonyms-substitution-based steganographic technique. For example, the use of "fatty–skinny", "tall–short", "hot–cold", "intelligent–stupid",

"fast–slow" and so on. Note that some of antonyms may also be rhymes, which makes sounding funny the goal of the joke. For instance, "happy bunny" can be "unhappy bunny", "fatty" can be "skinny", and so on. Antonyms that rhyme provide a more joking attitude, which legitimizes their use.

- *Meaning Substitution:* When a joke is retold, someone may communicate the meaning of a joke using different vocabulary and text. This legitimizes the use of meaning-substitution to camouflage data.
- *Other Common Steganographic Carriers:* Examples, Text-substitution-Based, Semantic-Substitution-Based, and Synonyms-Substitution-Based can also be used while the accuracy of the substitution will be a serious concern due to the fact that someone is just joking.

10.4 Conclusion

A novel steganography methodology that exploits textual jokes to conceal data, namely is demonstrated in this chapter. Automatic **Joke** Generation Based **Stega**nography (Jokestega) Methodology, Jokestega methodology takes advantage of recent advances in the field of Automatic Joke Generation (AJG) techniques to automate the generation of textual steganographic cover. Linguistically, in a corpus of jokes one may judge a number of documents to be the same joke although letters, locations, and other details are different. In addition, jokes and puns are commonly retold with totally different vocabulary, while still retaining their core identities. Therefore, Jokestega pursues the common variations among jokes to conceal data. Examples of ordinary variations among textual jokes may include different texts of the same joke, altering some words and letters without changing the core of a joke, taking advantage of unnecessary variations to follow the classic linguistic rules of writing, inserting nonlinguistc symbols, and many other factors and elements. Obviously, joking behavior is intrinsic; it is present in all humans regardless of race, nationality, or religion. Presumably, when someone is joking, anything may be said which legitimizes the use of joke based steganography. This makes employing textual jokes very attractive as a steganographic carrier for camouflaging data, especially since it also allows communicating parties to establish a covert channel without raising suspicions. It is worth noting that Jokestega follows the Nostega paradigm, which implies that joke cover is noiseless. As demonstrated and validated in this chapter, Jokestega is capable of achieving the steganographic goal and a superior bitrate to all other non-Nostega approaches.

11

LISTEGA

Steganography Methodology

The use of a textual list of items such as products, subjects, and books is widely popular and linguistically legible. This motivated the development of **List**-Based **Stega**nography (Listega) Methodology [29]. Listega uses textual lists to camouflage data by exploiting itemized data to conceal messages. Simply, it encodes a message then assigns it to legitimate items in order to generate a text cover in the form of list. The generated list of items, the text cover, can be embedded among other legitimate non-coded items for more protection based on a predetermined protocol among communicating parties such as read every other item, every fifth item, or any method other than the use of a particular sequence. Listega neither hides data in a noise (errors) nor produces noise. Instead, it camouflages data by manipulating a noise-less list of legitimate items. Listega establishes a covert channel among communicating parties by employing justifiable reasons based on the common practice of using a textual list of items to achieve the unsuspicious transmission of generated covers. The presented implementation, validation, and steganalysis of Listega demonstrate its robust capabilities of achieving the steganographic goal, the adequate room for concealing data, and the superior bitrate of roughly 1.32% up to 3.87% more than contemporary linguistic steganography approaches.

The remainder of this chapter is organized as follows. Section 11.1 explains the Listega methodology in detail. Section 11.2 demonstrates the Listega implementation. Finally, Section 11.3 concludes the chapter.

11.1 Listega Methodology

To illustrate Listega, consider the following scenario. Bob and Alice are on a spy mission. Bob and Alice run an online business similar to craigslist.org or yahoo.com to buy and sell items such as books, computer parts, music CDs, and movie DVDs. Before they go on their mission, which requires them to reside in two different countries, they plot a strategic plan and set the rules for communicating covertly using their online business as a steganographic umbrella. They agree on concealing messages in a list of items by naturally manipulating and fabricating this list in which they will embed data in such a way that the text cover (list cover) seems innocent. To make their plan work, Bob and Alice have the right to post or email the list cover (e.g., a list of books, computer parts, music CDs, or movie DVDs) to customers. In addition, Bob and Alice have the right to do business with each other, such as buying and selling, which legitimizes communications between them and enables them to deliver the list cover in an unsuspicious way. Covert messages transmitted in this manner will not look suspicious because of the legitimate relationship between Bob and Alice. Furthermore, Alice is not the sole recipient of Bob's list and vice versa. In addition, other non-spy customers also receive such lists, further warding off suspicion. These lists conceal data, but only Bob and Alice will be able unravel the hidden messages because they know the rules of the game. Their communications look legitimate and nothing is suspicious because of the legitimate relationship between the communicating parties. Alice and Bob are using real data from their business field to make their covert communications legitimate.

The above scenario demonstrates how Listega methodology can be used. Listega methodology is detailed in the remainder of this section.

11.1.1 Listega Architecture

Listega achieves legitimacy by basing the camouflage of both a message and its transmittal on a legitimate list of items. As stated earlier, in the above example of Bob and Alice, using a particular online business gives legitimacy for camouflaging both a message and its transmittal. The core idea of Listega methodology is basically camouflaging data in natural and legitimate itemized data. Obviously, such steganographic cover (text cover) in the form of a list of items is legitimate both linguistically and logically. The following is an overview of the Listega architecture, which consists of four modules as shown in Figure 11.1.

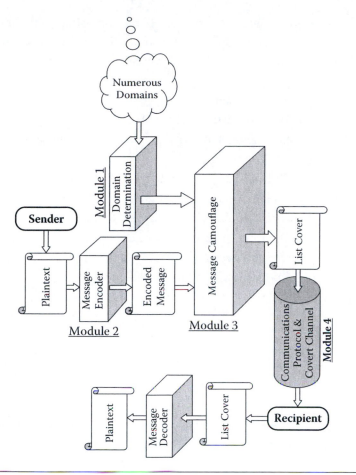

Figure 11.1 The architecture of Listega and the communications protocol.

1. *Domain Determination* (Module 1) determines an appropriate domain(s) for achieving the steganographic goal. One of the major factors for employing a particular domain is the use of legitimate lists. A domain such as an online business that naturally uses itemized data in lists of items (e.g., books, computer parts, music CDs, movie DVDs, or any other items) can be employed by Listega methodology. The process of Module 1 is only involved in the stage of constructing a Listega system.

2. *Message Encoding* (Module 2) encodes a message in an appropriate and required form for the camouflaging process (Module 3). The process of generating a list cover (Module 3) may influence the process of how a message should be encoded.

For example, a message may be encoded by slicing its binary string into a particular length of bits such as four bits, seven bits, or any required bit length as follows.

Message: *"Stop"*

Convert it to binary:

01010011011101000110111101110000

Then, slice the binary string into a particular length of bits such as four bits:

0101 0011 0111 0100 0110 1111 0111 0000

3. *Message Camouflager* (Module 3) generates the text cover (list cover), in which data are embedded by employing the output of Module 2. Simply, the text cover is a legitimate list of items.

4. *Communications Protocol* (Module 4) configures the basic protocol of how a sender and recipient would communicate covertly. Obviously, it includes the covert channel for delivering a list cover to the intended recipient and the decoder scheme to unravel a hidden message.

Once the Listega system is implemented, the covert communications will be accomplished in three steps. First, a message is encoded using the predetermined steganographic encoder (Module 2). Second, Module 3 camouflages the steganographic code (encoded message), which is generated by Module 2. Third, the message is sent based on the communications protocol (Module 4). The above modules are detailed in the following subsections.

11.1.2 Domain Determination (Module 1)

The chosen domain must be capable of concealing data. In other words, it must allow the process of embedding data without generating noise in order to achieve the steganographic goal. Listega mainly manipulates lists of items to camouflage messages. Therefore, Listega methodology can be applied to any domain that allows the use of lists of items such as books, computer parts, music CDs, movie DVDs, or other categories of items. In addition, the chosen domain must fit the communicating parties and provide some ground for justifying the communications. For example, a student would not post army aircraft stuff for free or sale on the craigslist.org website. Such communications would easily arouse suspicion because, while an individual such as a student may post his personal stuff for free or sale on an online website such as craigslist.org, the student cannot post army aircraft stuff.

Listega camouflages the delivery of a hidden message in a way that makes it appear legitimate and innocent. The scenario discussed above in Section 11.1 explains why the communication between Bob and Alice is not unusual because their mutual interest in an online business plays a role in camouflaging the delivery of list cover. A legitimate reason for sending, receiving, accessing, or obtaining a particular material can legitimize the covert communications among communicating parties. Therefore, selecting the appropriate domain can play an essential role for securing the steganographic communications by establishing an appropriate covert channel for delivering a steganographic cover regardless of its type.

11.1.3 Message Encoding (Module 2)

Implementing the message encoder follows a two-step process: first, determining the encoding parameters in the domain selected by Module 1, and second, defining a steganographic coding (e.g., binary, octal, or hexadecimal) based on these parameters. A parameter in this context means an aspect of a textual list that can be referred to using steganographic values in a list cover. Mainly, the itemized data that forms a list, such as books, computer parts, music CDs, or movie DVDs, can be exploited for concealing data.

The definition of the steganographic code will depend on the selected parameters. For example, encoding a message by using a list of books is different from encoding it using a list of computer parts or a list containing a combination of both books and computer parts. The encoding module of Listega exploits theses types of options and determines the parameters that will be employed to conceal messages. The popularity of certain list styles and types is an important factor in the selection. The unusual appearance of certain types of items may draw suspicion. For example, having a list of large airplanes on sale on eBay is an unusual practice. Another concern is when certain words are exploited for message encoding. An example of this would be using the word "planner" to mean "0," which in a set of items in a list might render the list suspicious. Listega methodology counters all of these concerns by simply imposing on the implementation of the Listega system the necessity of being made aware of such issues or potential for attacks. The domain selection is also crucial for justifying the inter-action among the communicating parties to establish a covert channel for delivering the steganographic cover (list cover). One would argue that the encoding parameters may actually influence the selection of a domain for the covert communication and should be done first. While this is a valid concern, the domain selection is crucial for justifying the interaction among the communicating parties, and is thus more affected by the criteria for establishing a covert channel.

Listega does not impose any constraint on the message encoder scheme as long as it generates a set of data values that can be embed-ded in a list cover. Given the availability of numerous encoding tech-niques in the literature that fit [3,23], the balance of this section will focus on the example that will be used in Section 11.2 to demonstrate the applicability of Listega. In the presented examples in Section 11.2, the encoding is done as follows: A message is first converted to a binary string. The string can be a binary of cipher text or a compressed representation. The binary string is then partitioned into groups of m bits. The value of m is determined based on the encoding param-eters that Listega exploits. In textual lists, the order of items, types of item, items' first letter, items' last letter, etc., can be exploited for concealing data. Note that the encoding scheme is just for illustration and many alternate and more sophisticated schemes can be employed, as demonstrated in Section 11.2.

11.1.4 Message Camouflager (Module 3)

As mentioned earlier, the high demand and popularity of using tex-tual itemized data by a wide variety of people render such text an attractive steganographic carrier. Listega takes advantage of such popularity and camouflages data in textual lists primarily by manipu-lating textual itemized data in order to embed messages without gen-erating any suspicious pattern. From a steganographic point of view, reusing or altering an existing text to hide data is not a recommended practice, since an adversary can reference the original text and detect the differences. In addition, the reuse of the same piece of text more than once may increase vulnerability of the covert communications. If

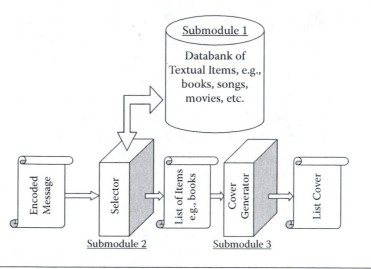

Figure 11.2 The architecture of message camouflager (Module 3).

an adversary intercepts the communications and sees a similar piece of text used over and over again between communicating parties, suspicion may be raised because the adversary will wonder about such use. This is not a concern in Listega methodology because reusing items or modifying textual lists of items is a common practice.

For example, an online business (e.g., online stores, online sellers) or online free stuff posted by individuals (such as on craigslist.org) may reuse and modify a list of items. Listega's strong feature eases the automation of a text cover (list cover). The automation process of list cover, as illustrated in Figure 11.1, is composed of three submodules, as shown in Figure 11.2:

1. *Databank of Textual Items (Submodule 1)* is simply a large database of textual items such as books, scientific subjects, nonscientific subjects, computer parts, music CDs, movie DVDs, or names, i.e., a huge collection of items that will be employed to conceal data. Implementing such a databank is accomplished by collecting the required textual items. This is initially developed by humans who are experts and capable of performing such a task. Thus, the list of items generated by such a bank of items is often linguistically legitimate given the rigor of the experts who developed the databank. For example, the wording of items in a test is often checked

a number of times to ensure clarity and accuracy. In addition, the reuse of items, which is a common practice as mentioned above, further strengthens them linguistically given the multiple review cycles that they go through. An example of such a databank is a database of business inventory. The document database does not have to be centralized though. A distributed implementation through a peer-to-peer system or web links can also be pursued. As noted earlier, updating such databases is continual and altering a list of items is not unusual and therefore would not draw suspicion. It is also worth noting that such a databank can encompass multiple domains or be limited to a particular domain.

2. *Selector (Submodule 2)* picks the elements from the bank of items (Submodule 1) that will form the list cover. The selection criteria are based on the domain and the message encoding scheme. For example, if the domain is selling books, the scope of the selection will be narrowed to that specific domain. If a list cover uses books, the Listega system will select a list of books that forms the list cover. The books chosen have to enable the concealment of the encoded messages. For example, if a message is to be concealed by using book prices, a set of authenticated book prices that matches the symbols (bit string) used in the encoded message has to be picked. The order of these picked book prices in the list-cover is handled by Submodule 3, as explained next.

3. *Cover Generator (Submodule 3)* is responsible for forming a list cover based on the textual items picked by the selector (Submodule 2) while embedding the encoded message. For some styles of list covers, the generator may be as simple as listing the picked textual items in an order that matches the encoded message. For example, if the encoded message is concealed in a particular set of textual items, the items are then sequenced according to the symbols or the bits of the encoded message. Other styles may require a slightly higher level of sophistication in order to generate a wrapper. For example, the use of a sample list of computer items as a list cover may require special formatting and the inclusion of preamble, header, and footer. Since the sender may mix list

cover among other legitimate documents, obviously, the basic configuration of the covert channel must include instructions enabling a recipient to decode only the right covers. For instance, the cover generator (Submodule 3) may put items of the list covers among similar but non-coded items. This can be accomplished by following a particular sequence, such as odd number, even number, every other 3, etc.; by placing list covers in a specific folder; or by using any other method that is a preagreed upon between sender and receiver.

11.1.5 Communications Protocol (Module 4)

The communicating parties configure the communications protocol of the Listega system, as shown in Figure 11.1, in order to communicate covertly by predetermining the following: 1) the particular specifications of the Listega system used including its decoder; and 2) the covert channel for securely transmitting list covers among communicating parties. Once the communications protocol is agreed upon, the intended parties are ready to communicate covertly with each other using Listega. The first item is the particular specifications of the Listega system to be used, including its decoder, which is addressed by Modules 1, 2, and 3. These are discussed in the previous subsections. The second item is a covert channel that mainly defines how the cover will be delivered to the recipient without raising suspicion. Covert transmittal of the steganographic cover (the material that contains the hidden message) is very crucial to the success of steganography. At the core of the cover transmittal issue is how to prevent the association between the sender and recipient from drawing suspicion. For example, exchanging email messages would automatically imply a relationship between the communicating parties. Similarly, downloading files from a website indicates an interest in the accessed material.

With advances in monitoring tools for network and Internet traffic, profiles of a user's access pattern can be easily established. An adversary most probably will suspect the presence of a hidden message, even if the content does not look suspicious, because of the observed traffic pattern and the lack of justification for the interest in the contents of such traffic. For example, if the pretended profession of a sender or recipient is that of an online bookseller and he sends or receives other suspicious documents such as list of huge airplanes, suspicions can easily be raised. A bookseller may send or receive only documents that are justifiable, such as a list of books. Therefore, it is very important to rationalize the sending and receiving of steganographic cover in order to avoid attracting any attention that may trigger an attack. Listega enables an effective solution for the issue of legitimizing a cover transmittal. The use of particular domains legitimizes the associations of communicating parties, and allows for the establishment of a covert channel. Thus, sharing a list cover would appear an ordinary practice. Textual itemized data is in high demand by a wide variety of people all over the world. Thus, the transmission of the list covers via email or posting them on web pages is a natural matter that does not raise suspicion.

11.2 Listega Implementation

This section demonstrates the feasibility of the Listega methodology and its distinct capability for achieving the steganographic goal with a higher bitrate than other contemporary linguistic steganography approaches. It is worth noting that the focus of this section is on showing how Listega achieves the steganographic goal rather than making it difficult for an adversary to decode an encoded message. Employing a hard encoding system or cryptosystem to increase the protection of a message is obviously recommended and straightforward using any contemporary encoder or cryptosystem. Similarly, employing compression to boost the bitrate can easily be accomplished by using the contemporary techniques in the literature. This section shows just a few examples of possible implementations following the steps outlined in the previous section.

11.2.1 Listega Configuration

This section first explains how Listega modules are employed and configured to construct the overall Listega system used by the communicating parties.

Determining Particular Domain(s) (Module 1): In this chapter two domains are employed, namely, songs and books. Obviously, these domains are just examples and any other domains may apply, as stated in Section 11.1.5. These domains are very popular worldwide among a wide variety of people. Such domains have no constraints for using any combination of items in a list, which render these domains suitable to be used by Listega.

Listega Encoder (Module 2): Listega encodes a message in a form that suits the camouflaging process. To increase the resilience against attacks, Listega introduces some randomness to the steganographic coding used. Therefore, a Latin square is used to define the random mapping of symbols to bit strings. The steganographic code in this Listega configuration works as follows:

1. Each item of list cover conceals a particular number of bits according to the steganographic code defined. In the presented examples, the length of the bit string (m bits), that can be concealed in a particular item is either four or seven bits. The coding is not dependent on the item though. Instead, the first letter of an item in the list cover contains a steganographic value according to a simple sequential steganographic coding. For example, using four bit coding, when an item starts with the letter "A," another starts with "B," another starts with "C," and so on. Then the steganographic code is "0000," "0001," "0010," and so on, respectively. On the other hand, for coding that uses seven bits as the length of bit string camouflages data in authenticated lists of item prices such as a legitimate price list of books, song CDs, or flowers. Note that the encoding is not the focus of this book and the encoding techniques that are used in this book are just simple examples to make it easy for the reader to follow.

2. Based on the agreed-upon protocol, a particular row or rows in the entire list cover are used in a particular order such as one row per message item.

Message Camouflage (Module 3): In the Listega system that is presented in this book, the list cover is mainly a list of items from the domains chosen by Module 1, such as the domains of songs and books. Obviously, these domains are just used as an implementation example and any other domains can be used. The camouflage module generates a text cover (list cover) by employing generic and specific (for a particular website) Internet search engines such as google.com or yahoo.com in order to generate lists of items that can conceal data. The selected items generated to camouflage data are picked based on either the first letter of the item or the price that matches the steganographic code value of an encoded message (the bit string of a message). As will be shown in the examples below, the use of first letters or authenticated item prices does not impose constraints on the employed implementation. Based on the presented Listega configuration, each item may conceal four to seven bits.

Communications Protocol (Module 4): This module configures the basic protocol of how a sender and recipient will communicate covertly. The basic communications protocol details the specifications of the Listega system that camouflages data, its decoder that unravels hidden messages, and the covert channel for securely transmitting list covers among communicating parties. The chosen domains can play an essential role in legitimizing the discernible communications between sender and recipient, such as the scenario of Bob and Alice detailed in Section 11.1. For instance, when a sender and recipient have a business or profession related to the chosen domains of songs or books, then it is a legitimate and common practice to receive, send, or otherwise obtain a textual list of items related to such domain. Generally, such a relationship can justify the discernible association between the communicating parties to legitimize the transmittal of a list cover. Once the communications protocol is agreed upon, the intended parties are ready to communicate covertly with each other using Listega. The following demonstrates examples of list cover.

11.2.2 Listega Examples

This section shows how the Listega system can be used to conceal messages. It describes the process of encoding a message and concealing the encoded message in the generated text cover, and also demonstrates samples of list cover.

- The plain text of two messages are *"get him"* and *"Stop"*.
- The Listega encoder converts the messages to a concatenated binary string using the ASCII representation of the individual characters, as follows:

     "get him" → 0110011101100101011101000010000001101
     0000110100101101101

     "Stop" → 01010011011101000110111101110000

- Listega encoder will then divide the above binary messages into slices of a particular size that match the steganographic coding used. It should be noted that the binary string could have been encrypted or compressed prior to this step. Nonetheless, the result is shown below:

     "get him" → 0110 0111 0110 0101 0111 0100 0010 0000
     0110 1000 0110 1001 0110 1101

     "Stop" → 0101 0011 0111 0100 0110 1111 0111 0000

- The camouflage module considers the sliced bit string of the encoded messages generated by the encoder, and maps every slice to an item. The item will conceal a part of the message according to Table 11.1. A slice of 4 bits will be assigned to each item. The samples of list cover are shown below.

Samples of List-Cover: The samples, based on the two domains used, demonstrate the effectiveness and efficiency of Listega. Table 11.1 demonstrates Sample 11.1 and Table 11.2 demonstrates Sample 11.2. However, the steganographic coding of Sample 11.2 in Table 11.2 adds a value of 1 to each value of steganographic code to alter the coding in order to avoid pattern detection. As shown in Tables 11.1 and 11.2, each item conceals 4 bits by selecting the item that starts with a particular letter to match the steganographic code. As observed, using a legitimate list of items such as products, subjects, or books is extremely common, linguistically legible, and unsuspicious. For example, one may consider the list of songs on the Internet as shown in Figure 11.3. Note, the list of songs in Figure 11.3 does not contain a hidden message and was just an innocent compilation created by people who like 80's music.

Table 11.1 Details for Camouflaging the Encoded Message *"get him"*

INDEX	BINARY STRINGS OF ASCII REPRESENTATION FOR ENCODED MESSAGE	FIRST LETTER OF SELECTED ITEM	LIST COVER LIST OF SONGS WITH SINGER NAMES [154,158]	LIST COVER LIST OF SONGS WITHOUT SINGER NAMES
1	0110	G or W →	Wicked Game—1989 Chris Isaak lyrics	Wicked Game
2	0111	H or X →	How Do I Live—1997 LeAnn Rimes lyrics	How Do I Live
3	0110	G or W →	Wonderful Tonight—1978 Eric Clapton lyrics	Wonderful Tonight
4	0101	F or V →	Faithfully—1983 Journey lyrics	Faithfully
5	0111	H or X →	Hero—2001 Enrique Iglesias lyrics	Hero
6	0100	E or U →	Endless Love—1981 Diana Ross & Lionel Richie lyrics	Endless Love
7	0010	C or S →	Careless Whisper—1984 Wham! Lyrics	Careless Whisper
8	0000	A or Q →	And I Love Her—1964 The Beatles lyrics	And I Love Her
9	0110	G or W →	Wild Thing—1966 The Troggs lyrics	Wild Thing
10	1000	I or Y →	Your Song—1971 Elton John lyrics	Your Song
11	0110	G or W →	Girl—1965 The Beatles lyrics	Girl
12	1001	J or Z →	Just Fine—Mary J. Blige	Just Fine
13	0110	G or W →	I Want You To Want Me—1979 Cheap Trick lyrics	I Want You To Want Me
14	1101	N →	Nobody Wants To Be Lonely—2000 Ricky Martin lyrics	Nobody Wants To Be Lonely

Note: The binary of this message is: 0110 0111 0110 0101 0111 0100 0010 0000 0110 1000 0110 1001 0110 1101.

Table 11.2 Details for Camouflaging the Encoded Message *"Stop"*

INDEX	BINARY STRINGS OF ASCII REPRESENTATION FOR ENCODED MESSAGE	FIRST LETTER OF SELECTED ITEM AFTER ADDING 1 TO ALTER THE STEGANOGRAPHIC CODE VALUES	LIST COVER LIST OF BOOKS WITH YEAR AND AUTHOR NAMES [154,159]	LIST COVER LIST OF SONGS WITHOUT YEAR AND AUTHOR NAMES
1	0101	G or W →	Warrior Heir (2006). Catherine Axelrad	Warrior Heir
2	0011	E or U →	Ever (2008). M. Fitzgerald	Ever
3	0111	I or Y →	Year of Fog (2008). Scott Sigler	Year of Fog
4	0100	F or V →	Vengeful Virgin (1958). Gil Brewer	Vengeful Virgin
5	0110	H or X →	Hunting Wind (2002). Melissa Smith	Hunting Wind
6	1111	Q →	Q is for Quarry (2002). Sue Grafton	Q is for Quarry
7	0111	I or Y →	Inventing the Abbotts (1987). Morag Joss	Inventing the Abbotts
8	0000	B or R →	Blood Is the Sky (2004). Steve Hamilton	Blood Is the Sky

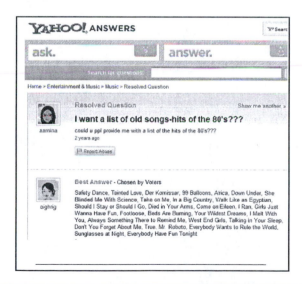

Figure 11.3 Shows the common practice of using textual lists of songs.

11.3 Conclusion

The presented **List**-Based **Stega**nography (Listega) Methodology conceals messages in textual lists of itemized data. The high demand for these kinds of lists by a wide variety of people allows the communicating parties to establish a covert channel to transmit hidden messages (list cover), rendering textual lists of items an attractive steganographic carrier. Listega neither hides data in a noise (errors) nor produces noise. Instead, it camouflages data in legitimate lists of items mainly by manipulating the itemized data (e.g., list of books, movie DVDs, music CDs, auto parts, etc.) in order to embed data without generating any suspicious pattern. The presented implementation achieves bitrates up to 3.87%. Such a bitrate is superior to contemporary linguistic steganography approaches found in the literature, confirming the effectiveness of the Listega methodology. Furthermore, Listega can be applied to all languages. The steganalysis validation has shown Listega methodology is capable of achieving the steganographic goal.

12

NOTESTEGA

Steganography Methodology

The wide use of notes in business, science, education, and news renders notes an attractive steganographic carrier that allows the communicating parties to establish a covert channel capable of transmitting messages in an unsuspicious way. The presented **Notes**-Based **Stega**nography (Notestega) Methodology takes advantage of recent advances in automatic note taking techniques to generate a text cover [31]. Notestega is based on the Nostega paradigm, thus it neither exploits noise (errors) to embed a message nor produces a detectable noise. Instead, it pursues the variations among both human note taking and the output of automatic note taking techniques to conceal data. Unlike machine translation and automatic summarizers, Notestega can embed nondirectly related elements to its output, including linguistic elements (e.g., sentences, words, abbreviations) and nonlinguistic elements (e.g., lines, stars, arrows, symbols). Thus the generated note cover (text cover) has ample room for concealing data. Such text generation is done carefully in order to avoid the introduction of a suspicious pattern while embedding a message. The presented implementation and steganalysis validation of Notestega demonstrate distinct capabilities for achieving the steganographic goal, adequate room for concealing data, and a bitrate of roughly 7.777%, which is superior to contemporary text steganography approaches.

The remainder of this chapter is organized as follows. Section 12.1 briefly highlights the related work of the automatic note taking field. Section 12.2 explains the Notestega methodology in details. Section 12.3 demonstrates the Notestega implementation. Finally, Section 12.4 concludes the chapter.

12.1 Automatic Note Taking

The field of automatic note taking has enjoyed significant advances in recent years. It is currently more active than ever and is still promising more in the future. Unlike machine translation and automatic summarization [190,191], automatic note taking can embed nondirectly related elements to its output, including both linguistic elements (e.g., sentences, words, and abbreviations) and nonlinguistic elements (e.g., lines, stars, arrows, and symbols). As will be discussed, such a feature makes automatic note taking a flexible scheme and provides adequate room for concealing data. According to Fister and Girju, automatic note taking techniques are investigated from two perspectives: linguistics and psychology [192]. Their study also pointed out that linguistics-based investigation has been minimal. A milestone of the linguistic analysis of note taking is traced back to a 1985 article by Richard Janda. Janda stated that "the purpose in taking notes is normally to have a potentially permanent record of at least the salient points of a lecture." This approach, from a note taking analysis point of view, treats a note as a register of human language [192,193]. Janda considered the note taking register for an adult talk versus a baby, and native versus non-native speakers of a language. He observed that the note talk has "no expressive, upgrading, or even clarifying processes."

Janda also conducted an experiment on an adequate collection of textual notes from a wide variety of lectures, topics, and students [193]. He observed ten various types of systematic grammatical reductions that occurred. It is also argued that notes retain linguistic and nonlinguistc contents. The nonlinguistic contents of notes may include the use of arrows, mathematical notations, and lines. In addition, the nonlinguistic contents of a lecture may also be transformed into linguistic contents. For example, the symbol of "=" can be written in a sentence using the word "equal" and so on. It is worth noting that this aspect of note analysis has been investigated and has led to significant advances in automatic note taking [194]. There are also other interesting automatic note taking approaches from the prospective of psychology mentioned in [192] and worth looking into. Nonetheless, from a steganographic point of view such note variations can be employed as steganographic carriers to conceal data.

12.2 Notestega Methodology

The main purpose of the Notestega methodology is to exploit the variations among human notes and the outputs of auto-note taking techniques to conceal data. A unique feature of automatic note taking that distinguishes it from machine translation and automatic summarization is that its output can be augmented with nondirectly related elements, both linguistic (e.g., sentences, words, abbreviations) and nonlinguistic (e.g., lines, stars, arrows, symbols) [192]. Such a feature enables great flexibility in concealing data in a note cover (text cover) and provides adequate room for that. Basically, Notestega manipulates human notes and the parameters of automatic note taking in order to generate legitimate various notes from the same inputs, employing some of the textual elements in one of the generated notes to embed a message without generating a suspicious pattern. The selected note for this procedure is pre-agreed upon by configuring, in advance, the Notestega system among communicating parties. For example, if the Notestega system can produce four different notes for the same inputs, then the system should be determined in advance that which one will be used. In other words, is it the note number 1, 2, 3, or 4? Note that the Notestega system generates different notes of the same inputs that make it feasible to make this designation. Moreover, the demand of using notes in business, science, education, and news renders notes attractive steganographic carriers and averts an adversary's suspicion when a note cover is transmitted among communicating parties.

To illustrate how Notestega can be used, consider the following scenario. Bob and Alice are on a spy mission. Before they start their mission, which requires them to reside in two different countries, they set the rules for communicating covertly using their professions as a justification. To make this work, they establish a business relationship as follows. Bob and Alice are students in two different schools, but taking the same course and they agree to use Notestega. This is like an online forum when students from different schools all over the world discuss a particular subject and exchange class notes. Bob and Alice generate notes concerning real topics to make their covert communications more legitimate. When Bob wants to send a covert message to Alice, Bob either posts notes online for authorized classmates or online student friends, or he send the notes to them via email. These notes conceal data. Covert messages transmitted in this manner will not look suspicious because Bob and Alice are students and their interaction is legitimate. The use of notes in both academic and non-academic spheres is natural given the time pressure experienced by people nowadays. This renders the activity innocent. Furthermore, Bob and Alice are not the sole recipients. Other non-spy students send and receive such notes, further warding off suspicion. However, only Bob and Alice will be able to unravel the hidden message because they know the rules of the game.

12.2.1 Notestega Architecture

Notestega camouflages both a message and its transmittal in a legitimate textual note. As stated earlier, in the above example of Bob and Alice, using a particular topic gives legitimacy for camouflaging both a message and its transmittal. The core idea of the Notestega methodology is basically camouflaging data in notes. Obviously, such steganographic cover in the form of notes is linguistically, logically, and scientifically legitimate. The following is an overview of the Notestega architecture, which consists of four modules as shown in Figure 12.1.

1. *Topics Determination* (Module 1) determines an appropriate topic(s) for achieving the steganographic goal. One of the major factors for employing a particular topic(s) is the use of note. The chosen topic(s) can be an academic subject (e.g., Psychology, History, Digital Design, etc.) or a nonacademic subject (e.g., real estate, driver jobs, construction, trading, etc.), either of which can be employed by the Notestega methodology. Module 1 is only involved in the stage of constructing the Notestega system.

2. *Message Encoding* (Module 2) encodes a message in an appropriate and required form for the camouflaging process (Module 3). The process of generating a note cover, by Module 3, may influence the process of how a message should be encoded. Therefore, studying and analyzing the output of Module 3 may be necessary for implementing an effective

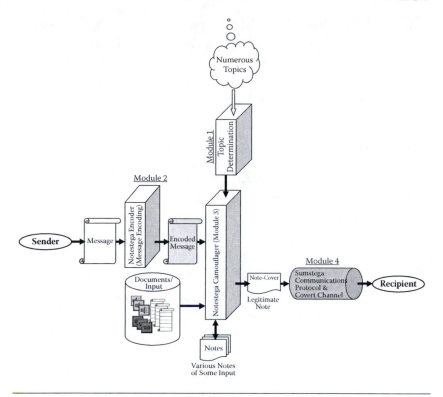

Figure 12.1 The architecture of Notestega and the communications protocol.

encoder. For example, a message may be encoded by slicing its binary string into a particular length of bits, e.g., four or seven bits, as follows.

Message: "*Stop*"

Convert it to binary:

01010011011101000110111101110000

Then, slicing its binary string into four–bit groups:

0101 0011 0111 0100 0110 1111 0111 0000

3. *Message Camouflager* (Module 3) generates the note cover (text cover) in which a message encoded by Module 2 is embedded. Simply, Module 3 exploits human notes and automatic note taking techniques to embed the output of Module 2, the encoded message, in the generated textual note. This is accomplished in such a way that the note cover looks legitimate like any ordinary note.

4. *Communications Protocol* (Module 4) configures the basic protocol of how a sender and recipient would communicate covertly. Obviously, it includes the covert channel for delivering a note cover to the intended recipient and the decoding scheme to unravel a hidden message.

12.2.2 Topic(s) Determination (Module 1)

The chosen topic must be capable of concealing data. In other words, it must allow the process of embedding data without generating noise in order to achieve the steganographic goal. Since Notestega mainly manipulates textual notes and automatic note taking techniques to camouflage messages, it can be applied to any topic that allows the use of notes. In addition, the chosen topic has to fit the communicating parties and provide some justification for the communications. For example, an uneducated person would not access, retain, exchange, or post atomic physics class notes. Such communications would easily raise suspicion because such an individual could not justify textual notes that fail to match his background and his interests. Notestega naturally camouflages the delivery of a hidden message in a way that makes it appear legitimate and innocent. The scenario discussed above (Section 12.2) demonstrates why the communications between Bob and Alice would not be unusual because their mutual interests play a role in camouflaging the delivery of note cover. A legitimate reason, for sending, receiving, accessing, or obtaining some particular material legitimizes the covert communications among communicating parties. Therefore, selecting the appropriate topic can play an essential role not only in camouflaging a message, but also in transmitting a steganographic cover. In another words, selecting a justifiable topic is essential for establishing an appropriate covert channel for securing the steganographic communications.

12.2.3 Message Encoding (Module 2)

Notestega creates an encoded representation of a message and then camouflages it in a note cover. The obvious constraint that Notestega imposes on the message encoder (Module 2) is to generate steganographic code that can be embedded in a note cover. Given the availability of numerous encoding techniques in the literature [25] that can fit the presented methodology, the scope of the encoding process in this chapter will focus on an example that illustrates how to meet the message encoding constraints. This example will be used in Section 12.3.2 in more detail to demonstrate the applicability of Notestega. In the example, the encoding is done as follows. A message is first converted to a binary string. The string can be a binary of cipher text or a compressed representation. The binary string is then partitioned into groups of m bits. The value of m is determined based on the number n of different notes that are produced, as specified by the encoding parameters (Module 3 in Section 12.2.4). Basically, m is set to $\log n$. If $n = 4$, i.e., four different notes, the bit pattern 00, 01, 10, or 11 will be implied if an element in the note cover uniquely matches that of the first, second, third or fourth generated note, respectively. Note that if the elements in the generated notes are not different from each other, then these elements imply null data bits. In other words, such elements will not be used to conceal data since Notestega employs only the variations among notes. Again, this encoding scheme is just for illustration and many alternate and more sophisticated schemes can be employed.

12.2.4 Message Camouflager (Module 3)

This module is responsible for generating a Notestega configuration that the sender and receiver must pre-agree upon so that the hidden message can be extracted. Numerous parameters to the auto-note taking process can be exploited to be steganographic carriers for concealing data. A parameter in this context means some input that a user may set to shape the generated note. Examples of these parameters include the desired linguistics such as sentences, words, expression, and abbreviations and also the nonlinguistic elements such as lines, circles, symbols, and arrows. This is similar to two students who both have different notes for the same class. The generated notes do not always look clear to everyone, but they are clear to the one who generated it or the one who is familiar with the same topic. Unlike machine translation and automatic summarizers, automatic note taking can embed nondirectly related elements to its output including linguistic elements and nonlinguistic elements [192], rendering the note cover (text cover) in such a way as to preserve plenty of room for concealing data. Simply, this module primarily exploits notes and the automatic note taking techniques to generate a set of notes for the same input. Each of these notes contains unique elements that will be used to embed a message. Then, based on a pre-agreed protocol, Module 3 selects a particular note to serve as the original note. Finally, it employs these uniquely different elements to embed the required elements from the original note (the selected one that was untouched) in order to embed the encoded message from Module 2. As will be explained shortly, Notestega will use the various notes to camouflage the data in a note cover.

12.3 Notestega Implementation

Due to space constraints, only high-level approaches are used to illustrate the implementation example of Notestega. This section demonstrates the feasibility of Notestega methodology and its distinct capability of achieving the steganographic goal with a higher bitrate than contemporary linguistic steganography approaches. It is worth noting that the focus of this section is on showing how Notestega achieves the steganographic goal, rather than making it difficult for an adversary to decode an encoded message. Employing a hard encoding system or cryptosystem to increase the protection of a message is obviously recommended and straightforward using any contemporary encoder or cryptosystem. Similarly, employing compression to boost the bitrate can easily be accomplished by using one of the popular techniques in the literature. This section shows just one example of a possible implementation following the steps outlined in the previous section.

12.3.1 Notestega Configuration

This section first explains how Notestega modules are employed and configured to construct the overall Notestega system used by the communicating parties.

Determining Particular Topic(s) (Module 1): In this chapter, one topic from the computer science field is employed; namely, the undergraduate class in Logic and Computer Design. Obviously, this topic is just an example and many other topics may apply as stated in Section 12.2.1. Such a topic is fairly popular among computer science students and professionals, and demonstrates the capability of using not only linguistic elements, but also nonlinguistic (e.g., lines, stars, arrows, and symbols). The topic has no constraints so that it is suitable for Notestega.

Notestega Encoder (Module 2): Notestega encodes a message in a form that suits the camouflaging process. The steganographic code in this Notestega configuration works as shown in Table 12.1.

Message Camouflage (Module 3): Based on the output of Module 1, the note cover is mainly a note from an undergraduate class fin Logic and Computer Design. Obviously, this topic is just used as an implementation example and many other topics can be used. The camouflage module employs human notes and automatic note taking techniques, and uses popular Internet search engines such as google.com in order to accommodate the note cover generation process. Module 3 in this implementation generates four different notes and uses special characters from Microsoft Word 97, as shown in Table 12.2. The steganographic carriers are picked based on what matches the steganographic code value of an encoded message (the bit string of a message). As will be shown in the example below, the first two bits are used for the note style and the second six bits for special contents that are popularly used. This process does not impose any constraint on the employed implementation.

Table 12.1   The Steganographic Code Used in This Chapter

TYPE OF NOTE TAKING GENERATION	1	2	3	4
Steganographic binary values for style and unique different elements	00	01	10	11
Special embedding such as sentences, words, character, symbols, etc.	000000–111111			

Note: The first two bits are employed for the steganographic carriers such as styles and unique different elements of various notes.

Table 12.2   The Steganographic Code Used in This Chapter By Note Samples

TYPE OF NOTE TAKING GENERATION	1	2	3	4
Steganographic binary values	00	01	10	11
Example style	False and False = False	0 & 0 = 0	F & F = F	F and F = F
Example special embedding	♣, *, #, →,☺, etc. can conceal 6 bits from 000000 to 111111			

Note: The first two bits are employed for the steganographic carriers such as styles and unique different elements of various notes.

Communications Protocol (Module 4): The chosen topic can play an essential role in legitimizing the discernible communications between the sender and the recipient such as in the scenario of Bob and Alice in Section 12.2. In this example, a sender and a recipient have a legitimate interest in the chosen topic, which justifies the communicating parties to receive, send, and obtain textual notes related to the topic. Once the communications protocol is agreed upon, the intended parties are ready to communicate covertly with each other using Notestega. The following demonstrates an example of note cover.

12.3.2 Samples of Note Cover

The presented sample is based on the chosen topic and demonstrates the robustness of Notestega. Table 12.3 demonstrates Sample 12.1 using Tables 12.1 and 12.2. As observed, the note cover below looks to be a legitimate ordinary note. Figure 12.2 shows what other notes that do not contain hidden data may look like in the Notetaking System [195].

Table 12.3   Virtual Example of Notestega Methodology

TYPE OF NOTE TAKING GENERATION →	NOTE TAKING GENERATION TYPE 2
Steganographic binary values	01
Example style	0 & 0 = 0
Example special embedding	011000 = →

Note: In this example, the letter "X", the binary string of which, in ASCII representation, is "01011000", will be concealed.

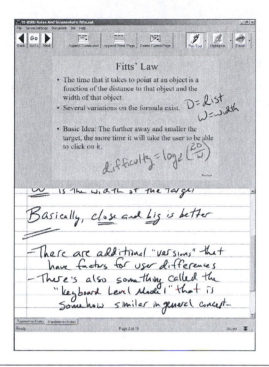

Figure 12.2   Screenshots from notes [196] that a student writes toward the bottom part of the writing surface and, as shown, more room is automatically created and scrolled to.

The following sample conceals the binary string "01011000" of the letter "X". Again, due to space constraints only high-level approaches are used to illustrate the implementation of Notestega. In addition, this can also be embedded among other Logic and Computer Design class notes.

Note-Cover Sample Conceal 8 Bits: "→ 0 & 0 = 0"

12.4 Conclusion

The presented **Note**s-Based **Stega**nography (Notestega) Methodology conceals data in textual notes. The high demand for textual notes by a wide variety of people allows the communicating parties to establish a covert channel to transmit hidden messages (note cover) rendering textual notes attractive steganographic carriers. Notestega neither hides data in a noise (errors) nor produces noise in the cover text. Instead, it camouflages data in legitimate notes by manipulating notes in order to embed data without generating any suspicious pattern. The presented implementation achieves a bitrate of up to 7.777%. Such a bitrate is superior to contemporary linguistic steganography approaches found in the literature, confirming the effectiveness of the Notestega methodology. Furthermore, Notestega can be applied to all languages. The steganalysis validation has demonstrated that Notestega methodology is capable of achieving the steganographic goal.

13
STEGANALYSIS VALIDATION

Steganalysis is the scientific art of defeating the steganographic goal [3,4]. As stated before, the steganographic goal is not to prevent an adversary from decoding a hidden message, but to prevent an adversary from suspecting the existence of hidden data [3]. Thus, when using any steganographic technique, if suspicion is raised the goal of steganography is defeated regardless of whether or not a plain text message is revealed [4,23]. As such, the aim of this chapter is to show the resilience to possible attacks of the several methodologies that are based on the Nostega paradigm. It is assumed that an adversary will perform all possible investigations. In addition, the adversary is also aware of Nostega, as a public paradigm, but he does not know the details of the Nostega-based system that the sender and recipient employ for their covert communication.

13.1 Traffic Attack

One of the possible attacks an adversary may pursue is to analyze the communications traffic and the access patterns to publicly available or exchanged documents, images, graphs, and files. For example, the intelligence community has a number of tools at their disposal for analyzing Internet traffic, tracking access to websites, monitoring checked out literature from public libraries, etc. The main goal of a traffic attack is to detect an unusual or questionable association between a sender and a recipient. Traffic analysis can intuitively identify who communicates with whom. The relationship between the communicating parties is then qualified based on the contents of the message. Traffic attacks can be applied to any contemporary steganography techniques regardless of the cover type (e.g., image, graph, audio file, or text) and can achieve successful results with relatively low cost. In the context of Nostega, the subject of the cover is checked rather than its validity and consistency. If someone sends, receives, or accesses materials without a legitimate reason for doing so, suspicion can be raised and further investigation may be warranted. The additional investigations will involve a thorough analysis of a steganographic cover, as detailed next.

Traffic analysis is deemed ineffective with Nostega-based methodologies because these methodologies camouflage the transmittal of a hidden message so that it appears legitimate and thus suspicion is averted. Nostega ensures that the involved parties establish a covert communication channel by having a well-defined relationship with each other. For example in Edustega, the transmittal of a hidden message (edu-cover) is camouflaged in a way that makes the delivery of the steganographic cover appear legitimate, thus averting suspicion. Basically, Edustega ensures that the involved parties establish a covert channel by having a well-plotted relationship with each other. Analyzing the traffic between them will not reveal any questionable association and will not trigger any further investigation. For instance, when a professor, teacher, or student sends, posts, or accesses educational material, e.g., exams, homework, exercises, or questions, which is relevant to his interests, suspicion is averted. In addition, the high demand by a wide variety of people for the material used as a steganographic cover, e.g., educational documents, chess games, graphs, or news summaries, creates a high volume of traffic that makes it impractical for an adversary to investigate all traffic. The voluminous traffic allows the communicating parties to establish a covert channel in order to transmit a Nostega-based cover without drawing attention, rendering it an attractive steganographic carrier. Finally, it is noted that if further investigations on a Nostega-based cover are triggered by traffic analysis, they will not be successful, as is explained next. In Nostega, differentiating between a Nostega-based cover that contains hidden data and other peer materials without a hidden message is not feasible.

13.2 Contrast and Comparison Attacks

One of the intuitive sources of noise that may alert an adversary is the presence of contradictions in the Nostega-based cover, such as finding inaccurate information in a particular cover, e.g., false information about a chess game or some naïve move made by a professional player. For instance, contradictions can be spotted when using data that indicates a clear violation of the rules in either a chess game or a graph. The use of authenticated or untraceable data as used in a graph cover will definitely counter such an attack. Untraceable data means data that matters only to a particular group or is shared privately, e.g., a game between two unknown amateurs, or numbers in a private chart that cannot be contrasted or compared. Meanwhile, noise in the context of comparison attacks reflects alteration of authenticated or previously used data. The goal is to find any incorrect and inconsistent data that may imply the manipulation of Nostega-based cover contents to include a hidden message. The vulnerability of Nostega-based cover to comparison attacks depends on how the cover is generated. Employing unaltered authenticated data makes the cover very resilient to this type of attack. For example, Chestega demonstrates how a non-steganographic tool like Chessmaster has allowed the selection of authenticated and appropriate moves and games that match an encoded message, and yet has facilitated the generation of the game description and analysis. An adversary cannot detect any discrepancy in a chess cover when examining the authenticity of the data and the consistency of the text with respect to the style of what Chessmaster usually generates.

It is worth noting that the traffic analysis, discussed earlier, can also be pursued as a base for launching comparison attacks in case the data is not publicly accessible. In that case, current data is compared to a record of old data in order to search for any inconsistency over some period of time. Countering such an attack is always a challenge because it requires consistency with data that was previously used over an extended period of time. Contradictions would surely raise suspicion about the existence of a hidden message. Nostega, as demonstrated through examples, is simply made contrast and comparison-aware. The flexibility in message encoding and the ability to employ more than one cover type enables Nostega to easily avert such attacks.

13.3 Linguistics Attacks

Linguistics attacks apply to Nostega-based methodologies, e.g., Chestega, Sumstega, and Edustega that employ text covers. Linguistics examination distinguishes the text that is under attack from normal human language. Distinguishing the text from normal human language can be done through the examination of meaning, syntax, lexicon, rhetoric, semantic, coherence, and any other issues that can help in detecting or suspecting the existence of a hidden message. These examinations are used to determine whether or not the text that is under attack is abnormal. Generally, the text produced by natural language generation (NLG) systems, like the one used in Chessmaster by Chestega, usually meets the expected properties of normal human language. This is due to the fact that such text is prepared in advance and is subject to careful review. Thus, employing NLG systems in cover generation prevents noises caused by linguistic flaws. For example, the chess cover shown in the implementation of Chestega is generated by contemporary non-steganographic tools such as Chessmaster and uses an NLG system which makes it linguistically sound (free of errors) [59]. Furthermore, if there are errors in the NLG engine, it should not be a concern for two reasons; first, it applies to all the generated text with and without a hidden message; second, nothing is concealed in errors. In addition, the use of contemporary, publicly known non-steganographic tools make it possible to fool an adversary into believing that the stenographic cover is just ordinary material. Other text-covers generated by schemes such as Sumstega and Edustega obviously have no unusual patterns to be detected because they look very similar to their innocent peers that carry no hidden data. Therefore, the Nostega paradigm is capable of surviving any linguistic attack by either human or machine examinations.

13.4 Statistical Signature

In this book, the statistical signature (profile) of a text refers to the frequency of the distribution of words and characters. An adversary may use the statistical profile of normal text that contains no hidden message and compare it to the profile of the suspected text in order to detect differences. An alteration in the statistical signature of normal text can be a possible way of detecting noise that an adversary would watch for. Tracking statistical signatures may be an effective means of attack because it can be automated. However, Nostega is resistant to statistical attacks as demonstrated by the experimental results in this section.

Three main schemes to capture the statistical profile are pursued for validating Nostega. Two of the validation schemes are based on fundamental concepts of Natural Language Processing (NLP), namely the Words Frequency Distribution (WFD) discussed in Section 13.4.1 and the Letters Frequency Distribution (LFD) detailed in Section 13.4.2. Finally, Section 13.4.3 demonstrates the results when using Kullback–Leibler Divergence (KLD) to assess the level of similarity between Nostega-based covers and normal text with respect to WFD and LFD.

13.4.1 Zipfian Signature

Human language in general and the English language in particular have been statistically investigated to discover their statistical properties. The most notable study on the frequency of words was done by George Kingsley Zipf [89,90]. Zipf investigated the statistical occurrence of words in human languages and, in particular, in the English language. Based on the statistical experimental research, Zipf concluded his observation in what is known as Zipf's law. Zipf's law states that word frequency is inversely proportional to its rank in an overall word frequency table, which lists all words used in a text sorted in descending order of their number of appearances. Mathematically, Zipf's law implies that $W_n \sim 1/n^a$, where W_n is the frequency of occurrence of the nth ranked word and a is a constant that is close to 1. Based on this mathematical relationship, a logarithmic scale plot of the number of times words appear and their rank will yield a straight line with a slope $-a$ that is close to -1. The value of a is found to depend on the sample size and mix. Zipf's law was originally observed on a huge bundle of textual collections containing numerous Domain Specific Subjects (DSS) written by different authors with different writing-styles, different writing-fingerprints, etc. Consequently, this huge bundle of textual collections is fairly blended, which causes the occurrence of approaching or reaching a Zipfian signature of -1. The following reports on the set of validation experiments for Nostega using the Zipfian signature of the covers. The first experiment is to compare the signature of texts based on a Domain Specific Subject

(DSS) to each other and to Zipfian's ideal value, as well to set the basis for evaluating Nostega-based cover. The second and third experiments examine Edustega and Sumstega methodologies, respectively.

Experiment #1: This experiment assesses the Zipfian signature of text documents about a particular Domain Specific Subject (DSS). The overall goal is to identify the basis for comparing Nostega-based covers to peers' texts that contain no hidden messages. The presented Zipf's observation in this book is based on diverse samples. However, small-sized documents focused on a specific subject may not exhibit the same behavior. Therefore, suspicion will be averted if a Nostega cover maintains the Zipfian signature of the text, regardless whether it conforms to Zipf's law or not. Therefore, Experiment # 1 investigates the Zipfian signature for the following texts:

1. Consumer Price Index (CPI) reports, as a text of a particular DSS (Matlist Cover), generated by a Natural Language Generation (NLG) template [59] which is also used by the Matlist system [27]. The size of the generated CPI text by the NLG is about one paragraph.
2. CPI reports generated by humans and collected from [91]. The size of this text is again about one paragraph.
3. Smoking cessation text used in smoking cessation counseling. This text is generated by humans and picked from the Internet [92]. The size of this text is roughly about one page.
4. Smoking cessation text also used in smoking cessation counseling but the text is generated by an NLG system using the NORMALS system to conceal data (NORMALS cover) [26]. The size of this text is roughly about one page.

Unlike Zipf's experiment, the Nostega experiment applied Zipf's law to a short piece of text with a unique Domain Specific Subject. Based on the experimental observation shown in Table 13.1, CPI text generated (Matlist cover) by the NLG template used by the Matlist system holds a Zipfian slope with an average of -0.87016 for 23 samples. On the other hand, the unaltered authenticated data of the same domain that are generated by humans holds a Zipfian slope with an average of -0.75611, as shown in Table 13.1, for 23 samples. Apparently, neither text fully obeys Zipf's law. The difference

Table 13.1 The Zipfian Distribution (Logarithmic Scale) of Three Different Types of Text

NO.	MATLIST COVER (FOR CPI NLG TEXT)			CPI TEXT BY HUMAN			SMOKING CESSATION TEXT BY HUMAN		
	EQUATION	R^2	$-a$	EQUATION	R^2	$-a$	EQUATION	R^2	$-a$
1	-0.8922x + 1.6735	0.9141	-0.8922	-0.8245x + 1.4915	0.9329	-0.8245	-0.7094x + 1.6976	0.9276	-0.7094
2	-0.8923x + 1.6595	0.8952	-0.8923	-0.8741x + 1.698	0.9467	-0.8741	-0.6596x + 1.4729	0.9237	-0.6596
3	-1.0243x + 1.7418	0.9145	-1.0243	-0.7412x + 1.266	0.9251	-0.7412	-0.618x + 1.3766	0.9113	-0.618
4	-1.0683x + 1.8115	0.9145	-1.0683	-0.8542x + 1.6855	0.9512	-0.8542	-0.7339x + 1.8687	0.9264	-0.7339
5	-1.1287x + 1.9761	0.893	-1.1287	-0.9557x + 1.8569	0.9559	-0.9557	-0.6922x + 1.6727	0.9304	-0.6922
6	-1.1287x + 1.9761	0.893	-1.1287	-0.737x + 1.4103	0.9201	-0.737	-0.6377x + 1.377	0.8922	-0.6377
7	-1.107x + 2.0269	0.9051	-1.107	-0.737x + 1.4103	0.9201	-0.737	-0.674x + 1.4475	0.9218	-0.674
8	-0.8459x + 1.4629	0.9165	-0.8459	-0.758x + 1.2825	0.9091	-0.758	-0.5745x + 1.3416	0.9012	-0.5745
9	-0.8068x + 1.4024	0.9107	-0.8068	-0.7493x + 1.428	0.9109	-0.7493	-0.7227x + 1.6441	0.9244	-0.7227
10	-0.8022x + 1.3283	0.892	-0.8022	-0.6697x + 1.4098	0.9173	-0.6697	-0.6558x + 1.388	0.9146	-0.6558
11	-0.7883x + 1.3009	0.885	-0.7883	-0.705x + 1.4186	0.9257	-0.705	-0.6141x + 1.4108	0.9145	-0.6141
12	-0.7521x + 1.1838	0.8818	-0.7521	-0.6559x + 1.2942	0.8882	-0.6559	-0.7221x + 1.6445	0.943	-0.7221
13	-0.6779x + 1.0286	0.8827	-0.6779	-0.7171x + 1.1889	0.9159	-0.7171	-0.8603x + 2.0621	0.9451	-0.8603
14	-0.7613x + 1.2248	0.9069	-0.7613	-0.6052x + 0.9868	0.8342	-0.6052	-0.8993x + 2.4766	0.9592	-0.8993

continued

Table 13.1 (continued) The Zipfian Distribution (Logarithmic Scale) of Three Different Types of Text

NO.	MATLIST COVER (FOR CPI NLG TEXT)			CPI TEXT BY HUMAN			SMOKING CESSATION TEXT BY HUMAN		
	EQUATION	R^2	$-a$	EQUATION	R^2	$-a$	EQUATION	R^2	$-a$
15	$-0.7607x + 1.1986$	0.8939	−0.7607	$-0.9121x + 1.5605$	0.9461	−0.9121	$-0.899x + 2.4759$	0.9591	−0.899
16	$-0.7804x + 1.2725$	0.8795	−0.7804	$-0.8504x + 1.3719$	0.9015	−0.8504	$-0.6942x + 1.5498$	0.9202	−0.6942
17	$-0.7881x + 1.2988$	0.8734	−0.7881	$-0.7116x + 1.3634$	0.8902	−0.7116	$-0.6432x + 1.4241$	0.887	−0.6432
18	$-0.7745x + 1.2665$	0.8774	−0.7745	$-0.7093x + 1.363$	0.9035	−0.7093	$-0.767x + 1.9058$	0.9409	−0.767
19	$-0.8885x + 1.5789$	0.9288	−0.8885	$-0.7352x + 1.329$	0.9185	−0.7352	$-0.7944x + 1.7776$	0.9282	−0.7944
20	$-0.8003x + 1.3395$	0.8722	−0.8003	$-0.7085x + 1.3469$	0.9021	−0.7085	$-0.7018x + 1.6793$	0.9279	−0.7018
21	$-0.859x + 1.497$	0.9162	−0.859	$-0.6697x + 1.4098$	0.9173	−0.6697	$-0.7441x + 1.9242$	0.9434	−0.7441
22	$-0.8617x + 1.5046$	0.9271	−0.8617	$-0.6603x + 1.2676$	0.8973	−0.6603	$-0.62x + 1.445$	0.8853	−0.62
23	$-0.8617x + 1.5046$	0.9271	−0.8617	$-0.671x + 1.3073$	0.9037	−0.671	$-0.8118x + 2.0752$	0.9449	−0.8118
	Average →		−0.8949	Average →		−0.75021	Average →		−0.7151

Note: The equation is a linear curve fitting the results. R^2 is the squared error. The blue shows the highest and lowest Zipfian values.

between both slopes is minimal at just −0.14477. In addition, it was noted that both texts fluctuate by similar values. To emphasize, the NLG text is very close to that generated by humans. The Zipfian values of NLG text fluctuate from −0.6779 up to −1.1287, and the CPI text by humans fluctuates from −0.6052 up to −0.9557. Similarly, Nostega's experiment applied Zipf's law directly to smoking cessation texts generated by humans. These have an average Zipfian value of −0.71518, as shown in Table 13.1, for 23 samples. Also it is observed that the Zipfian values of smoking cessation texts (text that is used in Smoking Cessation counseling) fluctuate from −0.5745 up to −0.8993, as shown in Table 13.1.

The NORMALS experiment applied Zipf's law directly to NORMALS cover, considering the worst case scenario that an adversary knows NORMALS methodology, knows there is a hidden message, and knows where the hidden message is concealed. Unlike Zipf's experiment, the NORMALS experiment applied Zipf's law on a short piece of text with a unique domain-specific subject. Based on the experimental observation, as shown in Figure 13.1, NORMALS cover (that contains a hidden message) holds a Zipfian slope of −0.8374. On the other hand, the unaltered authenticated data of the same domain, without a hidden message, holds a Zipfian slope with an average of −0.71518, as shown in Table 13.1. Furthermore, it is observed that there are two Zipfian regions, as shown in Table 13.1: the highest Zipfian region holds a Zipfian slope in the range of −0.8118 to −0.8993; and the lowest Zipfian region holds a Zipfian slope in the range of −0.5745 to −0.6942. In this experiment, the highest Zipfian region is in the range of −0.8118 to −0.8993 and is the closest to the ideal Zipfian of −1. Zipfian of the

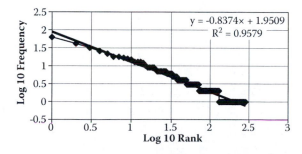

Figure 13.1   Illustrates the Zipfian signature for the presented NORMALS cover.

presented NORMALS Cover is −0.8374, which falls in the highest Zipfian region. As a result, NORMALS cover is on the safe side of both the ideal Zipfian of −1 and the Zipfian of the same domain. Similarly, the above observation was also seen, as shown in Table 13.1, with a different domain-specific subject—the Consumer Prices Index (unaltered authenticated data without hidden message)—where the Zipfian slope had an average of −0.74835 [1], the highest Zipfian region was in the range of −0.8245 to −0.9557 [1], and the lowest Zipfian region in the range of −0.6052 to −0.7493 [1].

The conclusion of the NORMALS experiment in word frequency is as follows. Since NLGS are based on a domain-specific subject, when applying Zipf's law, the NORMALS cover should have a slope similar to the Zipfian slope of its domain-specific subject (the unaltered, authenticated data of the same domain that contains no hidden message), and it should not be required to fully obey Zipf's law (Zipfian of −1). To emphasize, if the Zipfian slope of the NORMALS domain-specific subject (the unaltered authenticated data of the same domain that contains no hidden message) is equal to N value, then NORMALS cover should be either equal or close to that N value. Generally, it is feasible to avert any attack as long as the attack model is known, simply by constructing the steganographic scheme as attack-aware [25,26]. Furthermore, it is feasible to alter a natural language in a way that can fool Zipf's law if it is required. Simply, NORMALS can be designed as Zipf-aware [25,26] since the statistical model is already known. Obviously, NORMALS cover (contains hidden message) and the generated text that has no hidden message from the same NLGS will always hold identical Zipfian values.

The conclusion of the Zipfian Nostega experiment for the total of 69 samples of text is as follows. The Zipfian examination should be applied to texts of the same DSS. Yet, it is normal that a text that contains no hidden data may not fully obey Zipf's law (Zipfian of −1). For example, if a Zipfian value of DSS text is equal to −N, then the examined text should be very close to that −N value. Generally, it is feasible to avert any attacks, as long as the attack models are known, by simply constructing the steganographic scheme in an attack-aware manner. In regard to a Zipfian attack, it is feasible to alter the natural language in a way that can fool Zipf's law if it is required. Simply,

Nostega can be designed as Zipf-aware [13–15,25,28,35] since the statistical model is already known.

Experiment #2:   The aim of this experiment is to investigate the Zipfian signature of Edustega cover. Therefore, Experiment #2 investigates the Zipfian signature for the following texts:

1. Unaltered educational documents generated by auto-exam [69,70]. Generally, the size of this text is about 10 questions each.
2. Edustega covers which retain a similar size to the unaltered versions.

Basically, Zipf's law is applied to the edu-cover and the original text that contains no hidden data. Table 13.2 shows the results. It is observed that both the edu-cover and its peer, that contain no hidden data, have the same Zipfian values for 23 samples with an average Zipfian value of −0.82582. These Zipfian values fluctuate from −0.7195 up to −0.9758, which confirms the conclusion made by Experiment #1 above. Obviously, edu-cover can fully avert such an attack.

Experiment #3:   The objective of Experiment #3 is to inspect the Zipfian signature of Sumstega cover. Therefore, this experiment applies Zipf's law to summary cover versus its peer summaries that contain no hidden data. The following are considered:

1. Summaries that are generated by four automatic summarizers: AutoSummarize [82], SweSum [83], Automatic Text Summarizer [87], and Auto Summarizer [93]. The original texts used are collected from online news websites such as *TIME* Magazine [94] and *The New York Times* [94]. The summaries are short paragraphs, which range roughly from four to six sentences.
2. Sumstega Covers. The size of edu-cover is similar to the summaries, i.e., four to six sentences.

Table 13.3 shows the results of the experiment. The average Zipfian value of summary cover is −0.44159 for 23 samples. On the other hand, the average Zipfian value of peer summaries that contain no hidden data is −0.44372 for 92 samples, i.e., 23 documents [94,95]

Table 13.2   The Zipfian Distribution (Logarithmic Scale) of the Original Text That Contain No Hidden Data and Edu-Cover Hold Same Zipfian Values

	TEXT WITHOUT HIDDEN DATA			EDU-COVER		
TEXT #	EQUATION	R^2	SLOPE($-a$)	EQUATION	R^2	SLOPE($-a$)
1	$-0.7948x + 1.4646$	0.9111	-0.7948	$-0.7948x + 1.4646$	0.9111	-0.7948
2	$-0.7436x + 1.4305$	0.8933	-0.7436	$-0.7436x + 1.4305$	0.8933	-0.7436
3	$-0.8931x + 1.7267$	0.9549	-0.8931	$-0.8931x + 1.7267$	0.9549	-0.8931
4	$-0.8201x + 1.4454$	0.9285	-0.8201	$-0.8201x + 1.4454$	0.9285	-0.8201
5	$-0.8894x + 1.5987$	0.9052	-0.8894	$-0.8894x + 1.5987$	0.9052	-0.8894
6	$-0.9089x + 1.8336$	0.9419	-0.9089	$-0.9089x + 1.8336$	0.9419	-0.9089
7	$-0.7436x + 1.4128$	0.9371	-0.7436	$-0.7436x + 1.4128$	0.9371	-0.7436
8	$-0.7975x + 1.5543$	0.9234	-0.7975	$-0.7975x + 1.5543$	0.9234	-0.7975
9	$-0.7661x + 1.541$	0.9145	-0.7661	$-0.7661x + 1.541$	0.9145	-0.7661
10	$-0.7195x + 1.391$	0.9056	-0.7195	$-0.7195x + 1.391$	0.9056	-0.7195
11	$-0.7314x + 1.386$	0.8847	-0.7314	$-0.7314x + 1.386$	0.8847	-0.7314
12	$-0.8147x + 1.658$	0.9398	-0.8147	$-0.8147x + 1.658$	0.9398	-0.8147
13	$-0.8338x + 1.7116$	0.9542	-0.8338	$-0.8338x + 1.7116$	0.9542	-0.8338
14	$-0.7926x + 1.6032$	0.9219	-0.7926	$-0.7926x + 1.6032$	0.9219	-0.7926
15	$-0.9103x + 1.7424$	0.9434	-0.9103	$-0.9103x + 1.7424$	0.9434	-0.9103
16	$-0.8818x + 1.7571$	0.935	-0.8818	$-0.8818x + 1.7571$	0.935	-0.8818
17	$-0.7597x + 1.479$	0.9148	-0.7597	$-0.7597x + 1.479$	0.9148	-0.7597
18	$-0.7396x + 1.3786$	0.9201	-0.7396	$-0.7396x + 1.3786$	0.9201	-0.7396
19	$-0.9685x + 1.8276$	0.937	-0.9685	$-0.9685x + 1.8276$	0.937	-0.9685
20	$-0.7462x + 1.4402$	0.9206	-0.7462	$-0.7462x + 1.4402$	0.9206	-0.7462
21	$-0.9758x + 1.7782$	0.9286	-0.9758	$-0.9758x + 1.7782$	0.9286	-0.9758
22	$-0.8586x + 1.542$	0.9199	-0.8586	$-0.8586x + 1.542$	0.9199	-0.8586
23	$-0.9043x + 1.4876$	0.889	-0.9043	$-0.9043x + 1.4876$	0.889	-0.9043
	Average		-0.82582	Average		-0.82582

Note: The equation is a linear curve fitting the results (Slope [$-a$]). R^2 is the squared error.

each with four different summarizers generated using [82,83,87,93]. It is observed that the Zipfian values are similar to each other and the summary covers mainly hold Zipfian values that are in the range of peer summaries as shown in Table 13.3. Furthermore, both Zipfian values fluctuate. While the summary covers fluctuate from -0.3203 to -0.5599, peer summaries fluctuate from -0.2527 to -0.6238. To emphasize, while the fluctuation ranges are similar for both types of text, the fluctuation range of summary covers is within that of its peers. Thus, it confirms the above conclusion of the Nostega experiment, as shown in the Experiment # 1. Therefore, summary cover can easily pass an attack.

Table 13.3 The Zipfian Distribution (Logarithmic Scale) of Summary Cover and Its Peers That Contain No Hidden Data

TEXT #	PEER SUMMARIES EQUATION	R^2	SLOPE($-a$)	COVER #	SUMMARY COVERS EQUATION	R^2	SLOPE($-a$)
1	$-0.4721x + 0.8371$	0.8184	-0.4721	1	$-0.442x + 0.8056$	0.8128	-0.442
2	$-0.5095x + 0.9288$	0.8651	-0.5095				
3	$-0.4282x + 0.7806$	0.815	-0.4282				
4	$-0.4736x + 0.8485$	0.8487	-0.4736				
5	$-0.434x + 0.6567$	0.795	-0.434	2	$-0.3651x + 0.5949$	0.6624	-0.3651
6	$-0.4064x + 0.6584$	0.7663	-0.4064				
7	$-0.4632x + 0.834$	0.8155	-0.4632				
8	$-0.3674x + 0.6306$	0.7265	-0.3674				
9	$-0.5261x + 0.8299$	0.8426	-0.5261	3	$-0.4738x + 0.8283$	0.8477	-0.4738
10	$-0.5535x + 0.9973$	0.8919	-0.5535				
11	$-0.4782x + 0.8617$	0.8666	-0.4782				
12	$-0.5199x + 0.9315$	0.849	-0.5199				
13	$-0.5019x + 0.8749$	0.8405	-0.5019	4	$-0.5019x + 0.8749$	0.8405	-0.5019
14	$-0.5177x + 0.9141$	0.8131	-0.5177				
15	$-0.5098x + 0.9377$	0.8103	-0.5098				
16	$-0.4965x + 0.9418$	0.7874	-0.4965				
17	$-0.408x + 0.653$	0.7782	-0.408	5	$-0.411x + 0.6615$	0.7728	-0.411
18	$-0.4813x + 0.8491$	0.8526	-0.4813				
19	$-0.5692x + 1.1708$	0.8938	-0.5692				

continued

Table 13.3 (continued) The Zipfian Distribution (Logarithmic Scale) of Summary Cover and Its Peers That Contain No Hidden Data

	PEER SUMMARIES				SUMMARY COVERS		
TEXT #	EQUATION	R^2	SLOPE($-a$)	COVER #	EQUATION	R^2	SLOPE($-a$)
20	$-0.4447x + 0.8005$	0.7928	-0.4447				
21	$-0.4012x + 0.688$	0.8077	-0.4012	6	$-0.3975x + 0.6468$	0.7672	-0.3975
22	$-0.5095x + 0.8602$	0.8307	-0.5095				
23	$-0.4153x + 0.723$	0.8156	-0.4153				
24	$-0.3866x + 0.6568$	0.7716	-0.3866				
25	$-0.3321x + 0.5258$	0.76	-0.3321	7	$-0.4319x + 0.7599$	0.8376	-0.4319
26	$-0.4233x + 0.7193$	0.8291	-0.4233				
27	$-0.3973x + 0.686$	0.7838	-0.3973				
28	$-0.5471x + 1.0863$	0.8749	-0.5471				
29	$-0.445x + 0.7505$	0.8534	-0.445	8	$-0.4706x + 0.7829$	0.8508	-0.4706
30	$-0.3603x + 0.6105$	0.7105	-0.3603				
31	$-0.4729x + 0.7814$	0.8475	-0.4729				
32	$-0.3321x + 0.4788$	0.7739	-0.3321				
33	$-0.3264x + 0.4736$	0.7442	-0.3264	9	$-0.3607x + 0.5036$	0.7741	-0.3607
34	$-0.0592x + 0.0801$	0.2491	-0.0592				
35	$-0.5039x + 0.6719$	0.8231	-0.5039				
36	$-0.4093x + 0.5497$	0.7403	-0.4093				
37	$-0.4041x + 0.6762$	0.7779	-0.4041	10	$-0.4724x + 0.8296$	0.8597	-0.4724
38	$-0.4973x + 0.8613$	0.8711	-0.4973				

11	$-0.5158x + 0.8895$	0.8809	-0.5158
12	$-0.4855x + 0.8418$	0.8288	-0.4855
13	$-0.3203x + 0.5549$	0.7583	-0.3203
14	$-0.3843x + 0.6717$	0.7919	-0.3843
15	$-0.393x + 0.6923$	0.7534	-0.393
16	$-0.4801x + 0.795$	0.8638	-0.4801

39	$-0.3525x + 0.6202$	0.7977	-0.3525
40	$-0.4089x + 0.7255$	0.795	-0.4089
41	$-0.5058x + 0.8219$	0.8305	-0.5058
42	$-0.4303x + 0.7947$	0.839	-0.4303
43	$-0.5716x + 1.0711$	0.8343	-0.5716
44	$-0.5413x + 1.0708$	0.8257	-0.5413
45	$-0.5494x + 0.8683$	0.8622	-0.5494
46	$-0.5261x + 0.911$	0.8735	-0.5261
47	$-0.4014x + 0.7041$	0.7682	-0.4014
48	$-0.3863x + 0.661$	0.7526	-0.3863
49	$-0.377x + 0.6075$	0.7697	-0.377
50	$-0.3782x + 0.6113$	0.7887	-0.3782
51	$-0.2662x + 0.4488$	0.7251	-0.2662
52	$-0.4295x + 0.7628$	0.8194	-0.4295
53	$-0.4013x + 0.674$	0.7938	-0.4013
54	$-0.4294x + 0.761$	0.8497	-0.4294
55	$-0.4041x + 0.7241$	0.7952	-0.4041
56	$-0.4108x + 0.7338$	0.7805	-0.4108
57	$-0.3645x + 0.6219$	0.7727	-0.3645
58	$-0.5261x + 0.9381$	0.8856	-0.5261
59	$-0.4549x + 0.803$	0.8102	-0.4549
60	$-0.4842x + 0.8453$	0.8191	-0.4842
61	$-0.5081x + 0.8199$	0.8706	-0.5081

continued

Table 13.3 (continued) The Zipfian Distribution (Logarithmic Scale) of Summary Cover and Its Peers That Contain No Hidden Data

	PEER SUMMARIES				SUMMARY COVERS		
TEXT #	EQUATION	R^2	SLOPE($-a$)	COVER #	EQUATION	R^2	SLOPE($-a$)
62	$-0.5584x + 0.955$	0.8812	−0.5584				
63	$-0.3941x + 0.6544$	0.8249	−0.3941				
64	$-0.5111x + 0.8281$	0.8666	−0.5111				
65	$-0.5179x + 0.8442$	0.8115	−0.5179	17	$-0.4789x + 0.7794$	0.7917	−0.4789
66	$-0.5185x + 0.8675$	0.8464	−0.5185				
67	$-0.3852x + 0.624$	0.715	−0.3852				
68	$-0.429x + 0.7101$	0.7742	−0.429				
69	$-0.3745x + 0.617$	0.7545	−0.3745	18	$-0.396x + 0.6693$	0.8205	−0.396
70	$-0.4025x + 0.7021$	0.7049	−0.4025				
71	$-0.2527x + 0.4301$	0.6293	−0.2527				
72	$-0.4191x + 0.7456$	0.7672	−0.4191				
73	$-0.3556x + 0.6059$	0.798	−0.3556	19	$-0.3832x + 0.6863$	0.8182	−0.3832
74	$-0.3913x + 0.6791$	0.8204	−0.3913				
75	$-0.3236x + 0.5741$	0.7363	−0.3236				
76	$-0.3315x + 0.5791$	0.712	−0.3315				
77	$-0.4635x + 0.7874$	0.813	−0.4635	20	$-0.417x + 0.6999$	0.7992	−0.417

	Equation	R^2	Slope
78	$-0.3592x + 0.6174$	0.7976	-0.3592
79	$-0.462x + 0.763$	0.7798	-0.462
80	$-0.5181x + 0.8719$	0.7997	-0.5181
81	$-0.4961x + 0.7971$	0.8834	-0.4961
82	$-0.4878x + 0.8716$	0.8555	-0.4878
83	$-0.4386x + 0.777$	0.832	-0.4386
84	$-0.4688x + 0.8389$	0.8079	-0.4688
85	$-0.3971x + 0.626$	0.7874	-0.3971
86	$-0.4612x + 0.8344$	0.8362	-0.4612
87	$-0.4459x + 0.8148$	0.8198	-0.4459
88	$-0.4821x + 0.8897$	0.8082	-0.4821
89	$-0.6238x + 1.077$	0.9104	-0.6238
90	$-0.5642x + 1.0523$	0.8867	-0.5642
91	$-0.597x + 1.1247$	0.8954	-0.597
92	$-0.4999x + 0.9183$	0.8509	-0.4999
Average			-0.44372

	Equation	R^2	Slope
21	$-0.5204x + 0.8657$	0.8581	-0.5204
22	$-0.4953x + 0.8871$	0.8269	-0.4953
23	$-0.5599x + 1.0233$	0.8737	-0.5599
Average			-0.44159

Note: The equation is a linear curve fitting the results. R^2 is the squared error.

13.4.2 Letter Frequency Distribution

Human language can be defined as a set of characters. In modern languages, this set of characters represents the letters of a particular alphabet. Generally, in any language letters have different frequencies of usage. The following experiment has examined this phenomena, opting to identify distinct patterns that characterize text from different domains.

Experiment #4: Since Nostega is based on a DSS text, the objective of this experiment is to study the usage frequency of the various letters in the DSS text. Therefore, Experiment #4 examines the Letter Frequency Distribution (LFD) signature of the following English language documents:

1. General text representing a huge collection of different DSS texts. The document used is the entire text of the Graduate Catalog 2005–2006 University Of Florida [96], which contains about 1.5 million letters (exactly 1,482,338 letters).
2. The common letter frequency distribution [97,98].
3. Text of a broad domain about computer security, from [99], which contains subdomains such as authentication, cryptography, and key management. The examined text contains 44,232 letters.
4. Texts of three different domain-specific subjects:
   a. The first DSS text used is about the criminal law, collected from [100], which contains 13,438 letters.
   b. The second DSS text used is about queuing systems and is collected from an article [101] that contains 49,034 letters.
   c. Finally, the third DSS text used is from the Zoology domain (Zoology Postgraduate Handbook) from [102] that contains 40,208 letters.

Observation   It is observed in this experiment that in the English language the letters "E," "T," and "A" occur the most-frequently. "J," "Q," and "Z" occur least-frequently as shown in Figures 13.2, 13.3, and 13.4. This has also been confirmed by all other LFD figures in this section. However, in some domain-specific subjects the letters "J," "Q," and "Z" have an uncommonly high frequency. The following

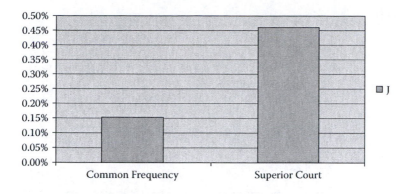

Figure 13.2   The letter frequency distribution (LFD) of the letter "J" in the superior court materials as the domain-specific subject [100] against the assumed common letter frequency distribution [98]. As shown in the figure, the letter "J" is used frequently in the domain-specific subject of superior court, far more than in the assumed common letter frequency distribution.

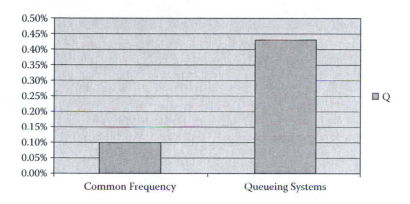

Figure 13.3   The letter frequency distribution (LFD) of the letter "Q" in queuing systems as the domain-specific subject [101] against the assumed common letter frequency distribution [98]. As shown in the figure, the letter "Q" is used frequently in the domain-specific subject of queuing systems, more often than in the assumed common letter frequency distribution.

words "judgment." "jurisdiction," "injured," "injuries," "judicial," "jury," and "subject" are used frequently in the domain-specific subjects of criminal law or court records, which gives "J" an uncommonly high frequency. Similarly, the letter "Q" in the domain-specific subject of a queuing system (in the telecommunications field) and the letter Z in domain-specific subjects such as Zoology have uncommonly high frequencies. Figures 13.2, 13.3, and 13.4 show the frequency of letters "J," "Q," and "Z" in these domains compared to the common relative frequency distribution in common English usage [97–99].

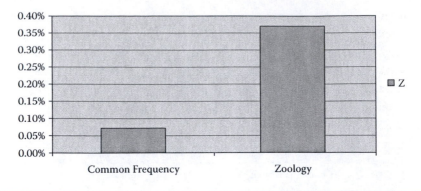

Figure 13.4   Illustrates the letter frequency distribution (LFD) of the letter "Z" in Zoology as the domain-specific subject [102] against the assumed common letter frequency distribution [98]. As shown in the figure, the letter "Z" is used frequently in the domain-specific subject of Zoology, far more than in the assumed common letter frequency distribution.

Result Analysis   The following discussion reflects on the above observations and analyzes the properties of an LFD as it relates to Nostega. Generally, the letters of any language build a word, words build a sentence, and sentences build speech or text. A letter can be repeated more than once in the same word and the same letter can be repeated numerous times in different words. Due to this fact, letter frequency is totally different from word frequency and, most likely, the letter frequency will always be balanced in the sense that the letter frequency will obey the characteristics of the letter frequency-plot-graph, as shown in Figures 13.5, 13.6, and 13.7. This is true regardless of whether it is a single or multiple DSS text.

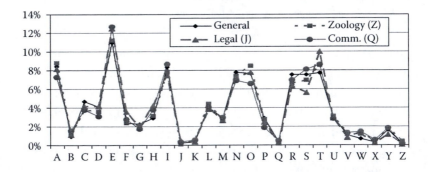

Figure 13.5   Distribution of letter usage in general and domain-specific literature [96].

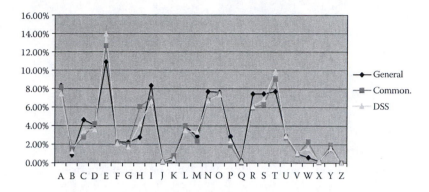

Figure 13.6 The letter frequency distribution (LFD) of three different sets of data. The first set represents multidomain-specific subjects [96], which contains around 1.5 million letters. The second set represents a wide domain-specific subject about computer security [99]. The third set represents the assumed common letter frequency [98]. The letter frequency distributions of three different sets of data are different but roughly obey the characteristics of the letter frequency-distribution-plot-graph of each other. In other words, the peaks and valleys of each plot of the LFD closely match each other. These three different sets of data are authenticated data and not used for concealing a message.

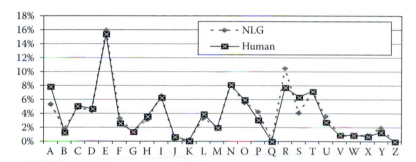

Figure 13.7 Illustrates the letter frequency distribution (LFD) of two different sets of data. The first set represents the average of the letter frequency distribution of text that is generated by an NLG template-based for DSS/CPI reports. The second set represents the average of the letter frequency distribution of the DSS/CPI generated by a human. The letter frequency distributions of two different sets of data are different but roughly resemble the characteristics of the letter frequency distribution-plot-graph of each other. In other words, the peaks and valleys of each plot of the LFD closely match each other.

To emphasize, the chances that a letter will occur as follows:

1. A single letter can occur alone in any language because of the linguistic rules, which is the grammar of the language. For example, in the English language the letter "A" can occur alone in a sentence.

2. A single letter can occur alone in any language because of a domain-specific subject such as math. Letters such as "X," "Y," or "Z" can occur alone in math, but not as a word.

3. A particular letter can occur in a word once.

4. A particular letter can occur in a word more than once. For example, the word "consists" contains the letter "S" three times.

5. A particular letter can occur numerous times in different words. For example, the letter "I" is repeated in the following words "university," "item," and "injury."

6. A set of entirely different letters can occur in different words. For example, all the letters in the word "consists" can be repeated in a different word such as the word "contains."

7. The letters that are commonly the least frequently used such as "J," "Q," and "Z" can be found in some domain-specific subjects with an uncommonly high frequency. However, in general cases, these letters are used in words, and when a particular word is frequently used its letters inherit the frequency as well as the word itself. For example, the following words "judgment," "jurisdiction," "injured," "injuries," "judicial," "jury," and "subject" are used frequently in domain-specific subjects of criminal law or court records, which give "J"s an uncommonly high frequency. Similarly, the letter "Q" in the domain-specific subject of queuing systems (in the telecommunications field) and the letter "Z" in some domain-specific subjects such as Zoology have an uncommonly high frequency. Moreover, these letters hold an uncommonly high frequency because these letters occurred in words that are frequently used in some domain-specific subjects. In detail, when the words that contain the letters "J," "Q," and "Z" are frequently used, all of the letters in these words inherit the high frequency, as well as the words themselves. In other words, when the words that contain the letters "J," "Q," and "Z" are frequently used, not only the letters "J," "Q," and "Z" gain high frequency, but also all the letters in the word gain that frequency. As observed by the experimental results, the following letters:

a. The letters that are the most frequently occurring letters
b. The letters that are the medium frequently occurring letters
c. The letters that are the least frequently occurring letters will remain relatively the same and will have the characteristics of the letter frequency of each other regardless of whether it is a different domain-specific subject or different multidomain-specific subjects, as shown in Figures 13.5, 13.6, 13.7, 13.8, and 13.9.

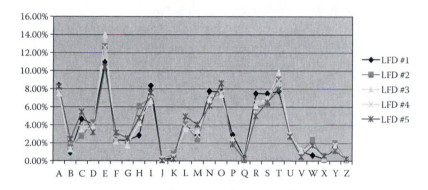

Figure 13.8   The letter frequency distribution (LFD) of LFD # 1, 2, 3, 4, and 5.

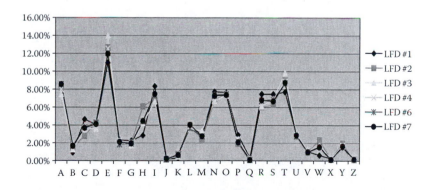

Figure 13.9   The letter frequency distribution (LFD) of LFD # 1, 2, 3, 4, 6, and 7.

Experiment #5:   The aim of Experiment #5 is to inspect the LFD of Edustega covers. Therefore, this experiment investigates the following:

1. Educational documents generated by auto-exam [69,70] that contain no hidden data. Generally, the size of these texts is about 10 questions each.
2. Edustega covers. The size of this edu-cover is similar to the previous one.
3. LFD of the original text before hiding data (the peers of edu-covers).
4. LFD #1 of a text [96] that contains about 1.5 million letters (exactly 1,482,338 letters). This is a general text representing a huge collection of different DSS texts. It is the Graduate Catalog 2005-2006 University Of Florida [96].
5. LFD # 2 is the common letter frequency distribution [97–99].
6. LFD #3 of text that represents a wide domain-specific subject about computer security, from [99], which contains sub domains such authentication, cryptography, key management, etc. This text contains 44,232 letters.
7. LFD # 4 is the average of LFD #1, 2, and 3.
8. LFD #5 is the average of Edustega's LFD, which retains the values of the original.

The following observations can be made about the results of Experiment #5, shown in Table 13.4:

1. LFD for both edu-cover and its original text before hiding data are exactly same and therefore LFD curves will be same for both.
2. LFD #1, 2, 3, 4, and 5 fluctuate; however, they have roughly the same characteristics of the letter frequency-distribution of each other as concluded by Experiment # 4 and also as shown in Figure 13.8.

Therefore, it is concluded based on the experimental results, as shown in this section, that edu-cover is capable of surviving an examination.

Table 13.4 The Letter Frequency Distribution (LFD) Values of Both Edu-Cover and Its Original Text That Contain No Hidden Data

LETTER	LFD #1	LFD #2	LFD #3	LFD #4	LFD #5
A	8.37%	8.17%	7.49%	8.01%	8.21%
B	0.92%	1.49%	1.30%	1.24%	2.39%
C	4.65%	2.78%	3.54%	3.66%	5.46%
D	4.08%	4.25%	3.62%	3.98%	3.17%
E	10.94%	12.70%	14.00%	12.55%	10.39%
F	2.33%	2.23%	2.18%	2.25%	3.11%
G	2.25%	2.02%	1.74%	2.00%	2.52%
H	2.84%	6.09%	4.23%	4.39%	4.78%
I	8.34%	6.97%	6.65%	7.32%	7.57%
J	0.21%	0.15%	0.27%	0.21%	0.04%
K	0.32%	0.77%	0.47%	0.52%	0.22%
L	3.98%	4.03%	3.57%	3.86%	4.95%
M	2.87%	2.41%	3.39%	2.89%	4.02%
N	7.74%	6.75%	6.74%	7.08%	6.15%
O	7.65%	7.51%	7.37%	7.51%	8.61%

continued

Table 13.4 (continued)   The Letter Frequency Distribution (LFD) Values of Both Edu-Cover and Its Original Text That Contain No Hidden Data

LETTER	LFD # 1	LFD # 2	LFD # 3	LFD # 4	LFD #5
P	2.89%	1.93%	2.43%	2.42%	1.86%
Q	0.33%	0.10%	0.26%	0.23%	0.24%
R	7.49%	5.99%	6.14%	6.54%	4.99%
S	7.48%	6.33%	6.95%	6.92%	6.53%
T	7.73%	9.06%	9.85%	8.88%	7.94%
U	2.99%	2.76%	3.00%	2.92%	2.73%
V	1.05%	0.98%	1.16%	1.06%	0.46%
W	0.63%	2.36%	1.69%	1.56%	1.73%
X	0.25%	0.15%	0.28%	0.23%	0.59%
Y	1.56%	1.97%	1.64%	1.72%	1.11%
Z	0.11%	0.07%	0.04%	0.07%	0.22%
Total	100%	100%	100%	100%	100%

LFD OF EDU-COVER # AND ITS ORIGINAL TEXT NUMBER THAT CONTAIN NO HIDDEN DATA

1	2	3	4	5	6	7	8	9	10	11	12
7.65%	7.32%	7.76%	8.66%	7.98%	7.98%	8.73%	8.97%	9.00%	8.74%	8.04%	8.63%
2.02%	2.53%	2.56%	2.84%	2.55%	2.50%	1.95%	2.62%	3.00%	2.26%	2.18%	2.21%
4.27%	5.23%	4.56%	7.61%	6.91%	6.00%	5.63%	4.99%	4.81%	5.30%	4.17%	5.28%
3.04%	2.79%	2.78%	4.03%	2.45%	3.36%	2.41%	3.55%	3.08%	4.03%	2.78%	2.81%
12.15%	11.42%	9.68%	10.45%	10.64%	9.43%	11.71%	10.58%	12.00%	12.38%	12.21%	10.57%
2.92%	2.62%	2.70%	4.33%	3.40%	3.43%	2.87%	3.30%	1.97%	3.05%	2.78%	2.54%
3.15%	2.88%	2.14%	0.90%	1.49%	2.77%	1.84%	3.64%	2.76%	1.96%	2.68%	4.28%
4.61%	4.18%	4.06%	5.67%	5.74%	5.67%	4.94%	4.06%	3.71%	4.13%	5.16%	3.75%
7.99%	7.67%	6.69%	6.27%	7.98%	7.45%	7.69%	7.36%	7.42%	7.66%	7.35%	7.42%
0.00%	0.17%	0.00%	0.00%	0.00%	0.00%	0.00%	0.00%	0.00%	0.00%	0.00%	0.13%
0.56%	0.09%	0.14%	0.00%	0.00%	0.40%	0.46%	0.34%	0.32%	0.39%	0.30%	0.13%
3.60%	5.06%	2.85%	5.22%	5.21%	4.61%	6.43%	5.08%	5.84%	5.21%	5.36%	4.82%
4.27%	4.27%	3.06%	3.43%	2.66%	5.01%	3.79%	4.65%	4.42%	3.44%	4.27%	4.62%

continued

Table 13.4 (continued)   The Letter Frequency Distribution (LFD) Values of Both Edu-Cover and Its Original Text That Contain No Hidden Data

					LFD OF EDU-COVER # AND ITS ORIGINAL TEXT NUMBER THAT CONTAIN NO HIDDEN DATA						
1	2	3	4	5	6	7	8	9	10	11	12
6.75%	5.75%	8.68%	5.22%	8.19%	4.55%	6.54%	6.26%	6.47%	5.70%	6.85%	6.29%
6.30%	7.93%	10.04%	10.00%	9.89%	9.36%	7.69%	7.45%	6.63%	7.27%	6.95%	8.36%
1.57%	2.53%	2.35%	1.79%	1.81%	2.31%	1.72%	1.18%	0.71%	1.96%	1.69%	1.94%
0.11%	0.17%	0.00%	0.00%	0.64%	0.07%	0.11%	0.17%	0.47%	0.39%	0.30%	0.07%
4.84%	4.53%	5.62%	6.42%	3.40%	4.61%	5.28%	5.50%	4.66%	5.30%	5.06%	4.01%
8.21%	7.24%	7.54%	6.27%	5.32%	5.60%	5.86%	5.33%	6.79%	5.89%	6.16%	6.22%
9.56%	8.81%	9.47%	5.97%	8.19%	6.92%	7.58%	8.38%	8.60%	8.45%	7.85%	8.56%
2.47%	3.05%	3.63%	2.54%	2.55%	2.83%	2.18%	2.28%	2.53%	1.87%	2.88%	2.88%
0.45%	0.52%	0.28%	0.60%	0.32%	0.46%	1.15%	0.68%	0.32%	0.39%	0.70%	0.40%
1.80%	1.48%	1.57%	1.34%	1.60%	2.24%	1.61%	1.86%	1.89%	1.67%	2.38%	1.67%
0.90%	0.17%	1.07%	0.00%	0.21%	1.05%	0.69%	1.18%	1.26%	1.08%	0.70%	0.60%
0.79%	1.48%	0.78%	0.45%	0.53%	1.25%	1.03%	0.51%	1.03%	1.38%	0.99%	1.61%
0.00%	0.09%	0.00%	0.00%	0.32%	0.13%	0.11%	0.08%	0.32%	0.10%	0.20%	0.20%
100%	100%	100%	100%	100%	100%	100%	100%	100%	100%	100%	100%

LETTER	13	14	15	16	17	18	19	20	21	22	23
A	8.75%	6.98%	9.65%	8.43%	8.12%	8.43%	8.12%	6.86%	8.35%	7.56%	8.20%
B	1.98%	2.54%	2.04%	1.87%	1.97%	1.87%	1.97%	2.55%	2.22%	2.52%	4.21%
C	4.60%	5.14%	4.25%	5.04%	4.68%	5.04%	4.68%	4.05%	8.67%	6.10%	8.65%
D	3.70%	2.28%	3.89%	3.39%	3.12%	3.39%	3.12%	2.46%	4.12%	3.05%	3.33%
E	9.71%	10.91%	7.35%	9.37%	10.99%	9.37%	10.99%	11.43%	7.93%	10.08%	7.76%
F	2.43%	2.79%	3.10%	2.95%	2.13%	2.95%	2.13%	3.17%	5.29%	4.51%	4.21%
G	3.26%	3.23%	2.74%	4.03%	2.46%	4.03%	2.46%	1.41%	1.27%	1.46%	1.11%
H	4.53%	4.25%	4.96%	5.26%	3.77%	5.26%	3.77%	4.40%	5.07%	5.44%	7.54%
I	8.68%	9.13%	9.03%	8.86%	8.20%	8.86%	8.20%	8.18%	5.60%	6.10%	4.21%
J	0.13%	0.00%	0.00%	0.14%	0.08%	0.14%	0.08%	0.00%	0.00%	0.00%	0.00%
K	0.13%	0.13%	0.18%	0.36%	0.00%	0.36%	0.00%	0.09%	0.63%	0.00%	0.00%
L	4.47%	4.19%	7.43%	5.19%	5.09%	5.19%	5.09%	3.61%	5.18%	5.17%	3.99%

continued

Table 13.4 (continued) The Letter Frequency Distribution (LFD) Values of Both Edu-Cover and Its Original Text That Contain No Hidden Data

| | LFD OF EDU-COVER # AND ITS ORIGINAL TEXT NUMBER THAT CONTAIN NO HIDDEN DATA | | | | | | | | | | |
LETTER	13	14	15	16	17	18	19	20	21	22	23
M	4.02%	4.25%	4.16%	3.89%	4.68%	3.89%	4.68%	3.87%	3.28%	4.64%	3.33%
N	6.64%	6.40%	4.60%	5.98%	5.25%	5.98%	5.25%	8.53%	6.13%	4.91%	4.43%
O	8.30%	7.61%	8.32%	7.71%	8.45%	7.71%	8.45%	9.67%	10.57%	10.08%	13.30%
P	1.66%	1.90%	1.86%	1.59%	1.97%	1.59%	1.97%	2.02%	1.06%	1.46%	4.21%
Q	0.19%	0.06%	1.42%	0.22%	0.41%	0.22%	0.41%	0.09%	0.00%	0.00%	0.00%
R	3.96%	5.14%	3.36%	3.46%	5.50%	3.46%	5.50%	5.45%	6.13%	7.16%	6.43%
S	7.28%	6.79%	6.73%	8.00%	7.14%	8.00%	7.14%	7.04%	5.60%	6.63%	3.33%
T	8.75%	9.58%	7.61%	6.84%	9.35%	6.84%	9.35%	8.62%	5.39%	6.23%	5.76%
U	3.00%	2.92%	3.36%	2.23%	3.12%	2.23%	3.12%	2.55%	3.07%	3.05%	2.44%
V	0.32%	0.13%	0.62%	0.50%	0.41%	0.50%	0.41%	0.88%	0.11%	0.40%	0.00%
W	2.11%	1.59%	1.50%	2.02%	1.39%	2.02%	1.39%	1.41%	1.80%	1.46%	2.00%
X	0.32%	0.51%	0.35%	1.01%	0.25%	1.01%	0.25%	0.18%	0.32%	0.27%	0.22%
Y	1.02%	1.52%	1.50%	1.59%	1.31%	1.59%	1.31%	1.23%	0.74%	0.66%	1.33%
Z	0.06%	0.06%	0.00%	0.07%	0.16%	0.07%	0.16%	0.26%	1.48%	1.06%	0.00%
Total	100%	100%	100%	100%	100%	100%	100%	100%	100%	100%	100%

Note: The LFD values are exactly the same for both edu-cover and its original text because the LFD values are the same.

Experiment #6:   The objective of Experiment #6 is to investigate the LFD signature of Sumstega cover. Therefore, this experiment investigates the following:

1. A total of 92 summaries generated by four automatic-summarizers: AutoSummarize [82], SweSum [83], Automatic Text Summarizer [87], and Auto Summarizer [93]. The original texts used are collected from online news websites such as *TIME* Magazine [94] and *The New York Times* [95]. The summaries are short paragraphs, which range roughly from four to six sentences.
2. A total of 23 Sumstega covers. The size of summary cover is similar to the previous one.
3. LFD # 1 is of a text [96] that contains about 1.5 million letters (exactly 1,482,338 letters). This is a general text representing a huge collection of different DSS texts. It is the Graduate Catalog 2005-2006 University Of Florida [96].
4. LFD # 2 is the common letter frequency distribution [97–99].
5. LFD # 3 is of text that represents a wide domain-specific subject about computer security, from [99]. It contains sub domains such authentication, cryptography, and key management. This text contains 44,232 letters.
6. LFD # 4 is the average of LFD # 1, 2, and 3.
7. LFD #6 is the average of the summary cover's LFD (Sumstega's LFD).
8. LFD # 7 is the average of the peer summaries' LFD.

It is observed, as shown in Table 13.5, that the LFD # 1, 2, 3, 4, 6, and 7 are different and this is the case for any text regardless of whether or not a message is hidden. However, the texts have roughly the same characteristics as the letter frequency distribution of each other, as confirmed also by Experiment #4. In other words, the peaks and valleys of each plot of the LFD closely match each other. Furthermore, the curves of both LFD #6 (the average of summary-cover's LFD) and LFD #7 (the average of peer summaries' LFD), as shown in Figures 13.9 and 13.10, are almost the same. Therefore, it is observed based on the experimental results, as shown in this section, that summary cover can easily pass an attack.

Table 13.5   The Letter Frequency Distribution (LFD) of the Average Values of Summary Cover (LFD # 6) and Its Peer Summaries (LFD # 7) That Contain No Hidden Data

Letter	LFD # 1	LFD # 2	LFD # 3	LFD # 4	LFD # 6	LFD # 7
A	8.37%	8.17%	7.49%	8.01%	8.58%	8.56%
B	0.92%	1.49%	1.30%	1.24%	1.67%	1.65%
C	4.65%	2.78%	3.54%	3.66%	3.76%	3.68%
D	4.08%	4.25%	3.62%	3.98%	4.29%	4.12%
E	10.94%	12.70%	14.00%	12.55%	12.05%	11.95%
F	2.33%	2.23%	2.18%	2.25%	1.85%	2.11%
G	2.25%	2.02%	1.74%	2.00%	1.95%	1.95%
H	2.84%	6.09%	4.23%	4.39%	4.42%	4.45%
I	8.34%	6.97%	6.65%	7.32%	7.32%	7.48%
J	0.21%	0.15%	0.27%	0.21%	0.23%	0.24%
K	0.32%	0.77%	0.47%	0.52%	0.67%	0.65%
L	3.98%	4.03%	3.57%	3.86%	3.64%	4.03%
M	2.87%	2.41%	3.39%	2.89%	2.75%	2.76%
N	7.74%	6.75%	6.74%	7.08%	7.38%	7.27%
O	7.65%	7.51%	7.37%	7.51%	7.48%	7.38%
P	2.89%	1.93%	2.43%	2.42%	2.17%	2.07%
Q	0.33%	0.10%	0.26%	0.23%	0.15%	0.10%
R	7.49%	5.99%	6.14%	6.54%	6.76%	6.81%
S	7.48%	6.33%	6.95%	6.92%	6.87%	6.68%
T	7.73%	9.06%	9.85%	8.88%	8.70%	8.75%
U	2.99%	2.76%	3.00%	2.92%	2.77%	2.86%
V	1.05%	0.98%	1.16%	1.06%	1.04%	0.97%
W	0.63%	2.36%	1.69%	1.56%	1.61%	1.53%
X	0.25%	0.15%	0.28%	0.23%	0.17%	0.13%
Y	1.56%	1.97%	1.64%	1.72%	1.56%	1.63%
Z	0.11%	0.07%	0.04%	0.07%	0.18%	0.16%
Total	100%	100%	100%	100%	100%	100%

Note: In addition, LFD # 1 is of a text [96] that contains about 1.5 million letters (exactly 1,482,338 letters), LFD # 2 is the common letter frequency distribution [98], LFD # 3 is of a wide domain-specific subject about computer security [99], and LFD # 4 is the average of LFD # 1, 2, and 3.

13.4.3 Kullback–Leibler Divergence

In probability theory and information theory, the Kullback–Leibler Divergence (KLD) [103–106] is considered a non-commutative measure. It measures the difference between two probability distributions P and Q; where P represents the true distribution of data, observations, or a precise calculated theoretical distribution, and Q represents

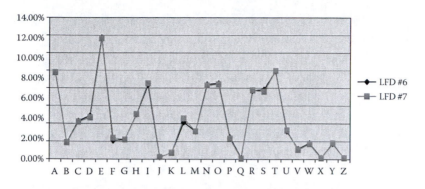

Figure 13.10   The letter frequency distribution (LFD) of LFD # 6 and 7.

a theory, model, approximation of *P*, or description. Therefore, KLD is employed in this book in order to compare the similarities of Nostega-based covers to normal text with respect to WFD and LFD. In this book, the KLD values may be considered a divergence between Nostega-based cover and other normal text.

To illustrate the interpretation of the KLD values, consider the following:

1. Zero KLD value means no divergence between a cover and its comparable normal text.
2. Small KLD value which cannot be considered as evidence of hidden data.
3. Large KLD value, which definitely raises suspicion.

For probability distributions *P* and *Q* of a discrete random variable the measure of K–L divergence of *Q* from *P* is defined to be

$$D_{KL}\left(P\|Q\right) = \sum_{i} P(i)\log\frac{P(i)}{Q(i)}$$

Experiment #7:   The aim of this experiment is to investigate the KLD between Edustega Covers and their peer texts. Therefore, Experiment #7 investigates the following:

1. Educational documents generated by auto-exam [69,70] that contain no hidden data. Generally, the size of the considered text is about 10 questions each.
2. Edustega covers. The size of this edu-cover is similar to the above one.

The Experimental Result Retain Zero KLD: The experimental results for all of these samples retain zero KLD on letter frequency distribution (LFD) and word letter frequency distribution (WFD). As shown in Table 13.2 (results of Experiment #2) and Table 13.4 (results of Experiment #5), the LFD and WFD for edu-covers versus the original text (the text that contains no hidden data) retain the same values; therefore, the KLD value is zero. This result is expected for both LFD and WFD since $D_{KL}(P||Q)$ zero if, and only if, $P = Q$ [103].

Experiment #8: The objective of Experiment #8 is to inspect KLD of WFD between Sumstega covers and their peer summaries. These KLDs are measured from their original texts, which are long documents before summarization.

Therefore, this experiment investigates the following:

1. A total of 92 summaries generated by four automatic-summarizers: AutoSummarize [82], SweSum [83], Automatic Text Summarizer [87], and Auto Summarizer [93]. The original texts used are collected from online news websites such as *TIME* Magazine [94] and *The New York Times* [95]. The summaries are composed of short paragraphs, which range roughly from four to six sentences.
2. A total of 23 Sumstega covers. The size of the summary cover is similar to the previous one.

The KLD's values are slightly different from each other and that is the case for any text regardless of whether or not a message is hidden within it. However, the KLD values of Sumstega covers are very similar to their peers, i.e., summaries that are generated by the four summarizers and that do not conceal data. Furthermore, the average of Sumstega's KLD, as shown in Table 13.6, is also very similar to the peers' average. In addition, the average of Sumstega's KLD is almost the same as the average of all peers, as shown in Table 13.6. It can be concluded based on the experimental results, as shown in this section and in Table 13.6, that summary cover is capable of averting such an attack.

Experiment #9: The objective of Experiment #9 is to inspect KLD of LFD between Sumstega covers and normal texts. Therefore, this experiment investigates the following:

Table 13.6 The KLDs on a WFD Level of Summary Covers and Peer Summaries That Contain No Hidden Data

INDEX	SUMSTEGA	SUMMARIZER #1	SUMMARIZER #2	SUMMARIZER #3	SUMMARIZER #4
1	0.354813878	0.377236243	0.341241948	0.361625134	0.395400394
2	0.65500777	0.699725911	0.665670103	0.497414631	0.60979046
3	0.437245498	0.517721119	0.385697716	0.405743394	0.390917031
4	0.396762057	0.396762057	0.389556202	0.360655445	0.349421236
5	0.505885726	0.534796306	0.380406385	0.231036797	0.38607999
6	0.450416421	0.409007628	0.387212822	0.41484822	0.456812196
7	0.338841051	0.453383203	0.391478281	0.385688121	0.209897585
8	0.310035332	0.31464009	0.262201274	0.312631204	0.856254701
9	0.496988813	0.448013283	0.580902899	0.630619242	0.526176392
10	0.413885375	0.459266859	0.464664119	0.468291529	0.434965616
11	0.432936903	0.441540021	0.3621624	0.30101569	0.29887798
12	0.45256566	0.518643007	0.444708352	0.480797538	0.492002612
13	0.868969817	0.691274912	0.77407164	0.842281494	0.744890203
14	0.371384462	0.414050667	0.350728131	0.337863603	0.35329571
15	0.320155145	0.351963381	0.306328524	0.316486447	0.367398389
16	0.48159655	0.522278399	0.446848235	0.579738782	0.509522925
17	0.28185726	0.305925769	0.28317241	0.356648517	0.307424174
18	0.64616599	0.703542061	0.619601434	0.728995475	0.522518272
19	0.365731318	0.464547517	0.400115936	0.374782073	0.399403911
20	0.522579408	0.646628326	0.565459411	0.5672476	0.519233893
21	0.304670342	0.334198172	0.235803956	0.24410068	0.244856277
22	0.369642927	0.563887987	0.373033843	0.334339968	0.354233064
23	0.21565294	0.307793824	0.183901945	0.180278434	0.216094016
Average	0.4345126	0.47290551	0.4171725	0.42231	0.4324116
Average of Sumstega versus average of all peers				0.434512637	0.43619991

Note: These KLDs were measured from their original texts (the long documents before summarization).

1. A total of 92 summaries generated by four automatic-summarizers: AutoSummarize [82], SweSum [83], Automatic Text Summarizer [93], and Auto Summarizer [91]. The original texts used are collected from online news websites such as *TIME* Magazine [94] and *The New York Times* [95]. The summaries are composed of short paragraphs, which range roughly from four to six sentences.
2. A total of 23 Sumstega Covers. The size of summary cover is similar to the previous one.

3. A text [96] that contains about 1.5 million letters (exactly 1,482,338 letters). This is a general text that represents a huge collection of different DSS text. It is the Graduate Catalog 2005-2006 University Of Florida [96].

4. The common letter frequency distribution [97–99].

5. A text that represents a wide domain-specific subject about computer security, from [99], which contains sub domains such authentication, cryptography, key management, etc. This text contains 44,232 letters.

The conclusion of Experiment #9 is that all KLD values and their averages are very similar, as shown in Tables 13.7, 13.8, 13.9, and 13.10. Therefore, it is obvious that Nostega-based Covers are capable of averting an attack.

13.5 Conclusion

This chapter shows the resilience of the Nostega paradigm. Nostega promotes camouflaging both a message and its transmittal. Nostega neither hides data in a noise (errors) nor produces noise rendering the generated cover noiseless. Instead, it conceals messages in the form of noiseless data in the generated cover using either unaltered authenticated data or untraceable data, thus avoiding a wide variety of attacks. The concealment process of Nostega has no effect on the linguistics of the generated cover if the text is used as a steganographic carrier rendering such text cover legitimate. Unlike other approaches such as translation-based, Nostega can be applied to all languages. For steganographic carriers, Nostega uses materials such as graphs, texts, and games, which have plenty of room for concealing data. Yet, Nostega is a public paradigm, which implies that it is resilient even when an adversary is well familiar with this new paradigm. As observed, the Nostega-based system is capable of fooling both machine and human examinations.

Table 13.7 The KLDs on an LFD Level of Summary Covers and Peer Summaries That Contain No Hidden Data

		KLD			
INDEX	SUMSTEGA	SUMMARIZER #1	SUMMARIZER #2	SUMMARIZER #3	SUMMARIZER #4
1	0.007	0.011	0.005	0.007	0.009
2	0.00889	0.01562	0.0099	0.01169	0.0068
3	0.01212	0.01591	0.00832	0.00664	0.00392
4	0.00471	0.00706	0.00441	0.00536	0.00334
5	0.00865	0.01242	0.01064	0.0087	0.0086
6	0.00932	0.00972	0.00698	0.0087	0.0081
7	0.0055	0.00715	0.0111	0.00567	0.00363
8	0.0083	0.00828	0.00601	0.00558	0.00602
9	0.01363	0.01661	0.00868	0.02722	0.01368
10	0.00509	0.00654	0.01209	0.01008	0.00471
11	0.00864	0.01446	0.00805	0.00595	0.00805
12	0.00936	0.01404	0.01004	0.00998	0.00642
13	0.00769	0.01167	0.01834	0.01608	0.00969
14	0.01482	0.0071	0.00828	0.00784	0.0057
15	0.0046	0.00374	0.00405	0.00594	0.00591
16	0.01553	0.00556	0.00666	0.01265	0.01376
17	0.0057	0.00953	0.00561	0.00703	0.00721
18	0.01064	0.0104	0.01142	0.00928	0.00827
19	0.00307	0.00791	0.00755	0.00534	0.00517
20	0.0087	0.00885	0.00641	0.00858	0.01055
21	0.00701	0.00615	0.00378	0.00496	0.00725
22	0.00579	0.00941	0.00308	0.00334	0.00393
23	0.00325	0.00703	0.00323	0.00422	0.00396
Average	0.008193	0.009833	0.007795	0.008601	0.007111
Average of Sumstega versus average of all peers				0.008193	0.008335

Note: These KLDs were measured from their original texts (the long documents before summarization).

Table 13.8   The KLDs on an LFD Level of Summary Covers and Peer Summaries That Contain No Hidden Data

		KLD			
INDEX	SUMSTEGA	SUMMARIZER #1	SUMMARIZER #2	SUMMARIZER #3	SUMMARIZER #4
1	0.017	0.029	0.017	0.018	0.022
2	0.02851	0.03061	0.03403	0.02293	0.01405
3	0.02302	0.04153	0.02154	0.02696	0.0182
4	0.0263	0.02806	0.03057	0.01834	0.01957
5	0.0261	0.03364	0.01572	0.01862	0.0227
6	0.01744	0.01527	0.02935	0.02182	0.02288
7	0.01807	0.01772	0.02072	0.0152	0.01478
8	0.02425	0.02807	0.02003	0.02038	0.02133
9	0.02395	0.0413	0.02554	0.03304	0.0415
10	0.01762	0.02013	0.02508	0.02129	0.01761
11	0.02887	0.03932	0.03076	0.01518	0.02893
12	0.01496	0.023	0.01943	0.01537	0.01165
13	0.01618	0.01902	0.02847	0.02266	0.01898
14	0.02259	0.01496	0.01955	0.01601	0.01541
15	0.02024	0.02179	0.01639	0.01921	0.02037
16	0.02639	0.0183	0.01933	0.02328	0.04247
17	0.03361	0.03381	0.0244	0.01953	0.03358
18	0.03374	0.02814	0.02972	0.02497	0.03683
19	0.02259	0.03021	0.02967	0.03206	0.03391
20	0.01893	0.02302	0.01812	0.02522	0.03872
21	0.01865	0.01581	0.00975	0.01001	0.01319
22	0.01372	0.01503	0.01095	0.01085	0.00765
23	0.01541	0.02435	0.01366	0.01513	0.01402
Average	0.022091	0.025750	0.022178	0.020247	0.023072
Average of Sumstega versus average of all peers				0.022091	0.022812

Note: These KLDs were measured from a text [96] that contains about 1.5 million letters (exactly 1,482,338 letters).

Table 13.9 The KLDs on an LFD Level of Summary Covers and Peer Summaries That Contain No Hidden Data

		KLD			
INDEX	SUMSTEGA	SUMMARIZER #1	SUMMARIZER #2	SUMMARIZER #3	SUMMARIZER #4
1	0.011	0.019	0.01	0.01	0.012
2	0.01048	0.02426	0.00952	0.0138	0.01191
3	0.0219	0.037	0.01549	0.01725	0.01518
4	0.01507	0.02103	0.01049	0.02161	0.01477
5	0.01981	0.02405	0.01419	0.02409	0.01873
6	0.01852	0.01709	0.01581	0.01353	0.01477
7	0.01775	0.01934	0.02272	0.01826	0.01178
8	0.0191	0.02735	0.02345	0.02194	0.02085
9	0.03005	0.0389	0.03167	0.0438	0.04136
10	0.01513	0.01281	0.02371	0.02095	0.00872
11	0.02649	0.03659	0.01636	0.01345	0.02172
12	0.03016	0.0373	0.03168	0.02588	0.0098
13	0.016	0.01741	0.02918	0.0268	0.01443
14	0.01022	0.01763	0.0144	0.01552	0.01153
15	0.01567	0.01417	0.01349	0.01629	0.01184
16	0.02365	0.01559	0.01037	0.01809	0.0153
17	0.0181	0.02223	0.01541	0.01419	0.01948
18	0.01199	0.01395	0.01564	0.01382	0.01115
19	0.01022	0.01596	0.00986	0.0112	0.0081
20	0.01336	0.01632	0.01332	0.01338	0.01795
21	0.02436	0.02146	0.01802	0.01825	0.02077
22	0.015	0.0232	0.00978	0.01136	0.01338
23	0.01344	0.02006	0.01341	0.01288	0.0113
Average	0.017716	0.022291	0.016868	0.018102	0.015514
Average of Sumstega versus average of all peers				0.017716	0.018180

Note: These KLDs were measured from the common letter frequency distribution [98].

Table 13.10   The KLDs on an LFD Level of Summary Covers and Peer Summaries That Contain No Hidden Data

		KLD			
INDEX	SUMSTEGA	SUMMARIZER #1	SUMMARIZER #2	SUMMARIZER #3	SUMMARIZER #4
1	0.01	0.023	0.009	0.011	0.015
2	0.01243	0.02753	0.01684	0.01894	0.00699
3	0.02352	0.04698	0.01482	0.01915	0.01756
4	0.01717	0.02202	0.01359	0.02021	0.01244
5	0.01904	0.02299	0.01304	0.01863	0.01574
6	0.0187	0.01527	0.01686	0.01756	0.01795
7	0.01521	0.01247	0.01904	0.01557	0.00751
8	0.01755	0.02445	0.01962	0.02035	0.01817
9	0.02541	0.03815	0.02624	0.0366	0.03691
10	0.01315	0.01229	0.02476	0.02183	0.00933
11	0.03024	0.04514	0.02245	0.01564	0.02614
12	0.02044	0.02368	0.02059	0.01956	0.0075
13	0.0138	0.01475	0.02483	0.02342	0.01234
14	0.01286	0.01598	0.01583	0.01185	0.01212
15	0.01608	0.01583	0.01376	0.01869	0.01518
16	0.01895	0.01248	0.01319	0.02225	0.02016
17	0.02213	0.02172	0.01484	0.01448	0.0232
18	0.02016	0.01748	0.02615	0.01484	0.02138
19	0.01286	0.01796	0.01597	0.02019	0.01752
20	0.01535	0.01732	0.01573	0.02266	0.02423
21	0.0194	0.01607	0.01501	0.01321	0.01972
22	0.0112	0.02182	0.00809	0.01064	0.00824
23	0.01458	0.02281	0.01437	0.01286	0.01183
Average	0.017414	0.022088	0.017167	0.018246	0.016383
Average of Sumstega versus Average of all Peers				0.017414	0.018471

Note: These KLDs were measured from a wide domain-specific subject about computer security [99].

14

CONCLUSION AND FUTURE WORK

This chapter concludes the book. It summarizes the contributions, reports on the current status of the work, spells out what remains to be done until the final book defense, and finally highlights directions for future research.

14.1 Contributions

The main contribution of the book is the novel **No**iseless **Stega**nography (Nostega) Paradigm [32,35]. Unlike all other approaches, Nostega neither hides data in a noise nor produces noise rendering the generated cover noiseless. Instead, it camouflages messages in the form of unquestionable data in the generated cover employing either unaltered authenticated data or untraceable data, thus avoiding a wide variety of attacks. The concealment process of Nostega has no effect on the linguistics of the generated cover if text is used as a steganographic carrier, rendering that text cover legitimate. Unlike other approaches such as translation-based, Nostega can be applied to all languages. Nostega is also capable of employing a wide variety of materials and cover-types such as graphs, games, and texts, which have plenty of room for concealing data. Based on this paradigm, several novel methodologies have been developed and validated. The implemented methodologies that are based on the Nostega paradigm are keyless schemes. Yet, Nostega is a public paradigm, which implies that it is resilient even when an adversary is very familiar with this new paradigm.

The following highlights the key features of these presented methodologies:

- *Graph Steganography Methodology (Graphstega):* Graphstega methodology is the science and art of avoiding the arousal of suspicion in covert communications by concealing a message in a novel cover type, namely graph cover [33,107]. It camouflages messages noiselessly as plotted data. Yet, graph covers can be applied to a wide variety of domains such as business, education, and news, rendering it a suitable Nostega-based cover. As such, it makes the investigation and detection of a hidden message infeasible.

- *Chess Steganography Methodology (Chestega):* Chestega exploits popular games such as chess, checkers, crosswords, and dominoes, to embed data in a steganographic game cover [30]. Chestega conceals messages in the related data of games including training documents, game analysis, and news articles by employing intrinsically authenticated or untraceable innocent data in the generated cover, which renders it noiseless. Unlike other approaches, the steganographic communications can be live when sender and recipient are playing or discussing an online-game.

- *Education–Centric Steganography Methodology (Edustega):* Edustega conceals messages in educational documents, primarily by manipulating the questions and answers (e.g., multiple-choice, true-or-false, fill-in-the-space, and matching) of exams, examples, puzzles, and competitions in order to embed data without generating any suspicious patterns [23]. For instance, multiple-choice questions can conceal data in the correct answers (choices) by placing the correct answers (choices) where they can represent a steganographic code of a message, e.g., choices from "A" to "D" can represent binary numbers from "00" to "11." In addition, wrong answers (wrong choices) can also conceal data. While these choices must be wrong, there is no real constraint on embedding data.

- *Summarization-Based Steganography Methodology (Sumstega):* Sumstega takes advantage of the recent advances in automatic summarization techniques to conceal messages in summaries generated by these techniques [23,34]. It pursues the variations among the outputs of auto-summarization techniques to conceal data. Basically, Sumstega manipulates the parameters of automatic summarization tools, e.g., the word frequency weights in the sentence selection, and employs other contemporary techniques such as paraphrasing and reordering to generate summary covers that look legitimate. The popular use of text summaries in business, science, education, and news renders summary an attractive steganographic carrier and averts an adversary's suspicion.

- *Mature Linguistic Steganography Methodology (Matlist):* Matlist employs Natural Language Generation (NLG) and template techniques along with Random Series (RS) values (e.g., binary, decimal, hexadecimal, octal, alphabetic, and alphanumeric values) of a Domain-Specific Subject (DSS) to generate noiseless text cover [27,107]. This type of DSS (e.g., financial, medical, mathematical, scientific, and economical) has plenty of room to conceal data and allows communicating parties to establish a covert channel such as a relationship based on the profession of the communicating parties to transmit a text cover. Matlist embeds data in the form of RS values, functions of RS, related semantics of RS, or a combination of these.

- *Normal Linguistic Steganography Methodology (NORMALS):* NORMALS takes advantage of recent advances in automatic Natural Language Generation (NLG) techniques to generate noiseless (flawless) and legitimate text cover by manipulating the input parameters of the NLG system in order to camouflage data in the generated text [26]. As a result, NORMALS is capable of fooling both human and machine examinations. Unlike Matlist, NORMALS is capable of handling non-random series domains.

- *Email-Header-Based Steganography Methodology (Headstega):* Headstega takes advantage of the frequent exchange of emails by a wide variety of people which generates a high volume of traffic and allows communicating parties to establish a covert channel without creating a suspicious pattern [24]. Headstega camouflages data in email header carriers (e.g., recipient's email addresses, names, and subject fields) in order to achieve the steganographic goal, while the email contents (the body of the email) are completely legitimate and do not conceal data.

- *Automatic Joke Generation Based Steganography (Jokestega):* Who does not joke? The obvious answer is no one. Yet, when someone is joking, anything can be said. This legitimizes the use of joke-based steganography. Jokestega methodology takes advantage of recent advances in Automatic Jokes Generation (AJG) techniques to automate the generation of textual steganographic cover [28]. Since jokes and puns can be retold with totally different vocabularies, while still retaining their identities, Jokestega pursues common variations among jokes to conceal messages and deliver them covertly.

- *List-Based Steganography Methodology (Listega):* The use of textual lists of items, e.g., products, subjects, and books, is widely popular and linguistically legible. Listega takes advantage of textual lists to camouflage data by exploiting itemized data to conceal messages [28]. Simply stated, it encodes a message then assigns it to legitimate items in order to generate a text cover in the form of legitimate list. Listega establishes a covert channel among communicating parties by employing justifiable reasons based on the common practice of using textual lists of items to achieve unsuspicious transmission of generated covers.

- *Notes-Based Steganography Methodology (Notestega):* The wide use of notes in business, science, education, and news renders notes as attractive steganographic carriers, and allows the communicating parties to establish a covert channel that is capable of transmitting messages in an unsuspicious way. Therefore, Notestega takes advantage of the recent advances in automatic note taking techniques to generate a text cover [31]. It pursues variations among both human-notes and the outputs of automatic-note taking techniques to conceal data. Unlike machine translation and automatic summarizers, Notestega can embed nondirectly related elements to its output including linguistic elements (e.g., sentences, words, and abbreviations), and nonlinguistic elements (e.g., lines, stars, arrows, and symbols). Thus, the generated note cover (text cover) has ample room to conceal data without creating a suspicious pattern while embedding a message.

The implementation, validation, and experimental results demonstrate that these methodologies are capable of achieving the steganographic goal.

14.2 Bitrate

The aim of this section is to compare the bitrate of contemporary linguistic steganography approaches to that achieved by the Nostega paradigm. The bitrate is defined as the size of the hidden message relative to the size of the cover. Table 14.1 shows the bitrate achieved in the implemented samples of Nostega-based methodologies. It is worth noting that the bitrate differs from one methodology to another and from one implementation to another as indicated in Table 14.1, which categorizes them based on the methodology used.

To put these bitrate figures in perspective, the bitrate of contemporary linguistic steganography approaches has been investigated. The following reports on the findings, categorizing them based on the pursued approaches. Table 14.2 provides a concise summary of these findings.

1. Statistical-based approach, namely mimic functions: An experiment has been conducted using 30 samples generated using Spam Mimic [38]. An average bitrate of 0.90% is observed.
2. Synonym-based approaches:
   - For the NICETEXT scheme, the samples in [9,11] are used to estimate the bitrate, which is found to be approximately 0.29%.
   - The Winstein scheme [39] roughly hides about 6 bits per sentence, which yields a bitrate of approximately 0.5% based on the sentences listed in these publications. However, this rate cannot be generalized since not every sentence in the text cover conceals data. In addition, the size of the sentences will affect the bitrate because there are short and long sentences. Nonetheless, the 0.5% figure is assumed given that it is based on the samples developed by the authors.
   - The capability of the scheme of Murphy et al. [47] again is reported as the number of bits per sentence. Based on the samples provided in their publication, the achievable bitrate is roughly 0.30% per sentence.

Table 14.1   The Linguistic Bitrate of the Implemented Samples of Nostega-Based Methodologies

	EDUSTEGA				MATLIST		NORMALS BITRATE	JOKESTEGA BITRATE	HEADSTEGA BITRATE
TOPIC	EDUSTEGA BITRATE	SUMSTEGA BITRATE	LISTEGA BITRATE	NOTESTEGA BITRATE	MATLIST BITRATE	DSS			
GRE Antonyms	3.26%				0.58%–1.02%	CPI			3.38–7.67%
Completion	1.46%	0.064%–0.20%	1.32–3.87%	7.777%	19.09%–21.51%	Elementary math	0.20% Using only external inputs	Up to 8 bits per a short joke	
Analogies	3.86%				1.35%–2.16%	Bookseller			
Chemistry Type 1	0.94%				2.424%	Chemistry			
Type 2	2.81%				18.4%	Discrete math			

Table 14.2 The Bitrate of Contemporary Linguistic Steganography Approaches

APPROACH	BITRATE	COMMENT
Mimic functions [7,8]	0.90%	Based on 30 samples generated at www.spammimic.com
NICETEXT [9,11]	0.29%	Based on the samples in the cited papers
Winstein [39]	0.5%	Based on the samples in the cited papers, and also confirmed in [47]
Murphy et al. [47]	0.30%	Average per sentence (as reported in [47])
Nakagawa et al. [44]	0.12%	As reported in [44], bitrate achieved in real application is only 0.034%
Translation-based [14]	0.33%	Noted by the authors in the cited papers
Confusing [50]	0.35%	Based on the samples in the cited papers

- Nakagawa et al. [44] have provided two samples for their scheme. The samples achieve bitrates of 0.06% and 0.12%, respectively. However, it has been noted that when tried in a real application, only a bitrate of 0.034% could be reached.
3. Noise-based approaches:
  - The bitrate for the translation-based scheme reported in [14] is roughly 0.33%.
  - Based on the examples in [50], the confusing scheme achieves a bitrate of approximately 0.35%.

The linguistic techniques of the SMS-based approach [51] is claimed to be capable of hiding few bits in a file of several kilobytes, which yields an extremely low bitrate.

Comparing Tables 14.1 and 14.2, it is obvious that Nostega-based methodologies achieve a far superior bitrate than all comparable approaches, making it a very effective steganography paradigm. The high bitrate also enables the use of reasonable cover sizes, which is a major concern for all steganography approaches whether linguistic or nonlinguistic techniques.

The only low bitrate that may appear with the Nostega paradigm is in the Sumstega methodology in [34]. Obviously, the bitrate may differ from one type of summarization technique to another and from one implementation to another. Nonetheless, the presented implementation of the Sumstega scheme may achieve a bitrate from roughly 0.064% up to 0.20%, with an approximate average of 0.12%. The bitrate may appear slightly lower than other approaches, e.g., mimic functions, NICETEXT, translation-based, etc., that are mentioned in Table 14.2. However, the text cover generated by Sumstega, as observed, retains superior qualities to contemporary approaches. In addition, this bitrate is limited to only the current implementation example, which employs only one type of summarization technique, namely an extraction technique. However, there are numerous summarization techniques [81,78–80] that can be employed by Sumstega, such as abstraction, revision, discourse, paraphrasing rule, semantic equivalency, information equivalency, cross-lingual, multi-document, and information retrieval. Obviously, employing such techniques can easily increase the bitrate.

The bitrates of nonlinguistic Nostega-based methodologies are as follows. The bitrate of Graphstega for concealing long and short messages is roughly 4.37 % and 1.0061%, respectively. On the other hand, Chestega may achieve 7-11 bits per move.

14.3 Final Conclusion and Future Work

This section highlights the following: in general, the fundamental concepts of contemporary steganography and the linguistic steganography approaches; in particular, the current state of the research, the technical concerns, and the future directions for constructing steganography schemes. Steganography is the science and art of camouflaging the presence of covert communications. The steganographic goal is not to hinder the adversary from decoding a hidden message, but to prevent an adversary from suspecting the existence of covert communications. When using any steganographic technique, the goal of steganography is defeated if suspicion is raised, regardless of whether or not a plain text is revealed. Contemporary approaches are often classified based on the steganographic cover type as image, audio, graph, text, and non-textual. Textual steganography has become more favorable in recent years since the size of non-textual covers is relatively large and is burdening the traffic of covert communications. Most of the published steganography approaches hide data as noise in a cover that is assumed to look innocent, embedding a message by altering a digital image or an audio file with noticeable degradation. However, such alteration of authenticated covers can raise suspicion and the message is detectable regardless of whether or not a plain text is revealed.

On the other hand, textual steganography approaches embed a message by imposing a steganographic process that generates a noisy text cover. Textual steganography approaches include using a series of words and characters, imitating the statistical profile of an existing text, exchanging synonyms, and exploiting errors in erroneous text. The vulnerability and concerns of these textual approaches, as explained in Section 14.2, can be summarized as follows. First, the textual cover introduces detectable flaws (noise), such as incorrect syntax, lexicon, rhetoric, or grammar when generating a text cover. Obviously, such flaws can raise suspicion about the presence of covert communications. Second, the content of the cover may be meaningless and semantically incoherent, and thus may draw suspicion. Third, the bitrate is very small. Since there is a limit to how many flaws a document may typically have, very large documents are needed to hide a few bytes of data. In fact, this applies to non-textual approaches as well. Fourth, the bulk of the efforts have been focused on how to conceal a message and not on how to conceal the hidden message's transmittal. In other words, the establishment of a covert communication channel has not been an integral part of most approaches found in the literature. Fifth, while these approaches may fool a computer examination, they often fail to pass human inspections. A successful textual steganography approach must be capable of passing both computer and human examinations. These concerns have motivated the development of the Noiseless Steganography (Nostega) Paradigm.

The Nostega paradigm overcomes the faulty steganographic issues just mentioned above by generating noiseless steganographic cover, e.g., text, game, graph, image, etc. Mainly, Nostega achieves the steganographic goal based on a DSS, which eases the process of generating a steganographic cover whether it is a linguistic or nonlinguistic cover. The main advantages of the Nostega system are as follows. First, it opts to use steganographic carriers that retain high volumes of traffic by a wide variety of people to allow establishing a covert channel and averting suspicion in the presence of covert communications. Second, Nostega does not imply a particular pattern (noise) that an adversary may look for. Third, the concealment process of Nostega has no effect on the linguistics of the generated text cover. Linguistically, Nostega-based cover is meaningful, rhetorically sound, semantically coherent, and legitimate, which renders it capable of passing both computer and human examinations. Fourth, all contemporary Nostega-based cover can be applied to all languages. Fifth, Nostega steganographic carriers have adequate room for concealing data and the Nostega system has a superior bit rate when compared to all contemporary steganography approaches found in the literature. The implementation and steganalysis validation demonstrate that the Nostega system is capable of achieving the steganographic goal. Hence, the Nostega paradigm is highly promising for future work. Nonetheless, the field of steganography is not popularly applied in the commercial community and is mostly employed for spying activities because of laws and bitrate issues. Therefore, improving the bitrate is also a subject for future work to enable applicability in practical systems such as online credit card transactions.

Finally, due both to the advances in the steganalysis field and the successful achievement of the Nostega paradigm, it is strongly recommended that the Nostega paradigm be adapted for constructing any future steganography scheme.

Bibliography

1. Kipper, G., *Investigator's Guide to Steganography*, CRS Press LLC, pp. 15–16, 2004.
2. Davern, P. and Scott, M., Steganography its history and its application to computer based data files, *Internal Report Working Chapter: CA-0795*, School of Computing, Dublin City University 1995, Available: http://computing.dcu.ie/research/chapters/1995/0795.pdf, accessed on August 03, 2006.
3. Johnson, N. F. and Katzenbeisser, S., A survey of steganographic techniques, in S. Katzenbeisser and F. Petitcolas, Eds., *Information Hiding*, MA: Artech House, Norwood, pp. 43–78, December 1999.
4. Kessler, G. C., An overview of steganography for the computer forensics examiner, An edited version, *Forensic Science Communications. Technical Report*, Vol. 6, No. 3, July 2004.
5. Martin, A., Sapiro, G., Seroussi, G., Is image steganography natural? *IEEE Transactions on Image Processing*, Vol. 14(12), pp. 2040–2050, December 2005.
6. Kahn, D., *The Codebreakers: The Story of Secret Writing*. Revised Ed., Scribner, December 1996.
7. Wayner, P., Mimic functions, *Cryptologia*, Vol. XVI/3, pp. 193–214, 1992.
8. Wayner, P., *Disappearing Cryptography*, Morgan Kaufmann, 2nd ed., 2002.
9. Chapman, M. and Davida, G., Hiding the hidden: A software system for concealing ciphertext as innocuous text, in the *Proceedings of the International Conference on Information and Communications Security*, Vol. 1334 of Lecture Notes in Computer Science, Springer, pp. 335–345, Beijing, P. R. China, November 1997.

10. Chapman, M., et al., A practical and effective approach to large-scale automated linguistic steganography. *Proceedings of the Information Security Conference (ISC '01)*, pp. 156–165, volume 2200 of Lecture Notes in Computer Science. Springer, Malaga, Spain, 2001.

11. Chapman, M. and Davida, G. I., Plausible deniability using automated linguistic steganography. In G. Davida and Y. Frankel, editors, *International Conference on Infrastructure Security* (InfraSec '02), volume 2437 of Lecture Notes in Computer Science, pp. 276–287. Springer, 2002.

12. Chapman, M. and Davida, G. I., Nicetext system official home page. Available: http://www.nicetext.com, accessed on August 03, 2007.

13. Grothoff, C., et al., Translation-based steganography, *Proceedings of Information Hiding Workshop (IH 2005)*, pp. 213–233. Springer-Verlag, Barcelona, Spain, June 2005.

14. Stutsman, R., et al., Lost in just the translation, *Proceedings of the 21st Annual ACM Symposium on Applied Computing (SAC'06)*, Dijon, France, April 2006.

15. Meng, P., Shi, Y.-Q., Huang, L., Chen, Z., Yang, W., and Desoky, A., LinL: Lost in n-best list, in the *Proceedings of 13th Information Hiding Conference*, May 2011 (in press).

16. Cvejic, N. and Seppanen, T., Increasing robustness of LSB audio steganography using a novel embedding method, in the *Proceedings of the International Conference on Information Technology: Coding and Computing (ITCC'04)*, pp. 533–537, Las Vegas, Nevada, April 2004.

17. Cvejic, N. and Seppanen, T., Reduced distortion bit-modification for LSB audio steganography, '04. In the *Proceedings of the 7th International Conference on Signal Processing (ICSP 04)*, Vol. 3 pp. 2318–2321, Beijing, China, August 2004.

18. Bender W., et al., Techniques for data hiding, *IBM Systems J.*, Vol. 35, Nos. 3 and 4, pp. 313–336, 1996.

19. Kirovski, D. and Malvar, H., Spread-spectrum audio watermarking: Requirements, applications, and limitations, in the *Proceedings of the 4th IEEE Workshop on Multimedia Signal Processing*, pp. 219–224 Cannes, France, October 2001.

20. Ansari, R., Malik, H., and Khokhar, A., Data-hiding in audio using frequency-selective phase alteration, in the *Proceedings of IEEE International Conference on Acoustics, Speech, and Signal Processing*, (ICASSP '04), Vol. 5, 17–21, pp. 389–92, May 2004.

21. Gruhl, D., Lu, A., and Bender, W., Echo hiding, in the *Proceedings of First International Workshop on Information Hiding*, Lecture Notes in Computer Science, Vol. 1174, Springer, pp. 295–316, Cambridge, UK, May 1996.

22. Desoky, A., Edustega: An education-centric steganography methodology, *International Journal of Security and Networks*, (in press).

23. Desoky, A., Sumstega: Summarization-based steganography methodology, *International Journal of Information and Computer Security*, Vol. 4, No. 3, 2011 (in press).

24. Desoky, A., Headstega: Email-headers-based steganography methodology, *International Journal of Electronic Security and Digital Forensics* (in press).
25. Desoky, A., Comprehensive linguistic steganography survey, *International Journal of Information and Computer Security*, Vol. 4, No. 2, pp. 164–197, 2010.
26. Desoky, A., NORMALS: Normal linguistic steganography methodology, *Journal of Information Hiding and Multimedia Signal Processing*, Vol. 1, No. 3, pp. 145–171, July 2010.
27. Desoky, A., Matlist: Mature linguistic steganography methodology, *Journal of Security and Communication Networks* (in press).
28. Desoky, A., Jokestega: Automatic joke generation-based steganography, *Journal of Information Security* (submitted).
29. Desoky, A., Listega: List-based steganography methodology, *International Journal of Information Security*, Springer-Verlag, Vol. 8, No. 4, pp. 247–261, April 2009.
30. Desoky, A. and Younis, M., Chestega: Chess steganography methodology, *Journal of Security and Communication Networks*, Vol. 2, Issue 6, pp. 555–566, March 2009.
31. Desoky, A., Notestega: Notes-based steganography methodology, *Information Security Journal: A Global Perspective*, Vol. 18, No 4, pp. 178–193, January 2009.
32. Desoky, A., Nostega: A novel noiseless steganography paradigm, *Journal of Digital Forensic Practice*, Vol. 2, No. 3, pp. 132–139, July 2008.
33. Desoky, A. and Younis, M. Graphstega: Graph steganography methodology, *Journal of Digital Forensic Practice*, Vol. 2, No. 1, pp. 27–36, January 2008.
34. Desoky, A., et al., Auto-summarization-based steganography, in the *Proceedings of the 5th IEEE International Conference on Innovations in Information Technology*, pp. 608–612, December 2008.
35. Desoky, A. Nostega: A novel noiseless steganography paradigm, PhD Dissertation, University of Maryland, Baltimore County, May 2009.
36. Petitcolas, F. A. P., Information hiding—A survey. *Proceedings of the IEEE*, Vol. 87, Issue: 7, July. Anderson, R. J. and Kuhn, M. G., pp. 1062–1078, 1999.
37. Shirali-Shahreza, M. H. and Shirali-Shahreza, M., A new approach to Persian/Arabic text steganography, in the *Proceedings of 5th IEEE/ACIS International Conference on Computer and Information Science (ICIS-COMSAR 2006)*, pp. 310 – 315, 10–12, Hawaii: Honolulu, July 2006.
38. Spam Mimic, Available: http://www.spammimic.com, Accessed on July 31, 2007.
39. Winstein, K., Lexical steganography through adaptive modulation of the word choice hash, January 1999. Secondary education at the Illinois Mathematics and Science Academy. Available: http://alumni.imsa.edu/~keithw/tlex/lsteg.ps, accessed on April 15, 2008.

40. Bolshakov, I. A., A method of linguistic steganography based on collocationally-verified synonymy. In Fridrich, J. J., Ed., *Information Hiding: 6th International Workshop*, volume 3200 of *Lecture Notes in Computer Science*, pp. 180–191. Springer, May 2004.

41. Bolshakov, I. A. and Gelbukh, A., Synonymous paraphrasing using wordnet and internet. In Meziane, F. and Metais, E. E., Eds., *Natural Language Processing and Information Systems: 9th International Conference on Applications of Natural Language to Information Systems, NLDB 2004*, volume 3136 of *Lecture Notes in Computer Science*, pp. 312–323. Springer, June 2004.

42. Calvo, H. and Bolshakov, I. A., Using selectional preferences for extending a synonymous paraphrasing method in steganography. In Sossa Azuela, J. H., Ed., *Avances en Ciencias de la Computacion e Ingenieria de Computo— CIC'2004: XIII Congreso Internacional de Computacion*, pp. 231–242, October 2004.

43. Chand, V. and Orgun, C. O., Exploiting linguistic features in lexical steganography: Design and proof-of-concept implementation. *Proceedings of the 39th Annual Hawaii International Conference on System Sciences (HICSS '06)*, volume 6, page 126b. IEEE, January 2006.

44. Nakagawa, H., Sampei, I., Matsumoto, T., Kawaguchi, S., Makino, K., and Murase, I., Text information hiding with preserved meaning—A case for japanese documents, *IPSJ Transaction*, 42(9):2339–2350, 2001. Originally published in Japanese. A similar chapter by the first author in English. Available: http://www.r.dl.itc.u-tokyo.ac.jp/ nakagawa/academic-res/finpri02.pdf, accessed on June 4, 2008.

45. Niimi, M., Minewaki, S., Noda, H., and Kawaguchi, E., A framework of text-based steganography using sd-form semantics model. *IPSJ Journal*, 44(8), August 2003. Available: http://www.know.comp.kyutech.ac.jp/ STEG03/STEG03-CHAPTERS/chapters/12-Niimi.pdf, accessed on June 03, 2008.

46. Topkara, U., Topkara, M., and Atallah, M. J., The hiding virtues of ambiguity: Quantifiably resilient watermarking of natural language text through synonym substitutions. In *MM&Sec '06: Proceeding of the 8th workshop on Multimedia and security*, pp. 164–174, New York, NY, USA, ACM Press, 2006.

47. Murphy, B. and Vogel, C. The syntax of concealment: Reliable methods for plain text information hiding, *Proceedings of the SPIE International Conference on Security, Steganography, and Watermarking of Multimedia Contents*, January 2007.

48. Atallah, M. J., Raskin, V., Crogan, M., Hempelmann, C., Kerschbaum, F., Mohamed, D., and Naik, S., Natural language watermarking: Design, analysis, and a proof-of-concept implementation. In Moskowitz, I. S., Ed., *Information Hiding: Fourth International Workshop, Lecture Notes in Computer Science, Springer*, volume 2137, pp. 185–199, April 2001.

49. Atallah, M. J., Raskin, V., Hempelmann, C. F., Topkara, M., Sion, R., Topkara, U., and Triezenberg, K. E., Natural language watermarking and tamperproofing. In Petitcolas, F. A. P., Ed., *Information Hiding: Fifth International Workshop, volume 2578 of Lecture Notes in Computer Science, Springer,* pp. 196–212, October 2002.

50. Topkara, M., Topkara, U., and Atallah, M. J., Information hiding through errors: A confusing approach, *Proceedings of the SPIE International Conference on Security, Steganography, and Watermarking of Multimedia Contents,* January 2007.

51. Shirali-Shahreza, M., et al., Text steganography in SMS *International Conference on Convergence Information Technology,* Vol., Issue, 21–23, pp. 2260–2265, Nov. 2007.

52. Hernandez-Castro, J. C., Blasco-Lopez, I., Estevez-Tapiador, J. M., Ribagorda-Garnacho, A. Steganography in games: A general methodology and its application to the game of go. *Computers & Security,* 25(1):64–71, February 2006.

53. Handel, T. G. and Sandford, M. T. Data hiding in the OSI network model, in *Information Hiding: First International Workshop, Proceedings,* vol. 1174 of *Lecture Notes in Computer Science,* Springer, pp. 23–38, 1996.

54. Anderson, R. J., Needham, R., and Shamir, A., The steganographic file system, *Proceedings of the Second International Workshop on Information Hiding,* vol. 1525 of *Lecture Notes in Computer Science,* Springer, pp. 73–82, 1998.

55. ScramDisk: Free hard drive encryption for Windows 95 & 98, Available: http://www.scramdisk.clara.net, Accessed on August 03, 2008.

56. Koblitz, N., *A Course in Number Theory and Cryptography,* Springer, 2nd Ed. 1994.

57. U.S. Bureau of Labor Statistics, Consumer Prices Index of July 2007 http://www.bls.gov/news.release/cpi.nr0.htm

58. Portable Game Notation (PGN), Available at http://www.very-best.de/pgn-spec.htm, accessed on June 03, 2008.

59. Reiter, E. and Dale, R., *Building Natural Language Generation Systems* Cambridge University Press, 2000.

60. http://www.csd.abdn.ac.uk/research/stop/onlineQ.htm, accessed on May 23, 2007.

61. TV show Who Wants to Be a Millionaire, Available: at http://en.wikipedia.org/wiki/Who_Wants_To_Be_A_Millionaire%3F, accessed on July 27, 2008.

62. Laywine, C. F., Mullen, G. L., *Discrete Mathematics Using Latin Squares,* Wiley-Interscience, 1st ed. Sep 3, 1998.

63. Dénes, J., Keedwell, A. D., *Latin Squares (Annals of Discrete Mathematics),* vol. 46, Elsevier Science Publishing Company Inc., North-Holland, Amsterdam, Jan 1, 1991.

64. Bammel, S. E. and Rothstein, J., The number of 9x9 Latin squares, *Discrete Mathematics,* Vol. 11, pp. 93–95, 1975.

65. Hoole, D., et al., A bank of chemistry questions on an on-line server, *Journal of Science Education and Technology*, Vol. 11, pp. 9–13, Number 1, March 2002.

66. An Online Exam Generator: Exams and tests such as GRE, SAT, etc., available: http://www.ets.org, accessed on July 27, 2008.

67. An Online Exam Generator: Graduate Management Admission Test (GMAT), available: http://www.mba.com/mba/TaketheGMAT, Accessed on July 27, 2008.

68. Exam Pro Software, available: http://www.exam-software.com, accessed on July 27, 2008.

69. testgenerator, available: http://www.testshop.com/content.php?id=63, accessed on July 27, 2008.

70. An Online Exam Generator at Department of Chemistry, Indiana University Northwest, available: http://www.iun.edu/~cpanhd/cgi-bin/generator/examgenerator.html, accessed on July 27, 2008.

71. An Online Exam Generator at Department of Chemistry, Ohio State University, available: http://lrc-srvr.mps.ohio-state.edu/under/chemed/qbank/quiz/bank1.htm, accessed on July 27, 2008.

72. An Online Exam Generator (GRE Antonyms), available: http://www.syvum.com/cgi/online/serve.cgi/gre/verbal/antonyms7.tdf?0, accessed on July 31, 2008.

73. GRE Sentence Completions, available: http://www.greguide.com/verbal.html, accessed on July 31, 2008.

74. GRE Analogies, available: http://greanalogies.blogspot.com/2008/04/analogies-91–95.html, Accessed on July 30, 2008.

75. Dictionary and Thesaurus—Merriam-Webster Online, available: www.merriam-webster.com, accessed on July 31, 2008.

76. Online Dictionary Net, available: www.online-dictionary.net, accessed on July 31, 2008.

77. Cambridge Dictionaries Online—Cambridge University Press, available: www.dictionary.cambridge.org, Accessed on July 31, 2008.

78. Microsoft Word 97, available: http://www.microsoft.com/en/us/default.aspx, accessed on July 31, 2008.

79. Mani, I. and Maybury, M. T., *Advances in Automatic Text Summarization*. Cambridge, MIT Press, 1999.

80. Marcu, D., *The Theory and Practice of Discourse Summarization and Parsing*, Cambridge: MIT Press, 2000.

81. Mani, I. *Automatic Summarization*, John Benjamins Publishing Company, 2001.

82. Jones, K. S., Automatic summarising: The state of the art, *Info. Processing Mgmt*, 43(6), pp. 1449–1481, 2007.

83. Microsoft Word 97, built-in AutoSummarize.

84. Hassel, M. and Dalianis, H. SweSum—Automatic Text Summarizer, http://swesum.nada.kth.se/index-eng-adv.html

85. Inxight Summarizer www.inxight.com/products/sdks/sum

86. SRA Corporation, DimSum Summarizer: http://sra.com

87. http://www.objectssearch.com/summary/index.jsp
88. LTRC, IIIT, Automatic Text Summarizer: http://search.iiit.net/~jags/summarizer/index.cgi
89. *TIME* Magazine: www.time.com/time/world/article/0,8599,1679108,00.html
90. Zipf, G. K. (1968). *The Psycho-Biology of Language: An Introduction to Dynamic Philology.* Cambridge, MA: MIT Press.
91. Li, W. (1992). Random texts exhibit Zipf's-law-like word frequency distribution. *IEEE Transactions on Information Theory*, 38(6), pp. 1842–1845.
92. Consumer Price Index (Archive): ftp://ftp.bls.gov/pub/news.release/History
93. Smoking Cessation, text retrieved July 22, 2008 from http://www.tobaccofree.org/quitpoints.htm
94. Auto Summarizer http://mskw.cipher-sys.com/Lectern/summary_submitter.asp
95. Articles from *TIME* Magazine: www.time.com
96. Articles from *The New York Times* http://www.nytimes.com
97. Graduate Catalog 2005–2006 University Of Florida, Gainesville: retrieved from http://gradschool.rgp.ufl.edu/current-files/current-catalog.pdf, accessed on February 2, 2006.
98. Stallings, W. (2003). *Cryptography and Network Security: Principles And Practices*, NJ: Prentice-Hall Inc., pp. 21–50.
99. Lewand, R. E. (2000). *Cryptological Mathematics.* Washington, DC: The MAA Inc., pp. 1–44.
100. Pfleeger, C. P. (2000). *Security In Computing.* NJ: Prentice-Hall Inc., pp. 21–65.
101. The Los Angeles Superior Court Civil—General Information http://www.lasuperiorcourt.org/civil/main.htm#3
102. University of Minnesota: Modeling and Analysis of Flexible Queueing Systems http://www.ie.umn.edu/faculty/faculty/pdf/nrl.pdf
103. University of Otago, Postgraduate Catalog of Zoology: http://www.otago.ac.nz/Zoology/pdf/postgraduate_handbook.pdf
104. Solanki, K., Sullivan, K., Madhow, U., Manjunath, B. S., and Chandrasekaran, S. Provably secure steganography: Achieving zero K-L divergence using statistical restoration, in *Proceedings of ICIP*, Atlanta, Georgia, USA, Oct 2006.
105. Kullback, S. and Leibler, R. A. (1951). On information and sufficiency. *The Annals of Mathematical Statistics* 22 (1): 79–86. doi:10.1214/aoms/1177729694. MR39968.
106. Kullback, S. (1959) *Information Theory and Statistics*, NY: John Wiley and Sons.
107. Kullback, S. (1987) The Kullback-Leibler distance, *The American Statistician*, 41:340–341.
108. Desoky, A. and Younis, M., PSM: Public Steganography Methodology, Technical Report TR-CS-06-07, Department of Computer Science and Electrical Engineering, University of Maryland, Baltimore County, November 2006.

109. Shirali-Shahreza, M. H. and Shirali-Shahreza, M., A new approach to Persian/Arabic text steganography in the *Proceedings of 5th IEEE/ACIS International Conference on Computer and Information Science (ICIS-COMSAR 2006)*, pp. 310–315, 10–12, Hawaii: Honolulu, July 2006.

110. Mani, I. *Automatic Summarization*, John Benjamins Publishing Company, 2001.

111. Mani, I. and Maybury, M. T., *Advances in Automatic Text Summarization*. Cambridge, MIT Press, 1999.

112. Marcu, D. *The Theory and Practice of Discourse Summarization and Parsing*, Cambridge: MIT Press, 2000.

113. Jones, K. S. Automatic summarising: The state of the art, *Inf. Process. Manage.*, 43(6):1449–1481, 2007.

114. Luhn, H. P., The automatic creation of literature abstracts, *IBM Journal of Research and Development*, vol. 2, no. 2, pp.159–165, 1958.

115. Microsoft, AutoSummarize built-in Microsoft Word (in this book version 97 used).

116. Hassel, M. and Dalianis, H. SweSum—Automatic Text Summarizer: http://swesum.nada.kth.se/index-eng-adv.html, accessed on December 25, 2007.

117. Inxight Software Incorporation, Inxight Summarizer (2000): http://www.inxight.com/products/sdks/sum, accessed on December 25, 2007.

118. IBM Intelligent Miner (1999): http://www.research.ibm.com/journal/sj/433/mack.html, accessed on December 25, 2007.

119. SRA Corporation, DimSum Summarizer: http://sra.com, accessed on December 26, 2007.

120. Leite, D. S., Rino, L. H. M., Pardo, T. A. S., and Nunes, M. G. V., Extractive automatic summarization: Does more linguistic knowledge make a difference? *TextGraphs-2: Graph-Based Algorithms for Natural Language Processing*, pp. 17–24, Rochester, New York, USA, 2007. Association for Computational Linguistics.

121. Okazaki, N., Matsuo, Y., Matsumura, N., and Ishizuka, M. Sentence extraction by spreading activation with refined similarity measure, *IEICE Transactions on Information and Systems* (Special Issue on Text Processing for Information Access), E86-D(9):1687–1694, 2003.

122. Ercan, G. and Cicekli, I. Using lexical chains for keyword extraction, *Inf. Process. Manage.*, 43(6):1705–1714, 2007.

123. Huffman, D. A. A method for the construction of minimum redundancy codes, *Proceedings of the Institute of Radio Engineers*, Vol. 40, No. 9, pp. 1098–1101, September 1952.

124. Storer, J., *Data Compression*, Computer Science Press, Rockville MD, 1988.

125. Liang, S. F., Devlin, S., and Tait, J., Investigating sentence weighting components for automatic summarisation. *Inf. Process. Manage.*, 43(1):146–153, January 2007.

126. Yu, J., Reiter, E., Hunter, J., and Mellish, C., Choosing the content of textual summaries of large time-series data sets, *Natural Language Engineering*, 13:25–49, 2007.

127. Nomoto, T., Discriminative sentence compression with conditional random fields, *Inf. Process. Manage.*, 43(6):1571–1587, 2007.
128. LTRC, IIIT, Automatic Text Summarizer: http://search.iiit.net/~jags/summarizer/index.cgi, accessed on December 26, 2007.
129. TIME Magazine: http://www.time.com/time/world/article/0,8599,1679108,00.html, Accessed on Fri, 2 Nov 2007.
130. Cremmins, E. T. *The Art of Abstracting*, Arlington, VA: Information Resources Press, 2nd ed., 1996.
131. Mana-López, M. J., De Buenaga, M., and Gómez-Hidalgo, J. M., Multidocument summarization: An added value to clustering in interactive retrieval, *ACM Transactions on Information Systems*, 22(2): 215–241, April 2004.
132. Sekine, S. and Nobata, C., A survey for multi-document summarization, In Radev, D. R., Teufel, S., Harman, D., and Iver, I., Eds., *Proceedings of the HLT '03/NAACL '03 Workshop on Text Summarization*, Edmonton, Canada, May 31–June 1, 2003. Association for Computational Linguistics.
133. Afantenos, S. D., Karkaletsis, V., Stamatopoulos, P., and Halatsis, C., Using synchronic and diachronic relations for summarizing multiple documents describing evolving events, *Journal of Intelligent Information Systems*, 2007.
134. Koumpis, K. and Renals, S., Automatic summarization of voicemail messages using lexical and prosodic features, *ACM Transactions on Speech and Language Processing*, 2(1), February 2005.
135. Auto Summarizer: http://mskw.cipher-sys.com/Lectern/summary_submitter.asp, Accessed on December 25, 2008.
136. *The New York Times*: http://www.nytimes.com/2008/12/11/world/europe/11britain.html?_r=2&hp, accessed on December 10, 2008.
137. Sjöbergh, J., Older versions of the rougeeval summarization evaluation system were easier to fool, *Inf. Process. Manage.*, 43(6):1500–1505, 2007.
138. Harnly, A., Nenkova, A., Passonneau, R., and Rambow, O., Automation of summary evaluation by the pyramid method, in Angelova, G., Bontcheva, K., Mitkov, R., Nicolov, N., and Nikolov, N., Eds., *Proceedings of the Fifth International Conference on Recent Advances in Natural Language Processing (RANLP '05)*, Borovets, Bulgaria, September 18–24, 2005.
139. Hobson, S. P., Dorr, B. J., Monz, C., and Schwartz, R., Task-based evaluation of text summarization using relevance prediction, *Inf. Process. Manage.*, 43(6):1482–1499, 2007.
140. Hirao, T., Okumura, M., Yasuda, N., and Isozaki, H., Supervised automatic evaluation for summarization with voted regression model, *Inf. Process. Manage.*, 43(6):1521–1535, 2007.
141. Reiter, E. and Dale, R., *Building Natural Language Generation Systems* Cambridge University Press, 2000.
142. Kukich, K., Design of a knowledge-based report generator, *In Proceedings of the 21st Annual Meeting of the ACL*, Massachusetts Institute of Technology, Cambridge, MA, pp. 145–150, June 15–17, 1983.
143. CoGenTex Inc., WeatherReporter http://www.cogentex.com/

144. Ana the Stock Reporter (StockReporter) http://www.ics.mq.edu.au/~ltgdemo/StockReporter/about.html
145. Consumer Price Index: December 2006: ftp://ftp.bls.gov/pub/news.release/History/cpi.01182007.news
146. U.S. Bureau of Labor Statistics, Full CPI: http://www.bls.gov/cpi/cpid0612.pdf
147. Elementary Math http://www.mathsisfun.com/mean.html
148. Elementary Math http://www.rbechtold.com/math4.html
149. Chemistry quizzes by the Department of Chemistry The Ohio State University http://lrc-srvr.mps.ohio-state.edu/under/chemed/qbank/quiz/bank1.htm
150. Grimaldi, R. P., *Discrete Combinatorial Mathematics, An Applied Introduction*, Addison Wesley Publishing Co., 3rd ed., 1994.
151. Consumer Price Index (Archive): ftp://ftp.bls.gov/pub/news.release/History
152. Kukich, K., Design of a knowledge-based report generator, *In Proceedings of the 21st Annual Meeting of the ACL*, Massachusetts Institute of Technology, Cambridge, MA, pp. 145–150, June 15–17, 1983.
153. CoGenTex Inc., WeatherReporter http://www.cogentex.com/
154. Ana the Stock Reporter (StockReporter) http://www.ics.mq.edu.au/~ltgdemo/StockReporter/about.html
155. Chessmaster: http://chessmaster.com
156. Email Generators, available: http://www.icontact.com, accessed on September 26, 2008.
157. Google Internet Search Engine, available: http://www.google.com, accessed on September 26, 2008.
158. Yahoo Internet Search Engine, available: http://search.yahoo.com/web?fr=fptb-msgr, accessed on September 26, 2008.
159. Live Search: Internet Search Engine, available: http://www.live.com, accessed on September 26, 2008.
160. Yahoo Email: https://login.yahoo.com/config/login_verify2?&.src=ym, accessed on September 26, 2008.
161. Google Email, available: https://www.google.com/accounts/ServiceLogin?service=mail&passive=true&rm=false&continue=http%3A%2F%2Fmail.google.com%2Fmail%2F%3Fhl%3Den%26ui%3Dhtml%26zy%3Dl&bsv=1k96igf4806cy&ltmpl=default&ltmplcache=2&hl=en, accessed on September 26, 2008.
162. MSN Hotmail, available: https://login.live.com/login.srf?wa=wsignin1.0&rpsnv=10&ct=1222960929&rver=4.5.2130.0&wp=SAPI&wreply=https:%2F%2Faccount.live.com%2Fsummarypage.aspx%3Fmkt%3DEN-US&lc=1033&id=38936, accessed on September 26, 2008.
163. Friedland, L. and Allan, J., Joke retrieval: recognizing the same joke told differently, *Proceedings of the 17th ACM Conference on Information and Knowledge Management*, October 26–30, 2008, Napa Valley, California, USA.
164. Joke Generator Project STANDUP, Available: http://www.csd.abdn.ac.uk/research/standup, accessed on August 01.

165. Joke Generator Project STANDUP, available: http://groups.inf.ed.ac.uk/ standup, accessed on August 01, 2009.
166. Waller, A., Black, R., O'Mara, D. A., Pain, H., Ritchie, G., and Manurung, R., Evaluating the STANDUP pun generating software with children with cerebral palsy, *ACM Transactions on Accessible Computing (TACCESS)* Volume 1, Issue 3, Article No. 16, February, 2009.
167. Manurung, R., Ritchie, G., Pain, H., Waller, A., O'Mara, D., and Black, R., The construction of a pun generator for language skills development, *Applied Artificial Intelligence*, 22(9) pp. 841–869, 2008.
168. Manurung, R., Ritchie, G., Pain, H., Waller, A., O'Mara, D., and Black, R., Adding phonetic similarity data to a lexical database, *Language Resources and Evaluation* 42 (3), pp.319–324, 2008.
169. Ritchie, G., Manurung, R., Pain, H., Waller, A., Black, R., and O'Mara, D., A practical application of computational humour, pp. 91–98 in *Proceedings of the 4th International Joint Conference on Computational Creativity*, ed. Cardoso, A. and Wiggins, G. A. London, 2007.
170. Black, R., Waller, A., Ritchie, G., Pain, H., and Manurung, R., Evaluation of joke-creation software with children with complex communication needs, *Communication Matters* 21 (1), pp. 23–28, 2007.
171. Manurung, R., Ritchie, G., O'Mara, D., Waller, A., and Pain, H., Combining lexical resources for an interactive language tool, In *Proceedings of ISAAC 2006, the 12th Biennial International Conference of the International Society for Augmentative and Alternative Communication* (CD), Düsseldorf, Germany, 9 July–5 August 2006.
172. O'Mara, D., Waller, A., Manurung, R., Ritchie, G., Pain, H., and Black, R., Designing and evaluating joke-building software for AAC users, In *Proceedings of ISAAC 2006, the 12th Biennial International Conference of the International Society for Augmentative and Alternative Communication* (CD), Düsseldorf, Germany, 29 July–5 August 2006.
173. Manurung, R., O'Mara, D., Pain, H. Ritchie, G., and Waller, A., Building a lexical database for an interactive joke-generator, In *Proceedings of LREC, the Fifth International Conference on Language Resources and Evaluation* (CD), Genoa, Italy, 24–26 May 2006.
174. Ritchie, G., Manurung, R., Pain, H., Waller, A., and O'Mara,D., The STANDUP interactive riddle builder, *IEEE Intelligent Systems*, 21 (2), March/April. Pp. 67–69, 2006.
175. Waller, A., O'Mara, D., Manurung, R., Pain, H., and Ritchie, G., Facilitating user feedback in the design of a novel joke generation system for people with severe communication impairment, In *Proceedings of HCII 2005* (CD), Vol. 5, G. Salvendy, Ed. Lawrence Erlbaum, NJ, 2005.
176. O'Mara, D., Waller, A., Manurung, R., Ritchie, G., and Pain, H., "I say, I say, I say…," *Australian Group on Severe Communication Impairment News*. Vol. 23, 2.
177. Manurung, R., Low, A., Trujillo-Dennis, L., O'Mara, D., Pain, H., Ritchie, G., and Waller, A., Interactive computer generation of jokes for language skill development, Conference of International Society for Humor Studies, Dijon, France, 2004.

178. O'Mara, D., Waller, A., Ritchie, G., Pain, H., and Manurung, R., The role of assisted communicators as domain experts in early software design, In *Proceedings of ISAAC, the 11th Biennial International Conference of the International Society for Augmentative and Alternative Communication* (CD), Natal, Brazil, 6–10 October 2004.

179. O'Mara, D., Waller, A., and Todman, J., The recognition and use of verbal humour by children with language impairment, presented as Emerging Scholar, Conference of International Society for Humor Studies, Dijon, France, 2004.

180. O'Mara, D. and Waller, A., What do you get when you cross a communication aid with a riddle? *The Psychologist* 16(2), pp.78–80. ISSN 0952-8229, 2003.

181. Binsted, K., Pain, H. and Ritchie, G., Children's evaluation of computer-generated punning riddles, in *Pragmatics and Cognition* 5(2):305–354, 1997.

182. Binsted, K., Machine humour: An implemented model of puns, PhD thesis, University Of Edinburgh, Edinburgh, Scotland, 1996.

183. MIT Project, Online Joke Generator System at, available at: http://scratch.mit.edu/projects/Ronan1888/4365, accessed on May 16, 2011.

184. Online Joke Generator System, available at: http://www.jokes2000.com, accessed on May 16, 2011.

185. Online Joke Generator System, Available at: http://www.thejokegenerator.com, accessed on May 16, 2011.

186. Online Joke Generator System, available at: http://www.pickuplinegen.com, accessed on May 16, 2011.

187. Dictionary and Thesaurus—Merriam-Webster Online, available: www.merriam-webster.com, accessed on July 31, 2008.

188. Online Dictionary Net, available: www.online-dictionary.net, accessed on July 31, 2008.

189. Cambridge Dictionaries Online—Cambridge University Press, available: www.dictionary.cambridge.org, accessed on July 31, 2008.

190. Microsoft Word 97, available: http://www.microsoft.com/en/us/default.aspx, accessed on July 31, 2008.

191. Mani, I., *Automatic Summarization*, John Benjamins Publishing Company, 2001.

192. Jones, K. S., Automatic summarising: The state of the art, *Info. Processing Mgmt,* 43(6), pp. 1449–1481, 2007.

193. Fister, A. and Girju, R., Preliminary investigation toward an automatic notetaking system. In the proceedings of *the 5th Midwest Computational Linguistics Colloquium (MCLC)*, Michigan, May 2008.

194. Janda, R. D., Note-taking English as a simplified register. *Discourse Processes,* 8(4):437–454, 1985.

195. Shuy, R. W. What we do with English when we take notes: Evidence from a civil lawsuit. Studia Anglica Posnaniensia: international review of English Studies, Adam Mickiewicz University Press. 1998.

196. Notetaking System, available: http://www.cs.umd.edu/~egolub/AVIAN/TE-BIRD, accessed on October 15, 2008.

Index